Medievalisms

STUDIES IN ENGLISH MEDIEVAL LANGUAGE AND LITERATURE

Edited by Jacek Fisiak

Vol. 21

PETER LANG

Frankfurt am Main · Berlin · Bern · Bruxelles · New York · Oxford · Wien

Liliana Sikorska (ed.)

With the assistance of Joanna Maciulewicz

Medievalisms

The Poetics of Literary Re-Reading

PETER LANG

Internationaler Verlag der Wissenschaften

Bibliographic Information published by the Deutsche Nationalbibliothek
The Deutsche Nationalbibliothek lists this publication in the
Deutsche Nationalbibliografie; detailed bibliographic data is
available in the internet at <http://www.d-nb.de>.

typesetting by **motivex**

ISSN 1436-7521
ISBN 978-3-631-57217-7

© Peter Lang GmbH
Internationaler Verlag der Wissenschaften
Frankfurt am Main 2008
All rights reserved.

Printed in Germany 1 2 3 4 5   7

www.peterlang.de

Contents

6   *Contents*

Medievalisms. An (unorthodox) introduction

When John Lydgate wrote his *Troy Book* (1412-1420) based on a medieval Latin version of the Troy story (1287), he paid tribute to Guido de Colonne, whose work was his major source of inspiration, but he was not particularly concerned with the original, if such a word can be used here, Homeric version. Lydgate addressed an elaborate dedicatory prologue to Prince Henry V. In this prologue, he called Mars, the classical god of warfare, the god of chivalry, praised writers for recording what would have died without them and suggested that only books tell the truth about men. Apart from apparent didacticism encapsulated by Lydgate's favorite image of the capricious goddess Fortuna and a number of digressions on malice, idolatry and on covetousness, Lydgate presents the ancient world in terms of chivalric virtues and common medieval vices. His *Troy Book* is an exemplary "mirror of the prince" rather than an epic work. His Troy is more medieval than classical, populated as it is with knights and unfaithful women, whose stereotypical portrayal augments Lydgate's typical medieval anti-feminism. His is not an isolated case. Medieval writers frequently used other writers' works for purpose of translation or, most commonly, adaptation, praising not the new but the rewritten stories as more valuable. They had a sense of their contemporary audiences, which required the old texts to be readily available in their own cultural context. Hence, William Caxton "Englishes" his *Boke of Eneydos* and Chaucer his tales in *The Canterbury Tales* told by different pilgrims and based on various European secular (Boccaccio) and religious (for example, hagiographic) sources. Lydgate also re-reads the story of Troy. Thus, instead of criticizing Lydgate for turning his war at Troy into a medieval romance, we, like his original audience, should praise his poetic and story (re)telling skills.

The literature of our time also constantly revises the medieval elements and there is not one way in presenting the Middle Ages, hence one should talk about medievalisms. From popular culture (film) to more serious reconsiderations of historical and religious studies, the Middle Ages inspire research into what we treat as the beginning of modern European culture. There are two seemingly competing currents of thought: the Middle Ages seen as either idealized through chivalry and courtly love, or de-idealized through the exploration of the history of medicine, law, geography and history. The Middle Ages are then offered either as the beginning of the modern world with the inventing of gun powder and spectacles, or as the dark ages of humanity, interminable wars and violence, witchcraft, alchemy and magic, at the expense of classical learning and the virtues of Greco-Roman culture. Postmodernism with its focus on marginal cultural phenomena brought the interest in religious minorities such as Jews, religious phenomena such as female mysticism, as well as in hitherto forbidden subjects of rape, incest, adultery, and homosexuality.

Already in the post-medieval period, the literature of each and every period after the Middle Ages returns to medieval motifs. The Renaissance used the medieval tradition in both drama and poetry; the Puritan period revised the great religious themes rewriting medieval religious motifs in the new Protestant context. The Enlightenment showed a rather ambivalent attitude toward medieval themes. On the one hand, the Enlightenment writers praise Chaucer by translating and imitating his works and style, but on the other, they see Chaucer's original genius in the context of the dark ages of English poetry and the Catholic religion. John Dryden saw the task of his and his contemporaries as that of translating Chaucer, and thus de-contextualizing and de-medievalizing Chaucer's works. Pre-Romantic and Romantic writers returned to the idealized Middle Ages of troubadour poetry, and in that of mysterious Gothicism, a force that linked the birth of national cultures with the elements of medieval folklore and popular culture. The discourse of nationalism was also used by Victorian writers and manifested in their interest in Anglo-Saxonism. For pre-Romantic writers, however, unlike for the Victorians, the quest for the pre-Christian bards was not connected with finding the forefathers of English nationhood, but the forefathers of English poetry. While Romanticism praised the non-rational elements in medieval culture and literature, Victorianism showed fascination with ideas of chivalry. Victorian writers searched for moral values and social order lost in the industrialized world of nineteenth-century England. Theirs was the search for the lost Grail epitomized in the reassessment of late medieval Arthurian romances. In modernism, the Grail, the universal symbol of unattained beauty, is contrasted with the barren land of the sick Fisher King, Eliot's waste land. Each and every period rewrites, revises, and alters the image of the Middle Ages, presenting its own version of the medieval, a tendency best exemplified in medieval(ist) films.

In the 1953 movie *Knights of the Round Table* (MGM) directed by Richard Thorpe, King Arthur marries Guinevere in full armor. Throughout the movie, all the knights treat battle armor as house clothes, despite its assumed weight. The misconception of weight of full battle armor results also in yet another mistake, as knights during and after the battle jump on and off their horses without any help, which is especially prominent in the last scenes with the dying Arthur. When Lancelot arrives home to Elaine, he opens the door, and for a split of a second, the audience anticipates: "Honey, I'm home". Robert Taylor in the role of Lancelot is closer to the speech mannerisms and behavior of cowboys than of medieval knights. And yet, what do we know about medieval knights to judge Taylor and his presentation? The literary works passed down to us are highly conventional. Medieval authors do not tell us about the ordinary life of knights and their wives, but of their adventures and, more stylized than real, courtly love. In the 1950s version of Malory's story the 1950s America is reflected and even foregrounded. *Le Morte D'Arthur* was written by Thomas Malory in the fifteenth century, but the story itself concerned half true and half mythical events taking place in Celtic

Britain of approximately fifth century. Malory's knights, however, are not fifth century Celtic warriors, but late medieval knights, whose ideal and idealized world of chivalry was slowly waning. Malory's Britain is not Celtic; it is the Britain of his day, with Arthur and his knights standing for the world, which we, the contemporary audience read and recognize as markedly our own.

So what is it exactly the medievalists would like to see in medieval movies? A faithful version of the original story, one can claim. But there is no original story in the case of King Arthur; there are only different versions of an unknown original, some anonymous and some signed, some shorter and some longer, alliterative and prose, French and English. Nevertheless, following Lydgate, literary scholars value written sources, assuming that our knowledge of the world is always textual; even archeological finds are always interpreted in writing, hence our stanch belief in written documents.

My father was an archeologist and a historian, a specialist in arms and defense strategies with a penchant for historical movies. Whenever we watched a movie, usually chosen by my father on the basis of their historical content, or simply watched a historical movie about Goths, Vikings, the Spanish Armada, Horatio Nelson, Napoleon or any other historical period or figure, my father would always complain about costumes and arms being inappropriate, and historical details far from being based on historical sources. I promised myself that I would never spoil the pleasure of watching a movie to anyone and yet ... I do exactly the same as my father did. Watching Jerry Zucker's 1995 *First Knight* (Columbia Pictures) with a friend of mine, I could not help laughing at the nice blue costumes the knights were wearing; neither could I stop complaining when at the end of the movie, the dying Arthur not only forgives Lancelot but also chooses Lancelot as his successor. We are not, however, privileged to see whether the succession is to the throne of Camelot, to the Round Table or to the bed of Guinevere. This friend of mine watched the movie for the Richard Gere and Julia Ormond love story and I for what historical and literary accuracy I could find. To cite yet another of my classroom dialogues: "What is wrong with this movie?" "Everything".

And yet, medievalists more than other literary scholars should be careful in demanding such historical accuracy. Although our knowledge of the Middle Ages, its cultural and literary background, is constantly growing, still one must assume, that most of our reading of the past is based only on pieces of a jigsaw and a lot of our reading is misreading, such as Umberto Eco demonstrated in his *Misreadings* (1993) or Peter Ackroyd in *The Plato Papers* (1999). In Ackroyd's novel, the comic handbook *Jokes and their relation to the unconscious* was found: "The meaning of the 'unconscious' is by no means clear, but it may be related to the idea of drunkenness, which even in our own time is the object of laughter" (1999: 59). Later, yet another archeological find is reported, that of a long strip of images embossed upon some pliable material. The researchers manage to reconstruct two words "Hitchcok" and "Frenzy" (1999: 70). Future Generations of Londoners understand the twentieth-century actions of drinking water and lighting a cigarette as: "the exile [i.e. major character of the film] pours liquid into a glass and swallows it in one gesture. This may be a form of awakening. He then places a tube of paper or cloth into his mouth and lights it; here we notice the worship of fire as well as water" (1999: 72). Thus, according to Ackroyd, any act of re-reading of older texts is necessarily an act of misreading. Many medievalists would agree with such claims but they would nevertheless complain about a "bad" presentation of the Middle Ages on film.

Such concerns are presented by Hans Sauer's paper on teaching the English Middle Ages on film and by Władysław Witalisz's paper on Mel Gibson's *Braveheart*. The most easily recognized medieval content is found in texts, in which authors conspicuously place the action of their works in the Middle Ages, such topics are addressed in Agnieszka Setecka's, Keiko Hamaguchi's, Dagmara Krzyżaniak's, and the first part of Małgorzata Milczarek's paper discussing the Renaissance play *The Witch of Edmonton*. The latter is based on a real life late medieval record of witch trial to demonstrate how the discourse of witchcraft was related to that of gender and power and how, in turn, the discourses of witchcraft and power are rewritten in contemporary feminist literature. Anna Czarnowus' paper concerns the revival of Anglo-Saxonism, both as a literary as well as cultural and political interest of Victorian Britain. The rest of the papers investigate models of medieval literature, which rewritten in various forms, still remain recognizable in contemporary post-medieval works. Thus, Andrzej Wicher's and Łukasz Hudomięt's papers search for the remnants of psychomachia, Jacek Fabiszak's paper depicts the figure of the she-vice in Renaissance drama as a continuation of medieval dramatic discourse, while Anna Warmuz traces echoes of the medieval beast fable in contemporary novels, and Marcin Cieniuch analyzes a contemporary novel which creates fictional Victorian poets, who purportedly write equally fictional medievalist poetry. Lindsay Clarke's paper and my paper on Lindsay Clarke's *The Chymical Wedding* discuss the unchangeable aspects of imagination, magic and love as encapsulated in medieval symbols, which provide the bridge between the medieval and the contemporary culture. Last but not least, Joanna Maciulewicz's paper recaptures the neoclassical debate over translation and imitation, in the context of Dryden's and Pope's modernizations of Chaucer.

In his preface to *Fables Ancient and Modern* (1700), Dryden recognizes Chaucer as the first poet who polished the language: "From Chaucer the purity of the English Tongue began..." (Dryden 1995: 217). He discusses the importance of Chaucer on several pages, and yet asserts: "I have ty'd myself to a Literal Translation but have often omitted what I judged unnecessary, or not of Dignity enough to appear in the Company of better Thoughts. I have presum'd farther in some Places; and added somewhat of my own where I thought my Author was deficient, and had not given his Thoughts their true Lustre, for want of Words in the Beginning of our Language" (1995: 275; capital letters original). With this preface, Dryden created a history of the reception of Chaucer in the post-medieval periods, while also initiating the fashion for the constantly repeated re-evaluation of the Middle Ages. The rewriting in contemporary culture results in films like Jerry Zucker's *The First Knight* (1995), a pseudo-medieval and yet somber rewriting of the Lancelot story; we may also add Brian Helgeland's *A Knight's Tale* (Columbia Pictures, 2001), equally pseudo-medieval but a work which acknowledges its arbitrary treatment of the times with contemporary music of Robbie Williams and Queen, contemporary language and sports in which jousting has nothing to do with chivalry but a lot to do with competitive sports of today. *A Knight's Tale* presents a late twentieth-century version of medievalism consciously without unveiling the contemporary perspective. By contrast, *The First Knight* attempts to recreate the medieval world, and in doing so fails miserably and becomes its own (post-modern) parody. And yet both films tell us something about ourselves, about our need to revise and rewrite. To use a quotation from Dryden's preface to *Fables Ancient and Modern*: "Another poet, in another Age, may take the same Liberty with my Writings if at least they live long enough to deserve Correction" (1995: 275). Let us take the words of John Dryden seriously and emphasize that not every rereading may be to our liking, yet all of them grant literary works textual survival.

References

Ackroyd, Peter
    2000   *The Plato Papers*. London: Vintage.
Eco, Umberto
    1993   *Misreadings*. London: Picador. (Translated from the Italian by William Weaver.)
Dryden, John
    1995   *The works of John Dryden*. (Edited by David Marriot.) London: Wordsworth Poetry Library.
Lydgate, John
  1906 [1996] Lydgate's *Troy Book*. (Edited by Henry Bergen.) Woodbridge, Suffolk: Boydell and Brewer.

Layers of fictionality. Reading Victorian medievalism in A. S. Byatt's *Possession*

Marcin Cieniuch, Poznań

For many readers, the basic and commonsensical distinction between scholarly or scientific and literary texts is that between fact and fiction. While the discourse of science and scholarship is treated as factual because of the assumed referentiality of the statements it makes, literature is deemed fictitious because of its conventional awareness and acceptance of the fictionality of its propositions. These distinctions are reflected in the different status of scholarship and literature: the former is recognised as a viable means for undertaking epistemologically oriented endeavours, the latter, as unsuited for any such ventures. In *Possession*, the Booker Prize winning novel of 1990, Antonia Susan Byatt challenges these discriminations and thematizes the representational crisis which results from them. In the novel's multi-layered, fictional world created out of a subtle and complex nexus of factual, literary and mythical discourses the novelist questions the commonly assumed invalidity of fiction as a medium for expressing past and present times and individuals. She sets the disparate discourses of contemporary literary scholarship and of Victorian historicist poetry against each other, focusing specifically on the Victorian rewriting of medieval myths and legends. While the supposedly factual, scholarly discourse of contemporary literary studies turns out to be too arbitrarily and narcissistically reflective of the interests of its authors, the metaphorical, non-representational medievalist poetry takes on the function of a positively informative source of knowledge about the past, serving at the same time as Byatt's general metanarrative commentary on the ability of literature to function in such a capacity. Thus, employing medieval motifs, Byatt's fictional poets give a metaphorical and encrypted, but nonetheless revealing and lasting expression of their forbidden romance and of the artistic, religious and moral concerns of their age; while the fictional contemporary scholars engage in a both emotionally and epistemologically rewarding encounter with the past not through their theoretically and critically oriented research but by reading the Victorian medievalist poetry itself.

Central to Byatt's discussion of the potential of fiction for fulfilling the role of a medium for representing the past are two Victorian poems written by her two fictional poets: Henry Randolph Ash's "Ragnarök" and Christabel LaMotte's "The Fairy Melusina". Importantly, both of these are based on a medieval myth and legend and have been written in a manner that seeks to retain the metaphorical, mythical quality of their originals: the Norse, pre-Christian myth of apocalypse and rebirth in the case of "Ragnarök", and the Breton legend of the tragic relationship between a water fairy and a mortal man in the case of "The Fairy Melusina". Their mythical, medievalist quality is crucial, for being at the furthest possible remove from the factual discourse of contemporary scholarship, they are Byatt's epitomes of the fabulous and fictional in literature. Despite this, however, in the fictional world of the novel they function as the source of relevant information about the actual events from the past, as LaMotte turns out to have invested her work with a previously unknown account of her secret love affair with Ash. For the world outside the novel, that is for the actual readers of *Possession*, both the content and form of "Ragnarök" and "The Fairy Melusina" function as Byatt's metafictional commentary on the primacy of art as the mode of human expression in general and on the ability of literature to represent the past in a metaphorical but still informative manner in particular. Moreover, as both the Victorian and contemporary plots of the novel unfold, they turn out to be structured according to the medieval legend rewritten by Byatt's Victorian poetess, which also is an implicit and subtle comment that not despite but thanks to its fictional character literature is a superior means of accessing and expressing the past. As the seemingly realistic novel becomes a postmodern *romance* in which the story from a medieval myth is played out first between Victorian poets and later between contemporary scholars, the established roles of scholarship and fiction are reversed.

Possession has a double narrative frame: one part of its plot is set in the contemporary reality of the late 1980s, which is when Byatt was writing the novel, the other part in the 1860s and 1870s, in the middle of the Victorian era. The book's contemporary world is that of literary scholars, some heartless or insensible in their appropriation of the past, others helpless or miserable in their struggle to really understand it. The past which they are trying to grasp is the Victorian age, specifically, the private world of thoughts and feelings of two fictional poets of that age, who, in turn, attempt to speak of their own present through an imaginative and artistic employment of medieval, mythical and legendary material. To Byatt, the poets' Victorian world is a meeting point in which the old myth – religion – becomes undermined and largely superseded by new ones – science on the one hand and spiritism on the other. Her poets utilise all these three myths in their poetry, which is the bottom fictional layer of the novel, giving voice to the experience of their entire age as well as of that of their own individual lives. Unlike her Victorians, Byatt's contemporary scholars seek to understand and represent the past rather than the present. Yet, the application of the twentieth-century critical apparatus to the study of the nineteenth-century poetry proves to be a flawed procedure: although their focus is the past, the scholars allow their contemporary interests, ambitions and expectations to impose themselves on the object of their investigations. Byatt compares these two, artistic and Victorian as opposed to scholarly and contemporary, methods and worlds, increasingly proclaiming, as her story develops to its sensational ending, her belief in the superiority of the literary, metaphorical mode of representation over the scientific, referential one.

The tension between literary and scholarly discourse, between the seemingly fanciful and the seemingly factual, organises *Possession* on all its levels. First of all, literary scholarship is what connects the novel's past and present, as both main contemporary characters are literary scholars with a professional interest in the literary production of the two Victorian characters: Roland Michell studies the poetry of Henry Randolph Ash, while Maud Bailey researches in the work of the poetess Christabel LaMotte. Also, although both pairs of characters are the fictional creations of Byatt's imagination, they have been firmly and meticulously set in the authentic historical background: a number of both contemporary and Victorian historical persons are present and active in the fictional world, resulting in the illusion of the historicity of the fictitious characters themselves. The illusion is further strengthened by the characteristic technique which Byatt uses for the presentation of the Victorian part of the plot. Her poets' lives, thoughts, and works, as well as the lives, thoughts and works of other Victorians, are accessible both to the fictitious researchers from the novel and to the actual readers of the novel almost solely through the textualised, seemingly authentic, remnants of the past: both poets' letters, other people's letters, fragments of private journals and diaries, a newspaper report, and even a suicidal note. To all this supposedly genuine historical material, in fact a laborious counterfeit by Byatt, the novelist adds also a number of similarly fictitious, contemporary writings on her two Victorian characters: some explanatory footnotes to their poems, the fragments of a seemingly authoritative biography (with references to both actual and fictitious critical and theoretical sources) and some critical articles. Nonetheless, the most important medium through which the Victorians are accessible both to the actual readers of the novel and to the fictional scholars is their poetry, especially the two medievalist poems which stand so conspicuously at odds with the discourse of the twentieth-century scholarship which seems to be dominating the novel. Thus, thanks to the constant juxtaposition of the two, the relationship between literature and literary scholarship, between fictional and factual discourse, becomes the major theme of the novel.

Byatt's rewriting of the Victorian epoch seems to be guided by her interest in the authentic historicist and medievalist Victorian poetry. Similarly as for her, for some historical Victorian authors, claims Margaret Gent, "[t]he use of the past in ... literature and art ... function[ed] as an important metaphor; the revitalisation of what is now dead serve[d] as a symbol of the artist's power" (Gent 1972: 35). In *Possession*, the artist's power consists primarily in his or her, and in art's ability to express the past, in their ability to relate to and to represent the actual world in as relevant a manner as do other, non-fictional kinds of discourse. On the basis of her critical essays on Robert Browning it appears that the very thematization of the connection between art and reality, or art and the past, was what drew the novelist to Victorian historicist poetry. Speaking of Browning's *The Ring and the Book* she says: "[a] writer who adopted a technique which gives ten different accounts of the same event in the twentieth century would almost certainly be reflecting on … the relativity of truth. Browning, on the other hand, appears to be insisting on the need to pursue and determine the truth as far as possible" (Byatt 1993: 35). *The Ring and the Book* was based on an actual historical event, while Byatt's fictional poets use medieval myths and legends as the sources of their poetry, in this way allowing the novelist to distance it even further from the referential diction of factual discourse, while still insisting on its meaningful relationship with the past of its origin. Medievalist and mythical as they are, "Ragnarök" and "The Fairy Melusina" allow their fictional authors to represent their experience in a manner similar to that in which Browning's "resurrected pasts … are … about Browning and the 19th century … [as well as being] … truly about … the New Testament … or Renaissance Christianity and Art" (Byatt 2001: 94). Moreover, and equally to Byatt's point, Ash's and LaMotte's epic-length poems are also a self-conscious commentary on the viability of art used for their own, and Byatt's, recreation of the past. In this, they are similar to the actual medievalist and myth-based poetry written in the Victorian times, especially to that by Alfred Tennyson.

Tennyson's medievalist poetry was on the one hand praised, and on the other criticised, for its other-worldly, dreamy, and self-contained quality[1] which was connected with the poet's wish to, rephrasing one of Arthur Hallam's comments, keep the feeling of art "ascendant in our minds over distressful realities" (quoted in: Hunt 1972: 90). Tennyson seemed to find the present too confused, "unreal and indistinct" (Tennyson in a letter to Emily Sellwood; quoted in: Hunt 1972: 91), to engage with it directly, without the distancing device of an artistically reordered past. Only through the use of the past, or through the even more secure, mythicised "setting largely outside time" (Fraser 2000: 130) of the Arthurian legends was he able to face the traumatic experience of his profound personal loss of his "another Arthur"[2] (Fraser 2000: 131), the deeply mourned Hallam, as well as present his ideological and moral support for his country.[3] It was this combination

---

1   See John. D Jump's collection *Tennyson. The critical heritage*. London: Routledge & Kegan Paul. A number of critical articles by Tennyson's contemporaries are reprinted there, among them: W. J. Fox's "On *Poems, Chiefly Lyrical* (1830)," A.H. Hallam's "On *Poems, Chiefly Lyrical* (1830)", Christopher North's "On *Poems, Chiefly Lyrical* (1830)", J. W. Croker's "On *Poems* (1830)", and J. S. Mill's "On *Poems, Chiefly Lyrical* (1830)" and "*Poems* (1833)".

2   Apart from *In Memoriam*, critics claim that the mourning after the loss of his friend was expressed also in other, mostly historicist, poems from the Laureate's *oeuvre*: Richards points to *Morte d'Arthur* (Richards 1988: 112), Fraser to "Ulysses" (Fraser 2000: 132-132), whilst Hunt speaks of "[t]he type of Christ-King Arthur-Arthur Hallam that the *Idylls* try to keep before us … [as of] another attempt … to establish for the poet a possible significance of his friend's life and death" (Hunt 1972: 117).

3   Despite the often repeated accusation that Tennyson's early poetry and *Idylls of the King* lacked "that larger [philosophical or ideological] scope that many Victorians desired" (Hunt

in Victorian historicist, medievalist and myth-based poetry of the three elements: the indirect expression of personal emotions invested in art by means of the past and myths, the commentary on the poets' broader present with the use of the same means, and finally, the self-conscious commentary on the power of art to lastingly serve the above two functions that drew the author of *Possession* to talk of fiction, of the past and present, through the Victorian medievalist poetry of her own creation. Yet, as her novel was written at the end of the twentieth century, its voiced belief in the artistic, mythical and metaphorical mode of representation is articulated jointly with a criticism of the seemingly referential discourse of science and scholarship.

Such a criticism was a trademark of a mindset which dominated the thinking of many theoreticians and artists in the final decades of the twentieth century, and which seems to have largely influenced *Possession*. A characteristic feature of postmodern thought was its specifically subversive attitude towards the culturally established ways of representing reality, in particular, towards those wishing to give a representation of the past. This is where Byatt's novel draws on the theoretical developments of postmodernism: its mistrust of scholarly discourse mirrors the movement's misgivings about historiography. In its scepticism about historiography's complacency about the factuality of its discourse, *Possession* is particularly congruent with the well-known conclusions of the research by Roland Barthes or Hayden White, the theoreticians whose work was seminal for the postmodern attitude towards textual renditions of the past. In 1967 Barthes attacked the status of historical facts as entities possessed of extra-textual existence, and observed that "historical discourse is in its essence an ideological elaboration, or to put it more precisely, an *imaginary* elaboration" (Barthes 1998: 121; emphasis original) on these purely textual constructs, thus undermining the claim to objectivity and veracity that historiography previously made. Hayden White continued this line of argumentation with his famous work *Metahistory* published in 1973. He claimed there that, at its most fundamental level, the scientific discourse of historiography was "generally poetic and specifically linguistic in nature" (White 1973: ix), and that it was subject to emplotment into the structure of four basic plot types: romance, tragedy, comedy and satire, characterised respectively by the four tropes: metaphor, metonymy, synecdoche and irony. In this way he effectively equated history writing with fiction writing. For postmodernists, however, this did not mean a cancellation of the possibility of knowing the past; it

---

1972: 95), some critics discern in them a strong ideological, even imperial message. Matthew Reynolds claims "The Idylls share ... the assumption that ancient heroism is an ideal towards which the present should aspire; that the past is, in this sense, a mirror for the future" (Reynolds 2001: 6) while Hilary Fraser stresses the fact that the "nationalistic legends of Arthur and his Round Table were traditionally read as an allegory of the historic virtue and authority of the British monarchy" (Fraser 2001: 131).

meant that the knowledge derived from, and through, fiction had a similar status to that gained from historiographic scholarship. In 1991 Elizabeth Deeds Ermarth, reiterated this belief, claiming that "[b]y refiguring fiction-making as the primary mode of consciousness … postmodern narrative emphasizes the power of invention and fabrication to the point … of making it the foundation of discourse, the subject of the book" (Ermarth 1998: 50). This is exactly what happens in *Possession*: fiction substitutes for scholarship as the means for representing the past and becomes the main subject of the book.

Factual discourse is embodied in *Possession* not so much by the works of Maud and Roland, but rather by the fragments of scholarly work by two other academics, both of them being leading experts on their chosen poets. The fragment which the readers of *Possession* get from Leonora Stern's acclaimed study of LaMotte's work is supposed to concentrate on natural imagery in her poems. Yet, Stern's analysis is presented as strikingly flawed and biased: as a contemporary scholar, a feminist and an outspoken lesbian, she only sees what she is predetermined to look for by her post-structural and psychoanalytic training on the one hand, and by her chosen ideology on the other. In the words of Roland: "Leonora Stern makes the whole earth read as the female body – and language – all language. And all vegetation is pubic hair" (*Possession*, 253).[4] He objects to such a reading of Victorian poetry knowing that when the post-Freudian literary scholars from the end of the twentieth century "see that everything is human sexuality" (*Possession*, 253) they impose their own psychological categories onto a mindset radically different from their own. Maud has similar misgivings about the supposedly authoritative biography of Ash penned by the famous Mortimer Cropper: "like many biographies … this was as much about its author as its subject, and … [b]y extension she found it hard to like Henry Randolph Ash, in Cropper's version" (*Possession*, 246). She discerns in Cropper's writing a good deal of vainglorious and self-loving aggrandisement of his subject, which barely hides the work's author's ultimate desire for self-aggrandisement.

Obviously, not all scholars from *Possession* are driven by such motivations, but all of them, Maud and Rolland included, are presented as trapped in the omnipotent contemporary episteme: Maud observes "[i]n every age there are truths people cannot fight whether or not they want to, whether or not they go on being truths in the future. We live in the truth of what Freud discovered. Whether or not we like it … [w]e aren't really free to suppose – to imagine – he could possibly have been wrong" (*Possession*, 254). This naturally translates itself into the purportedly transparent and factual scholarly discourse produced in our epoch. Roland is aware of the limitations this imposes on the epistemological value of contemporary scholarship, which claims for itself the status of objectivity and refer-

---

4   A. S. Byatt. 1991. *Possession*. London: Vintage. All the quotations from the novel are from
    this edition. References include the title and page number(s).

entiality, when he disconsolately points out "[e]verything relates to *us* and so we're imprisoned in ourselves – we can't see *things*. And we paint everything with this [Freudian/ sexual] metaphor" (*Possession*, 254; emphasis original). Thus, the contemporary, seemingly referential discourse is inevitably dominated by metaphors which, however, having been imposed by the present, conceal rather than reveal the past and its concerns. This is why, blinded by their own expectations and mental appropriations – before she learns the whole story of the Ash-LaMotte romance even Maud hopes that her poetess does not turn out to have been emotionally and intellectually involved with a typical Victorian male she believes Ash to have been – the contemporary scholars are for a long time unable to discern in Ash's and LaMotte's works the hidden reminiscences of their romance. Despite this, however, aware of the cognitive paradigm which dominates his own way of thinking, Rolland continues to research in Ash's poetry, for "Ragnarök" is "what stayed alive, when [he]'d been taught and examined everything else" (*Possession*, 55). Thus, he reveals an intuitive grasp of the lasting viability of Ash's reflection on his own, now past, Victorian world, as well as on the general primacy of art as the means for expressing human experience in general.

"Ragnarök" is recognised in the world of *Possession* almost on a par with Tennyson's *Idylls of the King* and shares with it the position of the Victorian poem on university syllabi. It is a long work, of which the readers of the novel get little more than 120 lines. The poem presents a nineteenth-century version of the Scandinavian myth of apocalypse, the final battle between Germanic gods and giants, which results in the death of almost all gods and in the destruction of the old world, but which leads to the world's recreation in a new form. The myth was written down around 1220 in Iceland in the work known now as the *Prose (or Younger) Edda*, created on the basis of earlier, both written and oral, sources by Sturluson. His work preserves the mythical history of the world of the northern Germanic gods – from the beginning of the world, created out of a body of a giant killed by the father of gods, through the creation of man, to Ragnarök, the apocalypse in which Norse gods heroically oppose the chaotic and destabilising force of the giants in order to win a chance of rebirth for their world. We learn from Roland Michell that the views of Ash's contemporaries on this poem were split: "some saw it as a Christianising of the Norse myth and some trounced [it] as atheistic and diabolically despairing" (*Possession*, 9). Indeed, even in the short fragment given to us, the inevitability of the ultimate catastrophe underlies the narrative, despite even the fact that it is the description of the creation of the world a long time before the apocalypse begins.

This interest in a pre-Christian myth of apocalypse and rebirth stems from the Victorian confusion caused by the changes in their perception of the world and man's place in it: "such destabilisation occurred as people began to examine the implications of both evolutionary science as it unfolded from Charles Lyell to Charles Darwin, and the new historicist biblical scholarship emanating from

Germany, which exposed the unreliability of the gospel narratives" (Fraser 2001: 117). Because of the poem's mixture of Christian and pagan elements, LaMotte admits in a letter to Ash: "'Ragnarök' was the occasion of quite the worst crisis in the life of my simple religious faith ... It seemed to me you made the Holy Scripture another Wonder Tale ... It seemed ... you were saying 'Such Tales men tell and have told – they do not differ, save in emphasis'" (*Possession*, 160). To this accusation of disbelief Ash replies that at the time of the creation of the poem he rather hoped to reinforce the meaning of "Biblical Certainties ... [by] a reassertion of the Universal Truth of the living presence of All-father (under whatever Name) and of the hope of Resurrection from whatever whelming disaster in whatever form" (*Possession*, 163). Nonetheless, with the benefit of hindsight, he is aware of the relativist potential in his poetic rendering of the "pagan Day of Judgement, and ... of the mystery of the Resurrection" (*Possession*, 160). He admits that "to say that the Truth of the Tale [the Bible] is in the meaning, that the Tale but symbolises eternal verity, is one step on the road to the parity of all tales" (*Possession*, 163). Moreover, the awareness of the relativist potential of "Ragnarök" comes for Ash to coincide with the actual loss of the previously accepted "Biblical Certainties". The only certainty which the poet is left with is that of the power of poetry: "the only life I am sure of is the life of Imagination. *Whatever the absolute Truth — or Untruth ... — Poetry can make ... man live for the length of the faith you or any other choose to give to him*" (*Possession*, 168; emphasis original). Thus, having lost his faith in the old kind of myth, in religion, but finding none other that could take its place[5] he willingly resorts to literature as the sole reservoir of meaning.

Out of this confusion, out of the newly developed distrust of both myth/religion and science, Ash tries to escape by believing in the power of art and imagination. Just as the original *Edda* is interested not only in myths but also in the manner of telling them – in addition to being a prose rendering of mythological and heroic lays whose origins probably go back to the first millennium, Sturluson's work is also a treatise on Icelandic skaldic poetry – Ash's work also con-

---

5   In *Possession* Byatt presents a number of other, not medievalist, poems by Ash. In two of them, "Mummy Possessed" and "Swammerdam", the poet deals with his private and his epoch's dilemmas concerning the loss of belief in man's central position in the world created and ruled by God. "Mummy Possessed" is a dramatic monologue of a medium who instructs her young and inexperienced aid in the art of cheating her customers who look for an opportunity to communicate with the dead, while "Swammerdam", another Browningian poem, refers to Jan Swammerdam, a seventeenth century Dutch microscopist and biologist, whose scientific work was profoundly influenced by his mystical religious convictions. "Mummy Possessed" is a work about the fallacies of spiritism as a substitute for religion while "Swammerdam" allows Ash to dramatise the clash between religion and science. For information on Swammerdam, see Matthew Cobb, 2000. "Reading and writing *The Book of Nature*: Jan Swammerdam (1637–1680)", *Endeavour* 24/3: 122-128.

tains his own, and Byatt's, metanarrative commentary. The fragment of "Rag-narök" given to the reader of *Possession* tells the story of the creation of the first man and woman, but in its metaphors Ash reflects on the nature of human perception and expression. Describing the newly created world, as yet existing before man's cognition of it, he points to the mental processes which humans will subject it to, and which are in themselves metaphorical and poetic:

> ... the sand breakers fell on the new sand
> With roar unheard, and curling crest unseen
> Like nothing else, for no man-mind was there
> To name, or liken them, in any way.
> They were themselves alone, and rose and fell
> Changing-eternal, new, not knowing time
> Which their succession measures for the mind.
>
> (*Possession*, 239)

Clearly, Ash suggests that the primary mode of human perception and expression is metaphorical, and when Honir, the Norse god of wisdom and thoughtfulness, gives the senses to the two logs of wood out of which he and his divine brothers, Odin and Loki, create the first human beings, he stresses that the world is experienced and meaningful primarily as a work of art, as poetry:

> ... if these could move and feel
> And see and hear, the *lines* of leaping light
> Would *speak* to ears and eyes. The garden's fruits
>
> Would render life to life. This lovely world
> Would be both known and loved, and so would live
> An endless life in theirs, and they should hear
>
> *And speak its beauties*, then first beautiful
> When known to be so.
>
> (*Possession*, 240; emphasis mine)

From the beginning, the first humans "...more than saw and less than saw" (*Possession*, 241) the natural elements of the world, which mirrors the claim made by Rolland that men cannot "see *things*" (*Possession*, 253; emphasis original), as well as comments on our inability to perceive and express either uncomplicated physical objects or complex social, ideological or artistic realities as simply themselves. Consequently, the very first action of the first humans created at the beginning of Ash's "Ragnarök" – their walk along the newly created, as yet "printless" beach – is compared to writing, to the creation of poetry, which becomes the first, that is basic and primary, means of expression:

> Then Ask [the first man] stepped forward on the printless shore
> And touched the woman's hand, who clasped fast his.
> Speechless they waked away along the line
> Of the sea's roaring, in their listening ears.
> Behind them, first along the level sand
> *A line of darkening prints*, filling with salt,
> *First traces in the world*, of life and time
> *And love, and mortal hope, and vanishing.*
>
> (*Possession*, 242; emphasis mine)

Ash's comments on poetry and imagination – both the explicit and the metanarrative ones – may be treated as Byatt's artistic manifesto in *Possession*. Numerous elements of the entire narrative and stylistic construction of the novel serve her to clash legend and literature with the supposedly factual discourse. The most important of these is the creation and slow unravelling of the two entwined stories which reflect one another in terms of both structure and narrative style, but which counter each other in terms of the mode of representation they embrace. Structure-wise, the romance between Ash and LaMotte mirrors that between Roland and Maud. Similarly, the two parts of the plot resemble each other in terms of style, the contemporary part of the novel is presented realistically while the Victorian one almost hyperrealistically, through the textual simulacra of the past. However, when it comes to the mode of representation significant for the Victorian and contemporary fragments, the medievalist, metaphorical Victorian poetry is juxtaposed with contemporary scholarship. Moreover, this Victorian, metaphorical discourse proves to be more informative than the seemingly factual work of the literary scholars from the twentieth century. Thus, Byatt reiterates her continuing belief in the power fiction for representing the past. Her ultimate expression of this power in *Possession* is the way she constructs the entire novel around the rewritten, medieval Breton legend of fairy Melusine.

The source of LaMotte's poem is also a medieval rendering of the folk tale of Melusine, the wife of a French aristocrat and the progenitor of his entire lineage, who, because of a curse, turns every Saturday into a half-woman-half-serpent. The author of the earliest extant version was a French *trouvère*, Jean d'Arras, who, in the second half of the fourteenth century, wrote his romance, *Roman de Mélusine*, as a part of his history of the Lusignan family from the French province of Poitou. The story of Melusine has all the elements, save one, of the tales belonging to the class of supernatural spouses: the heroes/heroines of this group of legends enter relationships with mortals setting up taboos which must not be violated, and Melusine marries Raimondin Lustignan on condition that she is always allowed to spend Saturdays entirely on her own. Typically, the relationships are broken due to the mortals' disobeying of the ban and Raimondin breaks the condition secretly observing his wife, half-woman-half-serpent, in a bath. Usually the breach of the taboo is followed by a separation and suffering, but final reunification of the lovers (Wicher 2003: 89). Reunification is what is missing in the tale of Melusine: on finding out that her husband broke the ban, she turns into a winged serpent or dragon and disappears, reappearing later only to foreshadow the deaths of the members of Lusignan family. Interestingly, according to Wicher, the lack of a happy ending is a typical feature of local legends or family sagas, such as the legend of Melusine: "[w]hat they have in common is precisely the lack of belief in the possibility of establishing bridges between this world and the other [supernatural] one. Hence the attempts to establish a romantic relationship with a fairy creature must be accompanied, in them, by death of disaster, and their atmosphere is gloomy enough" (Wicher 2004: 139).

In order to show how closely the fabulous literature, art and fiction are connected to reality Byatt constructs her novel in such a manner that the plot of the medieval legend is re-enacted within each of all the three – mythical, Victorian, and contemporary – layers of the plot of *Possession*. This is the ultimate expression of Byatt's attitude towards fiction. LaMotte may obviously have been aware of certain similarities between herself and the heroine of her chosen myth, yet it is Byatt who shapes her characters, the Victorian poetess and Maud Bailey, as well as their stories, in such a way as to make them congruous with the character and the story of Melusine. All three heroines share the features of a typical supernatural wife: they are enchanted into a seclusion and must be disenchanted from it by a relationship with a man. They also share a condition of duality: in Melusine it is the hybrid body of a half-fish-half-woman, in LaMotte it may be her half-English-half-Breton origin, in Maud, it is her unwillingness to uncover her hair, which may be connected with Melusine's body half submerged in water when her husband observes her in the bath (Wicher 2003: 94). The duality is further enhanced by the atmosphere of lesbianism which hangs about all three heroines. Moreover, all the three stories involve a meeting or meetings in a geographically remote place, which, according to Wicher (2004: 140) is a common element of the supernatural spouses type of folk tale. The central event in the story of Melusine, the catastrophic breach of the relationship between the supernatural being and the mortal caused by a violation of a taboo, is, however, reflected only in the Victorian plot. Once LaMotte and Ash's relationship crosses the barrier of his marital unfaithfulness and her loss of virginity, they must be separated, and the effect of their trespassing, the child who is to become Maud's ancestor, becomes to LaMotte a similar cause of grief and despair as her own lost children to Melusine. Similarly, after they are forced to leave their relationships both Melusine and LaMotte turn into voices: the former into the cry which foretells the death of members of the Lustignian family, the latter into her poems. The fact that the contemporary part of the novel evidently lacks these elements, might be somewhat pessimistically accounted for by the observation that Maud and Roland are at the end of the novel only at a preliminary stage of their relationship, and what fate has in store for them is beyond the scope of the novel.[6] Nonetheless, despite these missing elements in the contemporary part of *Possession*, it seems that on all the levels of the novel the same story is told. Within the novel, every layer of fiction prefigures the reality of those who read it. Outside the novel, Byatt also tries to convince her readers of the validity and relevance of fiction when her realistic novel turns into a romance, a romance derived from a Breton local legend or tale (German – *die Sage*, Polish – *podanie*) in which a fairy marries a mortal (Wicher 2003: 89).

Casting the French medieval romance in her own Victorian mode, LaMotte seeks to manifest her private experience as well as to generalise it into that of an independently-minded woman of her times, or, as the contemporary feminist critics from Byatt's novel would have it, of an independently-minded woman of any times. The legendary Melusine serves her to present a different kind of truth than that of Ash's religious and scientific considerations, the truth of her private experience, of her and Ash's romance, and of an unhappy and doomed motherhood, of which the contemporary scholars from the novel will try to learn from the poem. LaMotte and her fairy share common experience, the mythical Melusine is a mother who had to leave her children, like the poetess had to give away her and Ash's illegitimate child. Melusine is a woman alien to the world which surrounds her, like LaMotte, being an independent female artist is an alien to the Victorian reality in which she moves. In one crucial respect, however, "The Fairy Melusina" is similar to "Ragnarök": it also stresses the relevance of fiction as the expression of real, lived experience: writing of her poem is for LaMotte a veritable quest of self discovery and transcendence of traumatic personal past:

> And what was she, the Fairy Melusine?
> Were these her kin, Echidna's gruesome brood,
> Scaly devourers, or were those her kind
> More kind, those rapid wanderers of the dark
> Who in dreamlight, or twilight, or no light
> Are lovely Mysteries and promise gifts –
> Whiteladies, teasing dryads, shape changers –
> Like smiling clouds, or sparkling threads of streams
> Bright monsters of the sea and of the sky
> Who answer longing and who threaten not
> But vanish in the light of rational day
> Doomed by their own desire for human souls,
> For settled hearths, and fixed human homes.

---

6   The ambiguity remains as the final sentence of Maud and Roland's lovemaking scene is "In the morning the whole world had a strange new smell ... it was the smell of death and destruction, and it smelled fresh and lively and hopeful" (*Possession*, 507). As during the lovemaking Roland hears a distant cry of pleasure and triumph it may also suggest that in them, finally, the supernatural and mortal lovers will be reconciled.

...
Help me Mnemosyne ...
...
... O thou , the source of speech
Give me wise utterance and save conduct
From hearthside storytelling into dark
Of outer air, and back again to sleep,
In Christian comfort, in a decent bed.

(Possession, 292-293)

Here, LaMotte's Victorian belief in the connection between the fictional and the actual worlds is at its most conspicuous. LaMotte the author becomes Melusine herself. Her poetry becomes to her not only an expression of her actual experience but an attempt at its mastery, a mastery which could bring her back her lost belief in the old myth – "Christian comfort" of religion. Similarly, the discovery, through art and through poetry, of the truth of her own descent as well as of the truth of the passionate but transgressive romance of her chosen poetess becomes for Maud, the Melusine from the contemporary part of Possession, a mastery of her own experience. Importantly, all of this is done not through scholarship, but through fiction, fiction modelled on a medieval myth.

A. S. Byatt's *Possession* is a novel which thematizes the opposition between fact and fiction in scholarly and literary representations of the past. By creating a double narrative frame in which the characters from the past and from the present communicate with each other through the Victorian, metaphorical, non-referential, medievalist poetry on the one hand and through the contemporary, purportedly factual scholarly analyses on the other, and in which the stories of both groups are prefigured by a medieval legend, the novelist undermines the claims denying literary discourse any significance with regards to the possibility of expressing the past. Byatt uses Victorian medievalism, which in *Possession* epitomises art and literature in general, and her fictional contemporary critic's encounters with it in order to articulate her own belief, and to postulate a renewal of general belief, in the capacity of fiction for expressing both individual experience and the spirit of times, Victorian or contemporary. She makes the rewritten medieval legend as informative as contemporary scholarship, thus claiming that fictional and factual discourse are ultimately possessed of a similar epistemological status. Apart from this, she also rewrites Victorian medievalism simply to tell a pleasant story, a fairy tale, a romance with a gripping detective plot. Even if the enjoyment of her reader is immaterial in the debate about the ontological and epistemological status of fiction, for Byatt it still attests to the importance of fiction and literary discourse in general, as the validity of literature is what the novelist ultimately champions in *Possession*.

References

Alban, Gillian, M. E.
    2003   *Melusine the serpent goddess in A.S. Byatt's Possession and in mythology*. Oxford: Lexington Books.
Barthes, Roland
    1998   "The discourse of history", in: Keith Jenkins (ed.), 120-123.
Bradbury, Malcolm – David Palmer (eds.)
    1972   *Victorian poetry*. (Stratford-Upon-Avon Studies 15). London: Edward Arnold Ltd.
Bristow, Joseph (ed.)
    2000   *The Cambridge companion to Victorian poetry*. Cambridge: Cambridge University Press.
Byatt, A. S.
    1991   *Possession*. London: Vintage.
    1993   *Passions of the mind: Selected writings*. London: Vintage International.
    2001   *On histories and stories. Selected essays*. London: Vintage.
Cobb, Matthew
    2000   "Reading and writing The Book of Nature: Jan Swammerdam (1637–1680)", *Endeavour* 24/3: 122-128.
Ermarth, Elizabeth Deeds
    1998   "Why text?", in: Keith Jenkins (ed.), 47-64.
Fraser, Hillary
    2000   "Victorian poetry and historicism", in: Joseph Bristow (ed.), 114-136.
Gent, Margaret
    1972   "'To flinch from modern varnish': The appeal of the past to the Victorian Imagination", in: Malcolm Bradbury – David Palmer (eds.), 11-36.
Hunt, John Dixon
    1972   "The poetry of distance: Tennyson's *Idylls of the king*", in: Malcolm Bradbury – David Palmer (eds.), 89-122.
Jenkins, Keith
    1998   *The postmodern history reader*. London: Routledge.
Jump, John. D. (ed.)
    1982   *Tennyson. The critical heritage*. London: Routledge & Kegan Paul.
Kellog, Robert
    2001   "Introduction", in: Jane Smiley – Robert Kellog (eds.), xv-liv.
Krygier, Marcin – Liliana Sikorska (eds.)
    2004   *For the loue of Inglis lede*. Frankfurt am Main: Peter Lang.
Leglu, Catherine
    2005   "Nourishing lineage in the earliest French versions of the Roman de Melusine", *Medium Aevum* 2005, 1: [unpaged] (retrieved from Accessmylibrary database) (date of access 21st Nov 2006).
Michałowska, Teresa (ed.)
    2003   *Mediewistyka literacka w Polsce* [Literary medieval studies in Poland]. Warszawa: Wydawnictwo IBL.

Pins, Cyril de
    2006   The Fantastical Theology of Snorri Sturluson: A Reading of the Prologue of *Snorra Edda*. (Paper presented at the 13th International Saga Conference, Durham and York, 6th-12th August, 2006) (http://www.dur.ac.uk /medieval.www/sagaconf/sagapps.htm) (date of access 11th Jan 2007).

Reynolds, Matthew
    2001   *The realms of the verse. English poetry in a time of nation-building*. Oxford: Oxford University Press.

Richards, Bernard
    1988   *English poetry of the Victorian Period 1830-1890*. London: Longman.

Smiley, Jane – Robert Kellog (eds.)
    2001   *The sagas of Icelanders. A selection*. London: Viking Penguin.

White, Hayden
    1973   Metahistory. *The historical imagination in nineteenth-century Europe*. Baltimore – London: The John Hopkins University Press.

Wicher, Andrzej
    2003   "Wcielenia Meluzyny w literaturze średniowiecznej Anglii" [The incarnations of Melusine in the literature of medieval England], in: Teresa Michałowska (ed.), 88-100.
    2004   "The Breton lay and the tale of magic: A preliminary attempt at arriving at the internal unity and ideology of selected Breton lays", in: Marcin Krygier – Liliana Sikorska (eds.), 133-147.

The alchemy of imagination[1]

Lindsay Clarke

Generally speaking, we English are a sceptical lot, particularly the intellectuals among us, so the words "alchemy" and "alchemical" are rarely used in serious discourse these days except with metaphorical force. This isn't greatly surprising for even in the work of Isaac Newton and Robert Boyle, two of alchemy's most celebrated investigators, we can already see the tide of energy shifting away from the study of matter in the sacred tradition of the medieval world-view towards the new "sceptical chemistry" and the development of the scientific method of replicable experiment. The evolution of Enlightenment thinking was entirely opposed in spirit to the hermetic nature of alchemical assumptions, vocabulary and imagery, and if that tradition still holds sway in academic circles, it's not only among the strict minds of the scientific community.

Scholars of English literature, for instance, are comfortable enough with the satirical view of alchemy evinced in Chaucer's *Canon's Yeoman's Tale* - which may have furnished us with our derogatory term "crackpot" – as they are with the corrupt version of the alchemical art humorously portrayed in Ben Jonson's play *The Alchemist*. Many of them also delight in the use of alchemical imagery as the stuff of poetic conceits in the verses of John Donne and the Metaphysical Poets. But they tend to be less happy with the awkward fact that the interest shown in alchemical modes of thought by such undoubtedly great twentieth-century poets as W.B. Yeats and Ted Hughes was, for them, a matter of rather more than just literary importance. Indeed it seems to have been integral to their way of seeing, feeling, interpreting and re-creating their vision of how things are.

Now it's possible of course, to dismiss such apparent regression into a medieval way of thinking as a quaint eccentricity, a quirk of their creative imaginations – odd, yes, but forgivable as a perhaps necessary stratagem for the generation of new poetic energy. But I doubt that either poet would have been content with such a reductive view of what was, for them, a dynamic aspect of their personal experience and the very ground of the world-view out of which they wrote.

Nor is it just our poets who present such a problem. Novelists like James Joyce, Malcolm Lowry, John Cowper Powys, Patrick White and Doris Lessing, have all drawn deeply on hermetic modes of thought in order to articulate in fiction their experience of the world. In this respect they lie closer to the European tradition of hermetic writing achieved by such major figures as Wolfram von Eschenbach, Novalis, Goethe, Baudelaire, Rimbaud, Thomas Mann and Hermann

---

1   This paper is a transcript of Lindsay Clarke's lecture given at the Literature In English Symposium (LIES) held at Adam Mickiewicz University in Poznań on 22nd April, 2007.

Hesse than to the drier vision of sceptical academics. Not that we should glibly dismiss such scepticism, for even C.G. Jung himself, who did more than anyone to restore the dignity of alchemical enquiry, came away from his first encounter with the weird cavalcade of green lions, hermaphrodites and self-consuming serpents depicted in alchemical texts with the opinion that they were "something off the beaten track and rather silly". Only later, motivated by a powerful dream, did he return to them in a more committed spirit and begin to realize that the serious alchemists were not only his precursors in the evolution of psychology as a science of the soul but were also engaged in an imaginative enterprise towards the resacralization of what the orthodox Christianity of their time regarded as the fallen state of the material world.

It's part of Jung's heritage that the culture of the late twentieth century saw a revival of serious interest in the art of alchemy, and if, as I believe, such a development represents more than a recoil into quasi-medieval credulity, it seems that only a significant confluence of a slowly turning tide of cultural transition with the demands of sometimes urgent individual experience might lie behind it. Such was certainly the case with the growth of my own interest in alchemy, so I hope you will come to understand my reasons if I speak to my theme in personal terms before attempting a more generalized consideration of what its implications may be for a wider evolution of consciousness in our time.

Around twenty years ago my first novel was accepted for publication. Telling the story of a white man's ordeal of initiation through an encounter with a witch in West Africa, it had originally been a dense text more than 500 pages long entitled *Nigredo* after that arduous transitional phase of the alchemical opus in which darkness prevails and everything threatens to go wrong. But earlier disappointing responses from publishers had persuaded me to strip the novel down to half its length and change the title to *Sunday Whiteman*. In that form it proved acceptable to the editors at Jonathan Cape; but the book still had the look about it of the only egg this chicken might lay, so before the contract was signed I was asked whether I had anything else in progress. As it happened, I did have a couple of drafts of stories which had both got stuck at a relatively early stage. Conceived under the heavy influence of John Fowles' powerful novel *The Magus,* one of them told of an initiatory encounter between a young poet and an old poet and was a loose reworking of the medieval story of *Sir Gawain and the Green Knight.* The other idea I had begun to sketch out in the form of a novella based on the true story of the nineteenth-century alchemist Thomas South who insisted that his daughter Mary Anne burn all the copies of her own remarkable book *A Suggestive Enquiry Into The Hermetic Mystery* because, according to him, her text had revealed too much of the alchemical secret.

I was puzzling over which of these two still undeveloped ideas to submit when it occurred to me that the film of John Fowles' novel *The French Lieutenant's Woman* had done an interesting job of combining one story set in the nineteenth century with another set in the twentieth. Could I do something similar? So I re-wrote the openings slightly, sandwiched the start of the nineteenth-century tale between the opening two chapters of the twentieth, made up a list of chapter headings to give the impression that I knew exactly where this interwoven narrative device was taking me, and submitted it to Cape. The result excited them more than the first novel had done and I was committed to spending the next three years inside a bewildering hermetic labyrinth trying to find the way out. The book eventually became *The Chymical Wedding* which is the reason I was invited here today.

Now I have three reasons for sharing this somewhat disgraceful, confessional anecdote with you. Firstly – and I shall have more to say about this later – because the initially arbitrary conjunction of two apparently unrelated stories illustrates a principal theme of this talk – that something new can get made for life through the difficult process of the *mysterium coniunctionis* - the reconciliation of opposing forces.

Secondly, because it gives some sort of hint that one cannot begin to write imaginatively *about* alchemy without the writing itself becoming a work *of* alchemy. And even though I'm a novelist, not a practising alchemist, the alchemical theme on which I had chosen to write put me through a sometimes gruelling process of personal transformation before the work itself could be achieved. The end result may not have been pure gold but the struggle did give me some experience of what I'm trying to talk about. (I should perhaps add as a footnote – and as a caveat – that a talk about alchemy, if it is to be true to its theme, may also have something of the character of an alchemical treatise about it, proceeding not by the usual means of conceptual logic but through a sequence of images designed to elicit responses at levels deeper than that of the managerial intellect.) Lastly, I share the anecdote with you because it may give you an indication of the degree to which alchemy had begun to play an active part in the evolution of my personal consciousness long before I came to write the novel. But to say more about that I will have to speak more personally still.

Almost half a century ago I entered King's College, Cambridge as a woolly-minded, working class nature-mystic yearning to be a writer. I came away both with the conviction that there was not much hope of that, and with an alternative commitment to the tradition of sceptical humanist thought, which took me as a teacher to newly independent Ghana; then on, out of a profound conviction of the urgent need for social change, into work in Further Education with students on release from industry and commerce. Employing the heavily rational system of values I had acquired at Cambridge, I became a member of that gallant band of liberal minded intellectuals – a sort of unofficial lay clerisy – who believed they were transforming society by spreading the word of reason across the land.

At that time I became pretty good at convincing both myself and others that there was no meaning to life other than that imposed on it by the largely masculine exercise of human reason. And for a time I thought it was working. Suffice it to say that under a growing awareness of the contradictions in my work, the pressures of early marriage and fatherhood, and an abiding sense of personal failure, I was retreating into an ever falser, more withdrawn condition, when, aged 30, my embattled ego suffered the massive insult of discovering that my wife had responded to a larger feeling for life and my marriage was over. As my brittle world collapsed, I too went through a brief but intense episode of breakdown. It lasted for two days and three sleepless nights, during which time I was possessed by a frenzy of violent emotions such as no reasonable man likes to own as his. Long exiled feelings flooded back with a vengeance, and – beyond whatever words were spoken – I felt to be up against a cold, lunar principle, impervious to all but its own laws, against which my proprietorial ego raged in vain. At that point, while still awake, I dropped into the unconscious – or to use the kind of metaphor with which the medieval writers I had studied at Cambridge would have been comfortable, I made a journey into the otherworld. For the mythical fact is that, while still dimly aware of my external circumstances, I was elsewhere, in the interior, traversing an arduous terrain, and encountering some fearsome figures on the way. There are passages in my novels where I've tried to dramatize through fictional events something of the quality of that journey; but some truths are less credible than fiction and are largely unpublishable. Let me just say that, in exhausted acceptance of a kind of defeat, I eventually fell asleep, and when I woke up I found that the world had changed. It was as if frequencies of intelligence I had jammed for years were now beaming freely around me. I woke to the exhilarating sense that the unfolding flow of life was not only larger but richer in meaning and interest than my tightly managed model of it had been, and I felt an almost virgin taste for it. But the change was in me, of course, and it turned out that the alteration was both radical and lasting. Something had died, and with my head temporarily lopped off I was learning how to think with the heart. My collapsed ego would build back quickly enough, but the terms on which I lived my life had been irrevocably altered.

Out of the need to recognize more of the nature of that transforming journey for myself, and in the hope that it might help others to similar recognitions of their own, I felt I had to find both a context for it and a language. And through that search I eventually found my way into the rich store of emblems through which alchemy speaks of transformation. For guidance there I turned principally to Jung – not in therapy or analysis, just a process of free-ranging reading, following my nose. And, of course, like all who try to approach alchemical material through the analytic intellect, I quickly found myself confused by the twists and turns of that slippery fellow Mercurius Duplex, who dissolves into thin air just when you think you are about to pin him down. But what gradually emerged into focus for me was an enlarging sense of the beauty and subtlety of the alchemical vision and the degree to which it offered a vocabulary of images that confirmed the value of the more fugitive and elusive aspects of my recent experience and enabled me to relate to it in fuller recognition and with greater imaginative energy.

Much later I tried to convey something of the urgent excitement of that discovery in a longish speech I gave to the old poet Edward Nesbit in my novel *The Chymical Wedding*. Trying to persuade his sceptical young friend Alex Darken of the contemporary relevance of alchemy, Edward says:

> Materialism leaves us trapped in a world that won't hold together. It's centrifugal. It splits at every turn into the Ten Thousand Things each neatly labeled with a PhD thesis. In the meantime we become more and more obsessed with what we mistake for our real needs, hopes, fears, and more and more estranged from our birthright membership of a coherent universe... We can't live that way – not for much longer. And the world can't live with us – not like this. We have to change. We have to find a vision that will help us to change – that will restore dignity and meaning by altering our relationship to the delicate web that supports our life. Everyone knows it deep down; but we're lost, confused, complicit in our own bad dream. So how to realize a whole vision of life? Not some self-sealing intellectual construct; no shabby patchwork compromise, but a regenerative, transcendent change. One that reconciles matter with spirit, heart with mind, the female in us and the male, the darkness and the light. That was the problem which engaged the spiritual intellect of the true alchemist. That was the Elixir, the Stone, the Gold. They are all symbols for what cannot be said – only experienced. The alchemists, he declares, were part of a tradition that has always tried to see life whole, however painful the process of holding its contradictions together. They knew that matter and spirit are indivisible – that everything is translucent, permeable, infinite in its marvelous covenant of meaning.
>
> (*Chymical Wedding*, 179-180)

And he ends with the declaration that

> ... the Hermetic tradition has always offered a vision whereby men and women might recover their experience in its wholeness. It offers a technique for achieving that vision – and we need to know how to know it now, for that is how things deeply are, and not only human life depends on it.
>
> (*Chymical Wedding*, 179-180)

Now the language in which the old poet expresses himself may be a touch hectoring and over-dramatic but I believe that his heart is in the right place and there's a good deal of truth in what he has to say. So what were the main themes that emerged from my own investigations into alchemy at that time?

Firstly, what I drew from them was a vigorous confirmation of the visionary insight that had been borne in upon me immediately after my breakdown when I walked out into the quiet water-meadows of a sunlit morning to be met by a profound sense of the unitary nature of all being. The world felt one, singular and whole, and I was no longer apart *from* it but a part *of* it, my own soul resonating, as it had not done since I was a child, in answer to the living soul of the world around me. Everything else would follow from that experience, and perhaps nowhere outside the lines of the most sublime poetry was its unitary nature expressed more clearly than in the magisterial declarations of that seminal alchemical text, the Emerald Tablet of Hermes Trismegistus: "What is below is like what is above, and what is above is like what is below, for the performing of the marvels of the one thing".

Now as I have already suggested, Mercurius Duplex is the presiding spirit of the alchemical vision – an elusive figure embodying a complex of opposites, forever unchanging yet never quite the same, as unstable as quicksilver and impossible to pin down. So there could be nothing fixed and permanent about that insight into the unitary nature of being except the degree to which it had altered forever my way of perceiving things. Otherwise it kept, and still keeps, slipping back and forth across the boundary between consciousness and unconsciousness. And with this came the understanding that, though all things are interrelated through the great chain of being – "the delicate web that supports our life" – various phenomena are in quite different states of evolution towards consciousness.

Furthermore the insights of the alchemists suggested that all things are an interfusion of matter and spirit, each seeking to realize and celebrate its part in the union with the whole. And because we too are an integral part of that seamless process, we do to ourselves what we do to the world that appears to be outside us, and what we do to the world we are also doing to ourselves. Thus our inward condition will inescapably project itself onto our work with the world, and if there's an unholy mess out there, it mirrors the state of confusion inside us.

Yet the aspirations of the alchemists also seemed to demonstrate that by a proper use of the creative imagination we can raise the value of both inward and outward experience through a disciplined process of necessary change. But such work could only be done successfully, they insisted, by entering into right relations with the right material at the right time.

The various alchemical texts all agree that the one thing required to begin the work is the *Prima Materia;* they are, however, confusingly diverse in their assertions about just what that mysterious first matter is, even though some of them, like the *Gloria Mundi* of 1526, confidently assert that it is to be found everywhere and is therefore despised by all, though next to the human soul it is the most precious thing on earth. And the material was given so many disparate names – mercury, sulphur, salt, lead, earth, water, fire, dew, virgin, dragon etc. – that the alchemists were clearly speaking in symbolic terms rather than of some literal substance. By the same token, the secret fire that was needed for performing the alchemical processes – "a fire that does not burn" and which had to be extracted from the first matter and yet was also, and at the same time, the means of its extraction – was clearly not what we usually understand by the term.

Now I confess to having found the enigmatic nature of the alchemical texts as perplexing as the next man; and yet their language and emblems worked, and still work, a curiously exciting enchantment over my imagination, as though, like the often elusive images of dreams, they speak to something inside me deeper than the reach of the analytic intellect. And if their language is paradoxical it's because it strives to hold together apparently contrary forces, and that creative tension, it seems to me, goes to the very heart of the alchemical enterprise.

In describing the method of alchemical procedure, one formula tends to recur throughout the texts: *SOLVE ET COAGULA*, which in synoptic form instructs the would-be adept that the *prima materia* must first be dissolved into its constituent elements before it can be brought together again into a unified whole. Another version of this formula tells the alchemist "to make the fixed volatile and the volatile fixed". In chemical terms, this apparently refers to the process of reflux distillation by which liquid is heated until it evaporates into a gas which rises, cools and condenses into a liquid which is then fed back through the retort into the original liquid with transforming effect. If we translate this into psychological terms, it refers to the process by which consciousness arises out of the darkness of the unconscious, illuminating the conscious ego with insights that then allow for a more complete discrimination of unconscious contents into still larger consciousness. For the alchemists the two processes – one external and material, the other internal and spiritual - were identical; for the outer transformation could not happen without the same process working inwardly, thus affirming the essential unity of matter and spirit.

But as anyone who has seriously engaged with these processes will confirm, the effort required is long, arduous and at times extremely painful; for when one begins to dissolve a complex situation into its constituent parts by bringing them into the light of consciousness, one soon discovers that some of those elements are in a state of profound contradictory tension with one another; and to such a volatile degree that they continuously threaten to tear apart – or, in alchemical terms, to burst the crucible in which those tensions are held together.

A simple analogy might make the process clearer. A man and woman fall hopelessly in love in what they take for a blissful state of union which leads them into marriage. After a time uncomfortable aspects of their relationship of which they had previously been unaware begin to oppress them. Conflicts emerge and develop. When efforts to resolve those conflicts prove ever more difficult, the situation deteriorates until divorce begins to seem a desirable option. Only if a massive effort of honest self-disclosure along with mutual recognition and acceptance is undertaken and sustained, can true reconciliation and a new, more conscious union be achieved. It also requires a withdrawal of projections and a measure of self-sacrifice amounting at times to a kind of ego-death on both sides, and the difficulty of that process is evidenced by the divorce statistics of a world that remains largely uneducated in such transformational dynamics.

When the alchemists sought to speak of such matters as they saw them at work both in their alembics and in their own souls, they did so in archetypal terms, illustrating their procedures through the changing nature of the relationship between a King and Queen, for example, or of Sol and Luna, Sun and Moon, which represent the often combative relationship between the masculine and feminine principles, both inwardly and outwardly. Thus a marvellous illustration to the sixteenth century text called *Aurora Consurgens* depicts figures of the Sun and Moon jousting with one another, he armoured and riding a lion, she naked on a gryphon's back. Each seeks to unseat the other with a lance yet both are protected by shields, and the subtlety of the illustration consists of the fact that the Sun carries the emblem of the Moon on his shield, while the Moon is protected by the emblem of the Sun on hers.

The picture illustrates the first stage of the alchemical work in which the King and Queen, Sol and Luna, are in a volatile state of opposition with one another, a conflict which leads through the course of many distillatory circulations to a state of death and putrefaction – "a black blacker than black" known as the *Nigredo* - in which the opposed forces are dissolved so that each loses their separate identity. Out of that blackness a scintilla of white light eventually appears, heralding the cleansing stage known as the *Albedo*, through which, if the tension of contrary forces has been properly sustained, is eventually achieved the Royal Marriage of the *Rubedo* – the *Mysterium Coniunctionis,* in which all the contraries are reconciled and an enlarged sense of life, a newly unified state of consciousness – the Gold, the Elixir, the Philosopher's Stone itself - mysteriously arises.

These were the themes and processes I tried to explore in my novel *The Chymical Wedding,* which is, I suppose, a kind of alchemical text for our time presented as fiction. Its title, borrowed from a celebrated seventeenth-century text, is itself another emblem for the reconciliation of the opposites, and by structuring the book around two initially disparate stories set in different time frames but on a collision course, I sought to dramatize the process within the dual form of the narrative itself. The plain fact that I was largely unconscious of this aim when I first conceived the idea of the novel is an indication of the degree to which the three years of often bewildering work on the project mirrored my own struggle through into a larger degree of consciousness.

Now it's all very well for me to speak of the self-imposed tribulations of a novelist in this regard but I'm sure that among many of you the question will already have arisen as to whether the true alchemists were speaking in symbolic terms of mystical techniques for the raising of consciousness when they wrote of these things, or whether they were in fact offering a coded account of procedures by which base metal could indeed be transmuted into gold. As I said earlier, I'm not a practising alchemist so I'm not qualified to answer the question with any authority, but I would suggest that the divisive either/or terms in which it is posed may be missing the point, for it's quite possible that they were doing both.

As a pioneer of depth psychology, Jung tended to view the hermetic texts in psychological terms, interpreting the events that the alchemists observed in their alembics as projections of the unconscious contents of their minds. But in paragraph 394 of his great work *Psychology and Alchemy* he records how Martin Ruland's "astounding definition" of the imagination as "the star in man, the celestial or supercelestial body" suggested other possibilities. Imagination, he declared, "is perhaps the most important key to the understanding of the Opus", for it is "a physical activity that can be fitted into the cycle of material changes that brought these about and is brought about by them in its turn. In this way the alchemist related himself not only to the unconscious but directly to the very substance which he hoped to transform through the power of imagination".[2]

Thus, the alchemist is operating simultaneously in the psychic and the physical realms and changes are being brought about in both - an interaction of the observer and the observed which seems to prefigure in intriguing ways the relatively recent discovery of quantum physics that the behaviour of matter at molecular levels is conditioned by the approach of the scientist observing it.

What Jung was attempting to articulate here may not be easy to grasp but it lies, I would suggest, at the heart not just of alchemy but of all genuinely creative imaginative activity. And part of the difficulty we have in grasping it arises from the fact that our culture tends to reinforce only a limited understanding of the nature of the imagination. There is a tendency, when we try to grasp the imagination simply by thinking conceptually about it, to reduce it to a description of its various functions. We define it, for example, as the capacity to visualize things which are not actually present to our outward senses, so that I have only to say the word "elephant" and suddenly a large animal is present to your inner eye which was not there a moment ago. Or we can consider the way the imagination is able to transfigure things into forms other than those by which they usually present themselves to the senses. Magritte's painting of a pipe which insists that it is not a pipe makes us startlingly aware of this function. Or we might consider the metaphorical way in which the poetic imagination uses images drawn from one set of things to make statements about another, or to present them in an illuminating new perspective. Thus, an ordinary pair of boots or a stick-back chair remains just that until Van Gogh comes along with his oil paints and imagination and transforms these everyday objects into something visionary.

We might also consider the relationship of imagination to time. Doesn't imagination play such a large part in remembering what has happened in the past, for example, that one might wonder whether memory itself is an act of imagination? Certainly it's through the imagination that we try to envisage what will happen in the future; and at times it can turn against us by conceiving of fearsome things which might happen but probably won't, or of things which don't exist at

---

2   Ruland's text to which Jung refers is *Lexicon Alchemiae* published in Frankfurt in 1612.

all. For this, among other more sceptical reasons, Francis Bacon once declared that the imagination should be tied down with weights not given wing.

Such a pragmatic view seems to prevail in the general assumptions of a system of education where imagination is viewed only as a more or less useful adjunct to other more reliable and rationally accountable methods of intellectual procedure. But there is another, larger way of thinking about the imagination which certainly prevailed among the alchemists and has always been alive among the poets. For them, reality was not something fixed and impermeable, simply *there*, but a product of our vision and therefore porous to the transforming power of the imagination. Wasn't it something along these lines that Coleridge was thinking and feeling when he wrote in his *Biographia Literaria* that "the imagination is the prime agent of human perception?" (Coleridge 1997: 167). Wasn't William Blake rejoicing in this life-creating, world-endowing aspect of the imagination when he declared that "To Me This World is all One continued Vision of Fancy or Imagination?" (Blake 1971: 793). But this view of the imagination is much older than the romantic poets and philosophers, and when Ruland the Lexicographer defined imagination as the star in man he was affirming a creative link between human nature and the nature of the cosmos that goes back through the medieval world-view, to the Gnostics, to the mythopaeic imagination of the ancient world, and perhaps further to the primordial animistic vision of our inalienable involvement in the living intelligence of the universe.

It will already be clear that my own view of the imagination is allied to this ancient tradition. I regard the imagination as the means by which, with more or less psychic energy, we shape our vision of the world and our place within it, and also as the primary means by which we can transform it. But what matters, of course, is the degree to which we are conscious of what we are doing.

When I work with students in my writing classes I encourage them not only to *think* of the imagination this way but to try, through a kind of thought-experiment, actually to imagine the imagination. The first image I ask them to visualize is that of icon Earth, the planet's blue swirl of seas and continents and clouds as it was first seen from space by the astronauts. Then I ask them to drain it of colour until all that remains is a circle which represents the outside world – everything that is not them. For the next image I ask them to place a dot beside that circle – a dot which is them, alone and of minimal significance against all that vastness. Then I ask them to let that dot grow and open until it forms another circle beside the first and the same size as it. This represents their inner world, all that is only them – their thoughts, feelings, hopes, dreams, fears and anxieties, the entire realm of their inward experience. Lastly, I ask them to move both circles so that they overlap, with the circumference of each passing through the centre of the other.

You may recognize this last image as a Venn Diagram, but it is a very ancient symbol indeed, originally illustrating the meeting of Heaven and Earth through which life gets made. For this reason it forms the ground plan of many sacred sites, and was co-opted by Christianity as the Vesica Piscis, the Fish's Belly, as an emblem of Christ as the intersection of Heaven and Earth, Eternity and Time. But I ask my students to concentrate on the almond-shaped area of overlap between the two circles as the place where they actually live – that region where their inner world is in a permanent state of negotiation with all the intelligence that is reaching them from the outside world about what is real and true. That area of overlap is called the mandorla (from the Italian word for almond) though to the ancient Egyptians it was known as the hieroglyph *Ru,* which signified the female organ of generation and, by extension, a sacred portal through which new life enters. I think of it as the house of the imagination, as an image of the place where, all the time, our inner world merges with the outer world to shape the experience from which each of us builds our personal myth. For we don't just live in the public world around us, nor only in the private world within: we live in the mandorla where those two worlds meet and negotiate about reality with one another as a more or less vigorous exercise of the imagination. It's our gateway to meaning, and the problem is to keep it open so that the claims of both outer and inner world are honoured.

We all know people who live in narrow mandorlas by over-rating external quantifiable "facts" at the expense of inner values such as the feeling dimension of a given situation; or, conversely, people who are so lost inside private myths that they ignore all contrary evidence trying to reach them from outside. Nor are these things constant, for the scope of our mandorla fluctuates all the time; but the greater the area of overlap then the larger and more inclusive the embrace of our imaginative vision. If the two circles overlapped completely then one might have a sphere representing total knowledge, reminiscent of the medieval image of God as a circle whose centre is everywhere and circumference nowhere. But we are only human, betwixt and between creatures, caught up in contradictions, and the challenge is to keep the mandorla as open as possible.

The nature of the conflict and the challenge it presents was brilliantly defined by our late poet laureate Ted Hughes in an essay on *Myth and Education.* "The real problem", he says there,

> comes from the fact that outer world and inner world are interdependent at every moment. We are simply the locus of their collision...and whether we like it or not our life is what we are able to make of that collision and struggle. So what we need is a faculty that embraces both worlds simultaneously. A large, flexible grasp, an inner vision which holds wide open, like a great theatre, the arena of contention, and which pays equal respect to both sides. This really is imagination. This is the faculty we mean when we talk about the imagination of great artists. The character of great works is exactly this – that in them the full presence of the inner world combines with and is reconciled to the full presence of the outer world. And in them we see that the laws of these two worlds are not contradictory at all: they are all one inclusive system.
>
> (Hughes 1994: 150)

So the proper exercise of the imagination is an energetic process of negotiation between the outer world and the inner world through which we strive to hold together their often contradictory pulls. By engaging in that process we begin to work extraordinary changes, for it is through the meeting and reconciliation of opposites that something new can get made for life. In that respect, the Imagination is related to a word which comes from the same root – *magic* – the power to bring about those changes in the world which seem to defy the normal laws of causality. I would even go so far as to suggest that, in its conjuring and transformative power, magic is the active principal of the imagination.

Before you start imagining me as a member of some occult coven, however, let me add to what has already been said the importance of recognizing two different aspects of the imagination: firstly, its inventive aspect, by which we are free to make up the story of our life and world; and secondly its sympathetic aspect, by which it acknowledges the right of others to do the same. For it is through the activity of the sympathetic imagination that we perceive the world as others experience it, that we feel how things are for them in the world that they inhabit, and begin to relate to their sense of reality in a spirit of compassionate understanding. It seems to me absolutely vital that, in all aspects of our creativity, we strive to hold these two aspects of the imagination together, for when the inventive aspect loses touch with the ethical the results can be calamitous, and when the ethical aspect loses touch with the poetic then the work soon becomes dry, abstract, theoretical and dogmatic. Imagined in this way, as the conjunction linking all our lives, the imagination becomes an instrument of liberation, one to which we all have access and which, by its own intrinsic standards, serves not only to celebrate and enlarge our common humanity but also to invest with a newly heightened sensitivity our relationship to the living world around us.

It is in this way, as a continuous attempt to reconcile the contrary elements of our lives – inner and outer, spirit and matter, ego and soul, the masculine principle and the feminine, the conscious and unconscious regions of our being – that the alchemists understood the imagination as the truly creative principle of our lives and the secret fire that lay behind their work. In this respect I believe they still have a great deal to teach us – and not least in the example that their frequent failures give us of just how difficult the process of transformation is. As I tried to indicate earlier with the analogy of the married couple drifting towards divorce, alchemical procedures can offer us instructive metaphors for the process of individuation and for the creative conduct of our personal lives. By the same token they can illuminate the kind of imaginative energy required for the resolution of apparently intractable conflicts in the political domain – the kind of effort that is being made, for example, in Northern Ireland to draw that troubled province out of its dark history of sectarian violence into a new peaceable order.

But the contemporary relevance of alchemical imagery goes deeper than the attempt to find solutions for local conflicts. With their sensitive responsiveness to the soul of the world – the *Anima Mundi* – as a living and evolving intelligence, the alchemists prefigure the emergence of deep ecological thought in our own time – the kind that recognizes that short-term environmental fixes will not be enough and that what is required for the decent survival of our own and other species is a profound transformation of our relationship to the beautiful planet that sustains our life. And such a transformation will not come about without a change in the way we envision the natural world and our place inside it.

Against the onslaught of bad news that leaves us worrying that it may already be too late, there are two signs of hope: an unprecedented number of people worldwide are now engaged in imaginative search for greater self-knowledge; and along with that we have seen a rapid increase in the understanding of, and concern for, ecological perspectives. But the affairs of the world are still governed by an outworn patriarchal tradition of thought, infatuated by its own technological power, and in thrall to a dim materialism on the one hand and a literal-minded fundamentalism on the other. So great is the destructive power wielded by these forces that the changes we need may seem impossible. Yet, as the title of this conference insists, "Only the impossible is worth the effort". And there does appear to be a significant evolution of consciousness trying to happen in our time, one that may often falter in its attempts to find a language adequate to the demands of its own often confusing processes, yet at its best it represents not a regression into irrationality, but a movement through into trans-rationality – a new conjunction of solar and lunar modes of apprehending the world, one which values all the gains for consciousness that have been made by the discriminating methods of rational enquiry yet seeks to bring them into closer, creative relation with those less quantifiable aspects of our experience that have been undervalued. Those aspects are associated with the feminine principle that has long been neglected in western culture but seems now to be reasserting itself with renewed power and relevance. I mean such aspects as feeling, seen as a rational function by which we evaluate the facts of any given situation; intuition as a guide to understanding, and an alert response to the intelligence arising in poetry and dreams from the deep wellspring of the unconscious.

The imagination, both inventive and ethical, is the function through which we have access to these aspects of our being, and all artists sensitive to their own creative process will tell you that it is through its efforts to reconcile the often contrary pulls of the inner and outer worlds, and to allow something new to arise out of their conjunction, that new work gets made. Such a view of things would have been familiar, in their own terms, to the finest medieval poets and storytellers; and the most important alchemists too were artists of that creative order, attempting to bring about a practical conjunction of science and poetry in a transforming vision of the world. Their emblems of the royal marriage of Sol and Luna, and the new life arising from it, still offer imaginative guidance into the creative reconciliation of opposing elements. Having found in my own quest for self-knowledge, and for a deeper understanding of the critical issues we all face, that what alchemy offers us has been worth rather more to me than gold, I hope I've succeeded in sharing with you something of what I take to be its continuing relevance for our own transitional time. Thank you for listening so patiently.

Select bibliography

Blake, William
    1971   *Blake: complete writings*. Oxford: Oxford University Press.
Bacon, Francis
    1973   *The advancement of learning*. London: J. M. Dent and Sons.
Clarke, Lindsay
    1989   *The Chymical Wedding*. London: Jonathan Cape.
Coleridge, S. T.
    1997   *Biographia Literaria*. London: Everyman Paperback Classics.
Hughes, Ted
    1994   *Winter pollen: Occasional prose*. London: Faber and Faber.
Jung, C.G.
    1961   *Memories, dreams, reflections*. London: Collins Fontana.
Jung, C. G.
    1968   *Psychology and alchemy*. London: Routledge & Kegan Paul.

Artificial discourse of national belonging: the case of Anglo-Saxonism

Anna Czarnowus, Katowice

> *The old Anglo-Saxon race are the best breed in the world ... The absence of a too enervating climate, too unclouded skies, and a too luxurious nature ... has rendered them so superior to all the world*
> (Sir Charles Adderley)[1]

In the quotation above Matthew Arnold, the son of one of those whom Lytton Strachey named "eminent Victorians", is citing a fragment of the speech of Sir Charles Adderley. The lofty words were addressed to Warwickshire farmers, who were perhaps proud to hear they were descendants of the Anglo-Saxons. The Victorian enthusiasm for Anglo-Saxonism manifested itself not only in the literature of the time, to mention only Dickens' novels where some characters define the "English nation" in relation to this idea,[2] but also in visual arts. In high and late Victorianism the statues commemorating King Alfred were erected: first in 1877 in Wantage, Berkshire, the place of the king's birth, and then in 1901 in Winchester. The erection of the statues was preceded by the celebration of the millenary of his birth in 1849. In the Wantage statue Alfred's austere look ostensibly represents his intellectualism and philosophical interests, while his frame reflects the Victorian appreciation of robust masculine bodies shaped by adequate physical exercise. Thus, the figure of the legendary ruler symbolizes the perfect combination of an able mind with a fit physical form, which justifies his superiority in relation to more degenerate representatives of other nations. Hence, even on the basis of such representations, it may be noted that Victorianism was an era which put the figure of the king to the forefront, introducing it not only to the popular imagery of the time, but also combining it with the ideology of the Empire.

Nevertheless, Anglo-Saxonism was not a Victorian invention. Victorians merely continued the myth of Anglo-Saxon origin of the English nation and they consequently applied it for their own purposes. To cite Allen J. Frantzen and John D. Nilles, Anglo-Saxonism may be generally defined as "the process through which a self-conscious national and racial identity first came into being among the early peoples of the region that we now call England and how, over time, through

---

1   Matthew Arnold. *Essays in Criticism* (quoted in: Newsome 1997: 92).
2   Newsome quotes for example Dickens in: *Little Dorrit*, where Daniel Doyce states the following: " ... in truth, no man on earth can cheer like Englishmen, who do so rally one another blood and spirit ... that the stir is like the rush of their whole history, with all its standards flying, from Saxon Alfred's onward!" (quoted in Newsome 1997: 188).

both scholarly and popular promptings, that identity was transferred into an originary myth to a wide variety of political and social interests" (1997: 1). Nilles then correctly indicates Anglo-Saxons themselves as the first people who developed the myth of their originating from one ethnic group and forming one uniform nation (1997: 222). They accomplished it by means of, for instance, developing a lasting historiographic image of themselves in *The Anglo-Saxon Chronicle* and propagating the legend of King Alfred as a good ruler and, simultaneously, a poet and philosopher. In the ensuing epochs Anglo-Saxonism was further developed by scholars: Elizabethan writers such as, among others, Archbishop Matthew Parker and Laurence Nowell, or the eighteenth-century Elstobs, and particularly Miss Elizabeth Elstob, who contributed to the growth of that discipline.[3] In the nineteenth century the position of Anglo-Saxon scholarship was strengthened, but a very distinct political agenda started to be encompassed in the narrative of the Anglo-Saxon origin of the English nation.

The primary use to which Queen Victoria put that myth was the formation of a relationship between her as a ruler of German origin and the English nation. The idea was far from being new but the creation of a popular imagery associated with it obviously was a novelty. The first monarchs who had felt the necessity to establish a link between their ethnic identity and Britishness in order to legitimize their reign in England in that way were the Hanoverians. They were also the first ones to use the figure of King Alfred for strictly political purposes. One has to remember that James Thomson's *Ode: Rule, Britannia*, notorious for its nationalistic or even imperialist message, was written as a part of *Alfred. A Masque* in 1740. It was a play created for George III's father, Prince Frederick. Paradoxically, the ode was sung by an actor disguised as a Celtic bard. The words "Thee haughty tyrants ne'er shall tame" referring to "Britannia" were not true in the light of the conquest of the Celtic land performed by the Anglo-Saxons, but the phrase could be Alfred's possible motto in withstanding the Danish invasions (Thomson 1993: 2453). Yet, the debate about the role of Anglo-Saxons on English soil was nonexistent in the eighteenth century, as the official message entailed the image that king Alfred was not one of the conquerors, but a saviour of the land. The Hanoverians were probably very willing to identify themselves with such a legendary character.

However, the adjective "great" started to be commonly used in reference to Alfred as late as the nineteenth century,[4] while Queen Victoria inspired the perception of the Anglo-Saxon king as the founder of the British Empire (Keynes -

---

3   Borysławski's study (2000) includes an overview of many more Anglo-Saxon scholars who contributed to strengthening of the myth.

4   The epithet "the Great" was popularized by Sir John Spelman, the author of *Life of Alfred the Great*; its Latin version was published as early as 1678, while the English original in 1709 (Keynes - Lapidge 1983: 44).

Lapidge 1983: 49). Therefore, the Queen wanted to be seen as a continuator of the tradition in which a ruler of German origin introduced order in England and extended its territory. Spreading that image and hence creating the atmosphere of "naturalness" around the narrative was only a matter of time. The myth must have entailed numerous paradoxes, but the origin of all of those fallacies was rendered obscure and they were presented as facts to the general public. The statues of Alfred erected in the English provincial towns were therefore a natural continuation of gradually introducing that artificial discourse of national belonging into the social imagination.

Still, the Victorian Anglo-Saxonism cannot be analyzed in detachment from a wider perspective, according to which the Anglo-Saxon originary myth was a variety of medievalism.[5] In the nineteenth century the tendency to look on the Middle Ages in a two-fold way was strengthened. On the one hand, the medieval past was idealized as the Golden Age of Europe, and specifically of England. On the other, the Enlightenment idea of development, willingly adopted by Victorians and manifested also in their fascination with progress, made intellectuals perceive the Middle Ages as the time of worn-out ideas and obsolete social developments. The Victorian Anglo-Saxonism obviously idealized and romanticized the past, which led to the rise of economic and political medievalism within the movement. According to such radical politicians as William Cobbett, Reformation ruined the economic system which allowed the poor to live peacefully: it brought the dissolution of monasteries, which cared for the destitute, and led to the destruction of the manor and the erosion of the yeoman class (Newsome 1997: 180). Furthermore, the Young England Group (including Lord John Manners, George Smythe, and young Disraeli) visualized the Anglo-Saxon times as the epoch of unity between the aristocracy and the poor (Newsome 1997: 181). The central assumption of the Anglo-Saxon myth consisted in perceiving the Anglo-Saxon epoch as the cradle of democracy: it was generally maintained that England's liberties and its unique parliamentary institutions were started then (Newsome 1997: 187). However, the primary link between the Anglo-Saxon England and the British Empire in the Victorian era was the ideology of a "good conquest": it was maintained that Alfred civilized the post-Roman England after conquering it, while Victoria acculturated the colonized nations and hence led them out of their "dark ages".[6] Not surprising, the movement viewing the medieval past in the positive mode led to the emergence of what Ananya Jahanara Kabir calls "imperial medievalism" (2005: 184). Still, the medievalist metaphors were not employed consistently, but their usage depended on the ideological goal of the writer making the comparison, as it will be proved here later.

---

5   Another intriguing nineteenth-century variety of medievalism is its French scholarly version, nowadays discussed by the scholars as originating from modernist ideas (Bloch – Nichols 1996).
6   For an elaboration on the Victorian myth, see Simmons (1990).

Nevertheless, Victorians not only distorted the picture of the colonial reality in their opinions. Even their ideas about the Anglo-Saxon past originated from erroneous assumptions. When discussing the Anglo-Saxon times Victorians uncritically reiterated the statements of their predecessors; from the early nineteenth-century onwards writers and the public visualized the figure of Alfred as

> ... the lawgiver *par excellence*, the father of the British constitution and of the British navy, the reviver and patron of learning and literature, the ideal Christian monarch, an accomplished scholar and poet, and, above all, the founder of the British nation and preserver of its inherent liberties from the ravages of Danish invaders.
>
> (Pratt 2000: 139)

Even though Lynda Pratt is writing here about Joseph Cottle's *Alfred, an Epic Poem* (1800) and Henry James Pye's work by the same title (1801), the statements above also reflect the Victorian idea of Alfred as a perfect ruler. Obviously, in reference to conquest Victorians and their predecessors applied double standards to the history of colonization. The invasion of the Danes endangered civilization, while the Anglo-Saxons themselves were presented as those who had carried out a conquest beneficial to the formation of the English nation.

Still, one has to remember that Anglo-Saxonism was firstly a scholarly discipline and that research into Old English writings was continued in the nineteenth century. This aspect of the phenomenon was accompanied by the colonial ideology, which went hand in hand with Orientalism. If the latter discourse justified the conquest of the East by using the metaphor of subjecting the feminine Orient by the masculine Occident, Anglo-Saxonism would further confirm the superiority of the English nation over the colonized ones. The relationship between Orientalism and Anglo-Saxonism has not been sufficiently exploited in the criticism, but Allen J. Frantzen provides us with a thorough comparison of the two ideologies. He explains the critical silence over the relation between the two by stating that

> Orientalism is a recognized cultural phenomenon, while Anglo-Saxonism, its ideological partner, is not. Because Orientalism belongs to the category of "not Old English", its close association with the formation of Anglo-Saxon studies has been ignored.
>
> (Frantzen 1990: 29)

According to Frantzen the two share a common ground in the sense of being both scholarly disciplines and ideologies. Moreover, Orientalism used to function as a background for Anglo-Saxonism since it justified the English superiority by the fact that Western, more developed, languages originated from the Eastern, more basic, ones (Frantzen 1990: 29). Therefore, scholarship functioned in service of ideology, which continuously claimed that the Orient was inferior and had to be civilized as a consequence. Nonetheless, blaming the Victorians for such a state of things would be an exaggeration, since their "nationalistic outlook", as Frantzen calls it, was the same as that of the Elizabethans, also constructing their national identity in contrast with the "uncivilized" peoples (1990: 27). We have to bear it in mind that, as Benedict Anderson insists, the Renaissance was the time when the idea of the nation entered the public discourse, hence the epoch generated the first nationalisms.[7] Its English variety did not considerably differ from others at first, but with time the imperial project led to the development of its idiosyncratic versions.

Ananya Jahanar Kabir provides us with ample evidence that in the nineteenth-century both of the ideologies were used in the colonized countries. She diagnoses the colonial discourse as both Anglo-Saxonist and Orientalist (2005: 183-204). The sense of superiority over India led scholars to compare the nineteenth-century India to Europe in the Middle Ages (on the basis of language development), while the Muslim invaders of India were likened to Normans conquering the just and belligerent Anglo-Saxons. The metaphorization of India was not consistent: the Orientals could just as well be compared to Normans due to their despotic nature. Moreover, the English occupying India viewed themselves as descendants of Romans, who civilized the Celtic British Isles, which was clearly a continuation of the medieval tradition of *translatio imperii*. Research into linguistics was a point of departure for ideological statements which referred not just to languages, but also to cultures: linguistic colonialism would evolve into the cultural one. Characteristically, even though Victorian Anglo-Saxon scholarship could be divided into the popular and the learned variety, both of them were an aid in sustaining the myth of superiority (Kabir 2005: 183-204). If, according to Foucault, an equality mark can be placed between knowledge and power, the authority Anglo-Saxonists gained through their scholarly activities was used in order to construct an entirely inauthentic narration.

Thus, the past was manipulated through the construction of a narrative which led to nation formation, as such narratives always do. According to Homi Bhabha the idea of every nation is a narration created within a nationalistic discourse. Moreover, Bhabha claims that the issues whose existence cannot be denied are "the attempt by nationalistic discourses persistently to produce the idea of the nation as a continuous narrative of national progress, the narcissism of self-generation, the primeval presence of the Volk" (1990: 1). Anglo-Saxonism fulfilled the criterion of continuity, since it was started by Anglo-Saxons themselves and prolonged into the late Middle Ages, even though there emerged another discourse accompanying it and simultaneously trying to negate it, namely the myth of the Trojan descent of the English nation. The work treated as the starting point of that tradition was Geoffrey of Monmouth's twelfth-century *Historia Regum Britanniae*, which attributed the title of the founding father of the British nation to Brutus.[8] The latter narration at-

---

7　For a magisterial discussion of the nationhood formation through narration, see Anderson (1991).

8　On the story of Norman genealogy as a competing narrative of national belonging, see Thorpe (1966: 9-45); Geoffrey's imperialist project is discussed in depth by Warren (2000: 25-59).

tempted to suppress the Anglo-Saxon myth, but Anglo-Saxonism was preserved in the popular imagination due to the support provided by the scholars. The effects of their work denied any scholarly basis to the Trojan myth, hence it remained in the sphere of literary works, such as romances.

Bhabha's statement that "this cultural construction of nationness [is] a form of social and textual affiliation" (1990: 292) may also refer to the two-fold basis of Anglo-Saxonism. The English defined themselves in relation to the mythical Anglo-Saxon society, whose image remained vague, and felt affiliated to it through the textual area that embraced both scholarship and popular literature.[9] Apart from "affiliation", "appropriation" may be another key term in defining the process that led to the emergence and continuation of Anglo-Saxonism. John D. Nilles perceives appropriation as one of the primary processes of culture formation and he places it alongside acculturation and assimilation (1997: 214). Therefore Anglo-Saxons themselves started the process in which the mythical Anglo-Saxon past was incorporated into the narrative of the English nation. The temporality of the myth was negated and the kingdom of Alfred became a point of departure for the all-encompassing originary myth. Bhabha claims that all culture is, after all, local (by which he means "temporal"), which is its strength (1990: 292). Still, in the formation of the Anglo-Saxon story of nation creation the truth about the narrative being local was suppressed. Furthermore, the figure of king Alfred was artificially imposed on the consciousness of those who inhabited the regions historically not related to West Saxony in any way. The popular imagination was colonized as a consequence. Later Victorians tried to carry out a similar project in the colonies: they attempted to influence the consciousness of the colonial subjects of the Empire by imposing on them the sense of Anglo-Saxon superiority.

Victorians were not the first ones to use the ideologically-laden image of Alfred. Similar tendencies had appeared at the end of the eighteenth century and were related to the revolutionary ferment in Europe. The historical figure was appropriated by conservatives, who perceived the king as the guardian of traditional values, including the nationalistic ones. Strangely enough, revolutionaries also employed Alfred for their own purposes since they defined him as the prototype of an ardent patriot ready both to protect his country and to change it for the benefit of the whole nation (Pratt 2000: 141). The king was, after all, the one who established a state free from external intervention, which was ended by the mythical "Norman Yoke" (Newsome 1997: 187). The project of permanently incorporating Alfred into the world of politics was therefore an impossible one since his appropriation suited only the current purposes of a given political group. The political attempts may be now seen as incongruous, but the incongruity was also a feature distinguishing later manifestations of Anglo-Saxonism.

---

9   Representations of Anglo-Saxons and Normans in the nineteenth-century fiction are appropriate examples of the Romantic and Victorian textual affiliation, see Sanders (2000).

A good example of visualizing the political message is the so-called Theed tableau, now in the National Portrait Gallery in London.[10] The statue was executed by William Theed in 1868 and it portrayed Queen Victoria and (posthumously) Prince Albert as an Anglo-Saxon woman and her beau. The part of the representation verging on the absurd consisted in the two figures wearing Anglo-Saxon apparel and being partly stylized as simple country folk. This visualization of the political idea tried to deny the non-uniform identity of the sitters: they were of German origin and simultaneously British in the sense of occupying the important positions in the Empire, hence the uniform, Anglo-Saxon self they apparently represented belonged to the realm of pure fiction.

As for the statues of king Alfred in the midst of the countryside, their cultural unsuitability has recently become more and more acute due to the changing image even of the English provincial towns. Multiculturality ceased to be the principle reserved for the capital and other major cities, since it entered the communities which had hitherto been closed to the members of different ethnic groups. The tableau of Victoria and Albert in the museum is not as conflicted with the reality as the statues of Alfred, which introduce the artificial narrative about the Anglo-Saxon nation into the consciousness of the communities. Yet, the crucial event in the reinvention of Britishness should definitely not be a removal of the statues from the streets of Wantage or Winchester, but rethinking the Victorian (and earlier) Anglo-Saxonism as the ideology which might still produce anxiety on the part of the white British nowadays. As a matter of fact, this anxiety might be one of the factors contributing to the increasing xenophobia. Contemporary British society seems to have returned to the state of multiculturality which used to characterize it in the medieval times. Even though the ethnic identity of the groups contributing to that variegated identity differs from the ethnicities making up the "Englishness" of the past, Britain regained the cultural structure it had once had.

Due to the threat of new nationalisms the conclusion that Anglo-Saxonism is an outdated ideology which does not have any relevance for the present may be too hasty. T.A. Shippey claims that this variety of medievalism needs a very careful re-examination since it influences the presence and the future of Great Britain. As he insists,

> . . . the population of England (and the United Kingdom outside it) needs to come to terms with its pre-Imperial and pre-Union history in order to adjust to a post-Imperial (and conceivably post-Union) situation.
>
> (Shippey 2000: 235)

---

10   David Newsome ironically refers to the statue as "gratifyingly solid and therefore, one hopes, imperishable monument of Victorian medievalism and its looking back to Alfred and his kingdom of free-born men" (1997: 190).

Shippey suggests here a different perspective on the Anglo-Saxon past. He sees it as an ideology stifling the openness which is indispensable in the multicultural society and as the conception which questions not only the reality of external colonization, but also that of the internal one: England's relations with Scotland, Wales, and Northern Ireland. Anglo-Saxonism may function as the ideology providing the nationally frustrated population of England (or at least that part of it which is nationally frustrated) with a good excuse for xenophobic attitudes. Interestingly, the contagious nature of xenophobia leads to extending it to the new EU members, who are perceived as a real threat to the "indigenous" inhabitants of the island. The variety of medievalism in question is a force which might provide such people with a false memory of their glorious Anglo-Saxon descent.

Nonetheless, Shippey claims that even the historiographic assumptions of those who hail the superiority of the "modern Anglo-Saxons" over other groups may be wrong. As he proves, the term "Anglo-Saxon" itself was an invention of continental historians writing in Latin. The English authors simply adopted it from those who were not interested in the actual ethnic identity of the early medieval invaders of Britain (2000: 232). Shippey argues that the real "Anglo-Saxons" were highly diversified groups representing various ethnicities and cultures. The division into Angles and Saxons was a much later invention and its premises were altogether false, as there were more than just two ethnic groups among the newcomers (Shippey 2000: 215-236). Still, later historiography imposed this fallacy on the consciousness of the newly formed nation.

Medievalism may be treated as a means of psychoanalyzing oneself through improving one's self-image, which is particularly true of Anglo-Saxonism. The sense of superiority temporarily improves the way of thinking about oneself, but it has to be constantly reinforced once the process of using the past for such purposed has started. Anglo-Saxonism is yet more than just another variety of medievalism. It may pose danger similar to that of Orientalism, as it is a good ground for new nationalisms. The nationalisms in turn are generated also on the basis of xenophobia. It is debatable whether 9/11 was the starting point of those emerging nationalisms or perhaps they merely became more acceptable and hence more visible from that time onwards. From such a simplistic perspective postcolonialism was a phenomenon which sparked off the terrorist attacks. Such a view obviously does not take into consideration the beneficial influence of the post-colonial influence on the British culture, identity, or lifestyles.

Again, besides the false assumptions behind the myth of Anglo-Saxon origin, one has to do with an issue which has often been overlooked: Britain was also a post-colonial territory in the distant past. Nicholas Howe emphasizes this fact about the Anglo-Saxon times when he writes about England as a land which was firstly colonized by the Romans and with time abandoned by them, which left the inhabitants with an acute sense of treading on the footprints on the one-time Roman invaders (2005: 25-47). The Romans left numerous remnants of their material culture in Britain, which would return as a trope in the Anglo-Saxon poetry, to mention only *The Ruin* or those fragments of *Beowulf* where the Roman mosaic tiles at Hall Heorot are described. The material reminders of the past colonization were concrete and perhaps even generally recognizable, which introduces an unusual perspective into our view of Britain as the land of colonizers, not the colonized ones. Should not then the British feel that they have always lived in a post-colonial country?

Anglo-Saxonism may become the starting point of the debate about what it means to be British nowadays and what role ethnicity really plays in the construction of national identity. As an artificial discourse of national belonging, it should not be a factor impeding the smooth intermingling of the cultural phenomena acknowledged as "inherently British" with those which allegedly come from "the outside". Particularly if Michel Foucault was right to state that we are all Victorians, nowadays the Anglo-Saxonist medievalism that flourished in Victorianism should be realized and then rejected. Lynda Pratt writes that the figure of Alfred "was an essential component in the [early nineteenth-century] debate ... on the nature of Britishness itself" (2000: 141). The same figure may also become a point of departure for the debate nowadays, this time as a part of the political discourse still dangerous for Britain, with the multiple identities and identifications of the people inhabiting it.

References

Abrams, M. H. (ed.)
　　1993　　*The Norton anthology of English literature.* Vol. 1. New York – London:
　　　　　　W.W. Norton and Company.
Anderson, Benedict
　　1991　　*Imagined communities: Reflections on the origins and spread of nationalism.* London: Verso.
Bhabha, Homi K.
　　1990　　"DissemiNation: time, narrative, and the margins of the modern nation",
　　　　　　in: Homi K. Bhabha (ed.), 291-322.
Bhabha, Homi K. (ed.)
　　1990　　*Nation and narration.* London – New York: Routledge.
Bloch, R. Howard – Stephen G. Nichols (eds.)
　　1996　　*Medievalism and the modernist temper.* Baltimore – London: The Johns
　　　　　　Hopkins University Press.
Borysławski, Rafał
　　2000　　"Imperial Anglo-Saxonism: On the organic roots of the English sense of
　　　　　　superiority in the eighteenth and nineteenth centuries", in: Tadeusz
　　　　　　Rachwał – Tadeusz Sławek (eds.), 75-88.

Frantzen, Allen J.
  1990   *Desire for origins: New language, Old English, and teaching the tradi-
              tion*. New Brunswick – London: Rutgers University Press.
Frantzen, Allen J. – John D. Nilles
  1997   "Introduction", in: Allen J. Frantzen – John D. Nilles (eds.), 1-14.
Frantzen, Allen J.– John D. Nilles (eds.)
  2005   *Anglo-Saxonism and the construction of social identity*. Gainesville: Uni-
              versity Press of Florida.
Geoffrey of Monmouth
  1966   *The history of the kings of Britain*. (Edited by Lewis Thorpe.) Har-
              mondsworth: Penguin Books.
Howe, Nicholas
  2005   "Anglo-Saxon England and the postcolonial void", in: Ananya Jahanara
              Kabir – Deanne Williams (eds.), 25-47.
Kabir, Ananya Jahanara
  2005   "Analogy in translation: imperial Rome, medieval England, and British
              India", in: Ananya Jahanara Kabir – Deanne Williams (eds.), 183-204.
Kabir, Ananaya Jahanara – Deanne Williams (eds.)
  2005   *Postcolonial approaches to the European Middle Ages. Translating cul-
              tures*. Cambridge: Cambridge University Press.
Keynes, Simon - Michael Lapidge
  1983   "Introduction", in: Simon Keynes – Michael Lapidge (eds.), 9-58.
Keynes, Simon - Michael Lapidge (eds.)
  1983   *Alfred the Great. Asser's Life of King Alfred and other contemporary
              sources*. (Translated by Simon Keynes – Michael Lapidge.) Harmonds-
              worth: Penguin Books.
Newsome, David
  1997   *The Victorian world picture. Perceptions and introspections in an age of
              change*. London: John Murray.
Nilles, John D.
  1997   "Appropriations. A concept of culture", in: Allen J. Frantzen – John D.
              Niles (eds.), 202-228.
Pratt, Lynda
  2000   "Anglo-Saxon attitudes?: Alfred the Great and the Romantic national
              epic", in: Donald Scragg – Carole Weinberg (eds.), 138-156.
Rachwał, Tadeusz – Tadeusz Sławek (eds.)
  2000   *Organs, organisms, organisations. Organic form in nineteenth-century
              discourse*. Frankfurt am Mein: Peter Lang.
Sanders, Andrew
  2000   "'Utter indifference'?: The Anglo-Saxons in the nineteenth-century
              novel", in: Donald Scragg – Carole Weinberg (eds.), 157-173.
Scragg, Donald – Carole Weinberg (eds.)
  2000   *Literary appropriation of the Anglo-Saxons from the thirteenth Century
              to the twentieth century*. Cambridge: Cambridge University Press.

Shippey, T.A.
  2000   "The undeveloped image: Anglo-Saxons in popular consciousness from Turner to Tolkien", in: Donald Scragg – Carole Weinberg (eds.), 215-236.
Simmons, Claire A.
  1990   *Reversing the quest: History and myth in nineteenth century British culture.* New Brunswick, N.J.: Rutgers University Press.
Thomson, James
  1993   "Ode: Rule, Britannia", in: M.H. Abrams (ed.), 2453.
Thorpe, Lewis
  1966   "Introduction", in: Geoffrey of Monmouth, 9-45.
Warren, Michelle R.
  2000   *History on the edge. Excalibur and the borders of Britain 1100-1300.* Minneapolis – London: University of Minnesota Press.

The gender of the Vice: from the medieval she-vice to the Renaissance she-villain in Shakespeare's *Macbeth*[1]

Jacek Fabiszak, Poznań

The wilful evil-doer of the Renaissance culture is often associated with the figure of a scheming politician-turn-tyrant,[2] or a racial alien (a Moor or Jew), who is usually male. What was then the status of female villains and how did they evolve? is a question one may be tempted to pose when such perspective is assumed. Consequently, the paper is an attempt to contrast and compare figures from Middle English plays, both moralities and mysteries, and their developments in Renaissance drama by Shakespeare. The figures in question have a specified gender: they are female characters. The reasons for focusing only on one gender is that so far research into the gender of the vice/villain figure has been rather neglected, and, second, that the concept of femininity as a natural, as it were, milieu for the spread of evil in both the Middle Ages and the Renaissance, led to the conclusion that female characters were prone to become the seat of evil, as "the weaker vessels".[3] These metaphors are mentioned purposefully: the biblical idea of the imperfection of women and easy yielding to evil temptations must not be overlooked; characteristically, when it comes to male villains, at least in Renaissance plays, one is confronted with characters who willingly declare their villainous nature, as if they exerted control over it and had a genuine choice: such as Richard Gloucester in *Richard III*, or Barabas in *The Jew of Malta*. Female villains, albeit not lacking the qualities of their male counterparts – evil combined with comedy – seem to lack, however, the distance that male villains assume (as a result of their conscious

---

1   I would like to acknowledge the help I received when working on this article from my two distinguished colleagues: Professor Liliana Sikorska (aka Lilka) and Doctor Joanna Kazik (aka Kazik) who shared with me their expertise on English medieval literature and provided me with most valuable primary and secondary sources as well as critical remarks on the nature of this study. Also, I would like to thank yet another woman who patiently bore with me when I struggled to complete this work: Doctor Joanna Maciulewicz (aka Masia) for her patience and understanding when I struggled with both the early and final drafts of the work.

2   John Webster in his *Duchess of Malfi* (3.2) puts into the mouth of Bosola the following definition of a politician: "A politician is the devil's quilted anvil; / He fashions all sins on him".

3   This term can be found in the Bible; in The First Epistle General of Peter (1Pe 3: 7), the apostle admonishes Christian men that: "Likewise, ye husbands, dwell with *them* according to knowledge, giving honour unto the wife, as unto the weaker vessel, and as being heirs together of the grace of life; that your prayers be not hindered." (*The Holy Bible*. No indication of the date of publication. Authorized King James Version. London: Eyre and Spottiswoode Publishers.) Other translations, like the 1989 Bible, New International Version, conceive of a woman as "the weaker partner" (*The Bible. New International Version*. 1989. London: Hodder and Stoughton.)

choice) to their villainy. The apparent lack of distance may be the consequence of another stereotype, this time more prevalent in our times, of the woman's sense of responsibility (for the family, or the state) and her whole-hearted devotion to whatever she decides to do. As a result, there is hardly any room for cynicism or distance: the task must be accomplished, no matter what. Of course, as I will try to show below, it is not entirely true. Figures who seem to defy this stereotype include the Weird Sisters from *Macbeth* who remain detached from the events in which Macbeth is the protagonist and can be counted as villain figures. Noteworthy, however, is the fact that their sex / gender is questioned by other characters, and their humanity is also similarly dubious. The question then arises if Lady Macbeth, who is considered by many scholars to be the Fourth Witch, is also capable of assuming a distanced perspective as well? Again, this paper will try to look at her in the context of villainy in the play and the medieval traditions and stereotypes out of which she evolves. The reason for the choice of this figure is that she is involved in politics, plays an active role in it and is instrumental in bringing about the catastrophe in the fictional world. Furthermore, Lady Macbeth is perhaps the most widely known and at the same time quite controversial female villain in the Shakespearean canon.

The paper's structure will be threefold. First, aspects of female characters' villainy in the medieval tradition will be outlined. Here I will draw on some aspects of the medieval culture and drama. Second, villain characters and their nature in the English Renaissance will be discussed; here, the major point of reference will be of course Shakespearean Richard III and Macbeth, on the one hand, and Marlovian Machevill, on the other. Also, some minor female villain figures from the Shakespeare's plays will be mentioned in passim. Finally, in the third section the findings from the previous parts will be applied to an analysis of the figure of Lady Macbeth.

One of the earliest dramatic representations of a female villain was of course Noah's shrewish wife. It seems necessary, however, to voice a reservation at this point. What is considered "a villain" in the Renaissance did not necessarily have the same characteristics in the Middle Ages. For this reason, it is safer to speak about a shrew, a witch and Vice (the latter standing for the negative figures in the moralities) as sharing some features with a villainous character developed in the Renaissance (where the figure was after all far from uniform). Also, another significant element linking the shrew, witch and Vice with the villain is that the latter is a development of the former.[4]

Noah's wife is infamous for, on the one hand, letting the devil enter the ark and, on the other, her stubborn personality and reluctance to join her husband on the ark as well as constant grumbling. As Rosemary Woolf reminds us when referring to the N-Town Cycle,

---

4   On the development of villainous characters in medieval plays, see for example Schlauch
     (1956: 318-320).

The author of the *Ludus Coventriae* demonstrates obedience through a lyrical iteration of the theme: from the dramatic point of view the most effective way of treating submission to God's will ... was to contrast it with disobedience, thus showing how easy the refusal to submit one's own will might be. This is one of the many purposes served by the characterisation in the other plays of Noah's wife as a shrewish and obstinate woman. The suggestion for this seems to have derived from eastern legend and folktale that reached England through some unidentified intermediary. The legend falls into two parts. In the first part the devil, eager to discover and thwart the divine plan (which is concealed from him since God has instructed Noah to keep the building of the ark secret), approaches Noah's wife and advises her to offer Noah a potion, whereby he will be induced to tell her what the secret is: this she successfully does. In the second part the devil seeks a means to enter the ark and hovers by Noah's wife: he is able to enter when Noah, made impatient by his wife's hesitations, is driven to swearing and says something like, 'Come on board, you devil': the devil is similarly expelled from the ark when Noah, on the dove's return, exclaims 'Benedicite'.

(Woolf 1980: 136-137)

Woolf draws our attention to more than just two "vices" of Noah's wife. She rightly stresses the aspect of disobedience: on a micro-scale, in the patriarchal world of the Bible and the Middle Ages, of a wife to a husband; in other words, the "silent" wife must not contest the husband's words. Naturally, in the case of the Deluge play her disobedience runs counter not so much to Noah's plan, but the divine plan. Thus, it becomes a striking example of disobedience against God on a macro-scale. It is important to note that disobedience is a fundamental feature of villains in general; it appears that their vicious nature stems primarily from disobeying not only God, but also the laws and order prevalent in the society they live in, from even challenging them.

The disobedience has instant consequences. Noah's wife becomes susceptible to the devil's instigations, which – again – seems to result directly from her excessive talkativeness, her (in)ability to control her language. In the Chester Pageant of the Deluge Noah's wife is shown first of all as a character prone to gossip: she is talking to the wives of Noah's sons – Shem's, Ham's and Japhet's.

NOES WIFE
And wee shall bringe tymber to,
for wee mon nothinge ells doe–
women bynne weake to underfoe
any great travell.

SEMES WYFE
Here is a good hackestocke;
one this you must hewe and knocke.
Shall none be idle in this flocke,
ne nowe may noe man fable.

CAMES WIFE
And I will goe slytche,
the shippe for to clam and pitche.
Annoynte yt muste bee with stitche—
borde, tree, and pynne.

JAFETES WIFE
And I will gather chippes here
to make a fyer for you, in feare,
and for to dighte your dinnere,
agayne you come in.

(ll. 65-80)[5]

Stereotypically, the women talk rather than do actual work. Gossiping becomes actually one of the reasons why Noah's wife is unwilling to join her husband: "But I have my gossips everyechone, / one foote further I will not gone" (ll. 201-202). When Noah declares one of the purposes of building the ark: that he and his family will embark on it, his wife for the first time bluntly refuses to enter the ship:

NOE
Wife in this vessel wee shalbe kepte;
my children and thou, I would in yee lepte!

NOES WIFE
In fayth, Noe, I had as leeve thou slepte.
For all thy Frenyshe fare,
I will not doe after thy reade.

NOE
Good wiffe, do nowe as I thee bydd.

NOES WIFE
By Christe, not or I see more neede,
though thou stand all the daye and stare.

(ll. 97-104)

This passage confirms the major issue of disobedience. Let us note that Noah's wife considers her husband's plans nonsense (*Frenyshe fare*) and a figment of his imagination. There is a serious implication behind it, which puts Noah in a rather unfavourable light: apparently, he has had some such fantastic plans before. Be that as it may have, Noah's wife displays a feature which the Renaissance villains will share:

---

5   All quotations from *The Thirde Pageante of Noyes Fludd* come from the following edition: R.M. Lumiansky – David Mills (eds.) 1974. *The Chester Mystery Plays*. London – New York – Toronto: Oxford University Press, pp. 42-56. References include line numbers.

disobedience in general, challenging accepted values in particular. On a different plane, her disobedience has the form of standing up against her husband, of positioning herself as an equal partner in a male dominated world. Her equality amounts only, however, to the art of rhetoric: of *verbally* confronting her husband. Characteristically, Noah's response is to call his wife (and all women!) "crabbed" (l. 105), thus referring to the linguistic aspect of her conduct. Exasperated with her stubbornness, Noah swears, thus opening the way for the devil to get onto the ark: "Come in, wiffe, in twentye devylles waye, / or ells stand withowte" (ll. 219-220). When the woman is finally made to get on board, with her verbal skills thus subjected to the persuasive power, apparently a physical threat, of both Noah and his sons, she becomes more literal, but seems to respond in kind: "Have thou that for thy note" (l. 246), which probably means that she deals a slap; Noah's reaction seems to confirm it: "Aha, marye, this ys hotte" (l. 247). In a way, she thus assumes, albeit inadequately, male qualities, which – however – are a cry of despair. Women trying to be like men, even out-manning men, as it were, instead of keeping to their typically feminine nature had a tendency to become villains.

The significance that Noah's wife attaches to gossip (The Gossips, a character who is represented in the play) must not be overlooked. Gossip is hearsay spread by word of mouth. It is fiction based on truth. Or, it is truth which is filtered through one's fantasies. In the world of the Deluge Noah's wife takes her husband's decision to get on board the ark (not to build it, though) as his fantasy! The process to be reconstructed is as follows: God makes Noah build a ship. Noah makes his family build it. His sons, his wife and his sons' wives (in this order) volunteer to take part in it. Noah's wife does not treat it seriously; for her, it is just one of her husband's whims. No matter how hard her husband will insist, she will treat it as gossip: half-truth, half-false. The "false" in fact indicates *interpretation*, or the scope for it. Villainous figures like to interpret, or fit the world to their words. Lady Macbeth will so interpret her husband's letter in accordance with her needs.

Interpretation lies beyond control. Interpretation is thus subversive. The conduct of Noah's wife can also be classified as subversive. But perhaps the most seditious female figure in the Middle Ages (and the Renaissance, as a matter of fact) was a witch, who – like Noah's wife – was willing to yield to the devil's instigations. Lène Dresen - Coenders draws an interesting distinction between an actual witch and what she calls a sorceress: "The witches who began being persecuted in the 15th century must be distinguished from the sorceresses who had been operating within and without Christian culture down the ages and who used their magic powers for good or evil purposes" (1987: 59). This distinction is between women who did use magic, or were believed to do so (irrespective of what they really were capable of), and those who either proved too independent or too challenging for the patriarchal system. The former are not necessarily linked with Christianity; the latter are an integral element of the Christian culture. The distinction, naturally, comes from what is perhaps the most notorious "treatise" on witches, *The Hammer of Witches* (*Malleus Malefi-carum*, 1487), in which the latter category of witches is referred to as "modern witches". These, as Dresen - Coenders reminds us "in contrast to the witches of earlier times ... freely consecrate themselves to the devil with body and soul" (1987: 59). Thus, it is not only thinking that runs counter to the dominant ideol-ogy but also conduct which is not accepted in the society, that is debauchery, and – to make things even worse – sexual encounters with man's arch-enemy, the devil![6] Let us note in passim that although Noah's wife is not shown copulat-ing with the devil, yet her shrewish nature to a large extent depends on her rela-tion with the fiend.

Women who were prone to yield to the temptation of the incubi were so suscep-tible for different reasons. The authors of *The Hammer* list three categories of such women and their reasons, including married ones. Consequently, the devil could suc-cessfully affect the sanctity of the sacrament of marriage. However, according to *The Hammer*, "this was permitted because of the repugnance of the sexual act. This act had of course always been connected with lust since the sin of Adam and Eve and had at the same time transmitted original sin to their descendants" (Dresen - Coenders 1987: 61-62). The stress is then on the sexual aspect of marriage, on lust, a point not to be missed in the discussion of the villainy of Lady Macbeth.

Other features of "modern witches" include "the killing of the unborn and newly born children, preferably unbaptized, along with the dedication to the devil of those children who do live. ... [Here] midwives ... have special power with regard to the unborn and recently born" (Dresen - Coenders 1987: 60). Again, it is worth noting that midwives traditionally slipped out of the men's control as, indeed, the whole process of labour and giving birth. The fear of women getting out of control, or – as Dresen - Coenders saw it, "the fear of the power of women" was also roused by the "power of mothers over unborn and newly born babies, but also ... [by] their power over children's upbringing, especially when it came to girls. Thus, the daughters of witches were always suspect" (1987: 63).

What emerges from the brief remarks concerning the perspective on "modern witchcraft" voiced in *The Hammer of Witches* coincides, as I have been trying to show, with general views of women as the weaker vessel, of women reduced to their bodies (although by no means deprived of cunning), of, finally, women who break the social rules. As Renée Pegeaud put it with reference to the continental urban morality, "Literature, drama and the visual arts all reinforced and propa-

---

6   By no means is it to say that only women were prone to copulate with the devil. According to
     Dresen – Coenders "[t]here are also some men who enter into the unholy pact but their num-
     ber is smaller..." (1987: 59). On a different, yet related, note in the early modern period
     witchcraft, although "largely understood as a woman's crime ... Of those indicted, 93 per
     cent were women [the rest including men]" (Mendelson – Crawford 2003: 45).

gated this morality by portraying woman as a dangerous temptress and demonstrating how famous men had met their downfalls through their mistresses" (1987: 39).[7] Naturally, the downfall was caused by excessive indulging in bodily pleasures, and the negative stereotype of a woman was that of a prostitute, who traded her *body*, and an adulteress, who used her body in a dishonourable way (Pegeaud 1987: 43). The stigma of abusing one's body was further transmitted onto the illegitimate children. Again, according to Pegeaud, "[a]ll categories of dishonourableness have in common the connection with the bodily, the organic and the animal element in man" (1987: 43).

These stereotypes did not change much in the course of time and they remained pretty much the same in the Renaissance, albeit assuming different shapes. As Dresen - Coenders aptly remarked,

> There are indications that during the transition from the Middle Ages to the modern era (1400 – 1600) people were just as preoccupied with the role of woman as they are at the present day. It was the period of growing persecution of witches on the one hand and of new idealized images on the other.... Literature and the visual arts vied with one another to present examples of the good women, but more especially of the bad, who were lecherous, domineering or crafty.
>
> (Dresden – Coenders 1987: 7)

A similar stance is echoed in Mendelson and Crawford: "The stereotypical choices were particularly polarized. Women could be good, proceeding from virginity to marriage and maternity, and die after a virtuously spent widowhood. Or they could be wicked: scolds, whores, or witches. What they could not be, in theory, was independent, autonomous, and female-oriented" (2003: 17). In the last sentence, Mendelson and Crawford refer to the fear of woman power, which is linked with their independence. It is also combined with the inexplicable; here, one could note an interesting change in the perception of the female mind: "The theoretical links between women and hysteria were stronger at the end of the early modern period. Earlier, a woman was more likely to be labelled as a witch than as insane. Madness as a label for 'deviance' filled the place of witchcraft in the eighteenth century" (Mendelson - Crawford 2003: 29-30). Certainly, what we would call today madness may have been believed to be caused by the contact with evil forces; alternatively, it may have suggested such propensity in a woman (or a man, for that matter).

---

7   An example of which could be numerous stories relating women's stratagems to seduce men. In the Middle Ages such stories were to be found in *El Libro de Los Enganos e Los Asayamientos de las Mugeres* [The Book of the Wiles of Women] from 1253 or – with reference to English literature – in Chaucer's *The Canterbury Tales*. Characteristically, the editor of an anthology of medieval literature about women, marks such texts as "antifeminist tales", see Alcuin Blamires (1992: 130-135).

Nevertheless, as signalled above, changes between the stereotypical negative image of a woman were rather insignificant in the Renaissance. It seems appropriate to follow here the lead of Mendelson and Crawford (2003: 69-71) who speak of three types of women: the scold, the whore and the witch: "All challenged patriarchal control. Each built on specific fears: the scold, of the power of women's tongues; the whore, of unbridled sexuality; the witch, a mirror reversal of all that the patriarchy deemed good in a woman" (Mendelson – Crawford 2003: 69). Naturally, the scold developed from the stereotype that women were excessively talkative. Scolds were not merely a stereotype, irritating but laughable creatures, but they were considered "disturbers of their neighboures" (Mendelson – Crawford 2003: 70) and, as a result, were legally punished: from imposing fines to "duck[ing] in a pond or river on a device known as cucking stool" (Mendelson - Crawford 2003: 70) and (that was illegal, though) to "the public parading of a woman through a town wearing an iron device, the scold's bridle, over her head and tongue" (Mendelson – Crawford 2003: 70).[8] The image of a scold is very much like that of a shrew; after all, Shakespeare in his *The Taming of the Shrew* has Petruchio describe the Shrew, Katherina in the following words: "I know she is an irksome brawling scold" (1.2.186).[9] Interestingly enough, the *OED* lists the meaning of the shrew as a scold only in the third place, the first two being occupied by "1 [a] malevolent or mischievous person; a villain, a rascal" and "2 [a]n evil and troublesome act, circumstance, or other thing".[10] Putting the shrew on a par of with a scold combines a grumbling and possibly bad-tempered woman with a villain, an evil and dangerous person.

Likewise, the medieval conception of a lewd woman and a prostitute does not differ much from the stereotype of a whore. "Prostitution was constructed as sexual disorder, a form of deviance, rather than as work" (Mendelson – Crawford 2003: 70-71).[11] The name "whore" was not, however, reserved only for women of

---

8   Interestingly, the woman's lavish use of language, outside the context of a shrew (although not entirely), is in a way confirmed in Marlowe's *Edward II*. When Isabella agrees to plead with the barons to have Gaveston return from exile thanks to Isabella's intercession with the barons, Edward happily showers his wife with promises of reward: "For thee, fair queen, if thou lov'st Gaveston, / I'll hang a golden tongue about thy neck, / Seeing that has pleaded with so good success" (1.4.229-331). Christopher Marlowe. 1986. "Edward II", in: *The complete plays*. (Edited by J.B. Steane.) Hardmondsworth: Penguin Books, 431-533.

9   The quotation is taken from the following edition: William Shakespeare. 2000. *The Taming of the Shrew*. (Edited by Brian Morris.) (The Arden Shakespeare edition.) London: Thomson Learning.

10   *The new shorter Oxford English dictionary on historical principles*. (Edited by Lesley Brown.) Vol. 2. Oxford: Clarendon Press.

11   For documents illustrating the nature of prostitution in both medieval and Early Modern England see P.J.P. Goldberg (ed.). 1985. *Women in England c. 1275-1525*. Manchester – New York: Manchester University Press, 210-222.

lower social status. "[B]rave satirists occasionally attacked even the kings' mistresses", as Mendelson and Crawford (2003: 71) remind us. There existed a "natural" link between a whore and a witch which was related to the woman's alleged promiscuity. The desecration of the woman's body as a result of the copulation with the devil was considered the most repulsive. Especially in view of the fact that "the stereotype of the witch focused on women who were old, or widowed" (Mendelson – Crawford 2003: 71).

The villainous character of both the scold/shrew and a witch was dramatically and theatrically informed by the figure of the Vice. The Vice (called a whole variety of related names) betrays a significant feature that was lacking in both the cultural representations of the negative images of women and their dramatic transformations in mystery plays: self-awareness. Arguably, it, at least partly, results from the overtly didactic tone of the moralities as distinct from the rather descriptive nature of mysteries or miracles. Consequently, the spectator must not be confused: s/he must clearly know the nature of the characters, which is so significantly defined by the characters themselves, in soliloquies and dialogues.

Perhaps the most representative and best known Vice figure is the Mischief from *Mankind*. This character betrays a feature that is so often associated with Renaissance villains: self-awareness and meta-theatricality. This is already visible in the first lines Mischief utters. Naturally, the context is important here: Mischief constitutes a foil to Mercy, who delivers the opening monologue. Mischief (definitely a "he", who heterosexually recalls the kisses of the wife of a jailor in Scene III, see below) interrupts Mercy's flow and ridicules it; thus, he displays a linguistic awareness of the power of language:

> MYSCHEFFE. I beseche yow hertyly, leue yowr calcacyon.
> Leue yowr chaffe, leue yowr corn, leue yowr dalyacyon.
> Yowr wytt ys lytyll, yowr hede ys mekyll, 3e are full of predycacyon.
> But, ser, I prey þis questyon to claryfye:
> Mysse-masche, dryff-draff,
> Sume was corn and sume was chaffe,
> My dame seyde my name was Raffe;was Raffe;
> Onschett yowr lokke and take an halpenye.
>
> *(Mankind,* 1.45-52)[12]

---

12 All quotations from *Mankind* are taken from the following edition: Mark Eccles (ed.). 1969. *The Macro Plays*. London – New York – Toronto: Oxford University Press, pp. 153-184. References include the title followed by act number and line numbers in this particular edition. For an electronic version of this play see http://www.umm.maine.edu/faculty/necastro/drama/Mankind_Basic.txt (date of access: 17th March 2007).

Interestingly, Mischief first attempts to discredit the linguistic skills of Mercy, both by questioning his argument ("leue yowr calcayon") and his ability to reason ("Yowr wytt ys lytyll"), to suggest that Mercy speaks nonsense ("Mysse-masche, dryff-draff"). It appears that Mischief tries to confuse Mercy and prove his linguistic superiority. He then mimics the preaching nature of Mercy's speech by using Latinate expressions:

> MYSCHEFF. For a wynter corn-threscher, ser, I haue hyryde,
> Ande 3e sayde þe corn xulde be sauyde and þe chaff xulde be feryde,
> And he prouyth nay, as yt schewth be þis werse:
> 'Corn seruit bredibus, chaffe horsibus, straw fyrybusque.'
> Thys ys as moche to say, to yowr leude wndyrstondynge,
> As þe corn xall serue to drede at þe nexte bakynge.
> 'Chaff horsybus et reliqua,'
> The chaff to horse xall be goode provente,
> When a man ys forcolde þe straw may be brent,
> And so forth, et cetera.
>
> *(Mankind, 1.52-63)*

Mischief shows here his command of Latin, or – in general – his linguistic mastery. Mischief is perfectly aware of the stylistic and rhetoric nuances of language, a trait that a typical villain is characteristic of. Mercy realises the nature of Mischief's meddling and interruppts him sharply, simultaneously chiding him: "Avoyde, goode broþer! 3e ben culpable / To interrupte thus my talkyng delectable." (1.64-65). Similarly to the figure of the shrew, especially Noah's wife, Mischief calls on the devil:[13] "I say, ser, I am cumme hedyr to make yow game. / 3et bade me not go out in þe Deuyllys name / Ande I wyll abyde." (*Mankind*, 1.69-71). Obviously, Mischief here also shows his skills of manipulation and scheming, so characteristic of a villain.

Although Mischief's master is the devil, he himself, being the arch-villain, as it were, is the master of other villainous characters: New Guise, Nowadays and Nought, who suffer from the hands of Mercy:

> MYSCHEFF. I, Myscheff, was here at þe begynnynge of þe game
> Ande arguyde wyth Mercy, Gode gyff hym schame!
> He hath taught Mankynde, wyll I haue be vane,
> To fyght manly ageyn hys fon.
> For wyth hys spede, þat was hys wepyn,
> Neu Gyse, Nowadays, Nought hath all to-beton.

---

13 A point also noted by G.A. Lester in his comment on Mischief's words addressed to Mercy: "i.e. since you did not invoke the devil (Mischief's master) in bidding me go out, I will remain. In medieval legends of *Noah* the devil is able to enter the Ark when Noah invokes his name in swearing at his wife" (1972: 136-137).

> I haue grett pyte to se þem wepyn.
> Wyll 3e lyst? I here þem crye. Clamant
> Alasse, alasse! cum hether, I xall be yowr borow.
> Alac, alac! ven, ven! cum hethere wyth sorowe!
> Pesse, fayer babys, 3e xall haue a nappyll to-morow!
> Why grete 3e so, why?
>
> NEU GYSE. Alasse, master, alasse, my privyte!

(Mankind, 2.417-429)

Finally, the last feature of Mischief which brings him close to the figure of a witch this time is lust and crime. Here, Mischief reports how he got away from captivity:

> MYSCHEFF. I was chenyde by þe armys: lo, I haue þem here.
> The chenys I brast asundyr and kyllyde þe jaylere,
> 3e, ande hys fayer wyff halsyde in a cornere;
> A, how swetly I kyssyde þe swete mowth of hers!

(Mankind, 2.642-645)

Preventing Mankind from performing religious rites and inciting him to crime and is naturally yet another trait of a villain:

> MYSCHEFF. On Sundays on þe morrow erly betyme
> 3e xall with ws to þe all-house erly to go dyn
> And forbere masse and matens, owres and prime.
> 'I wyll,' sey 3y.
>
> MANKIND. I wyll, ser.
>
> MYSCHEFF. 3e must haue be yowr syde a longe da pacem,
> As trew men ryde be þe wey for to onbrace þem,
> Take þer monay, kytt þer throtys, thus ouerface þem.
> 'I wyll,' sey 3e.
>
> MANKIND. I wyll, ser.

(Mankind, 2.710-717)

Interestingly, the last command concerns also robbery; a Shakespeare reader definitely finds here affinities between Mischief and Sir John Falstaff from *Henry IV*. Naturally, similarities between these two figures have long since been commonplace in Shakespeare criticism.

This brings us to the nature of villainy in Renaissance drama. One can find a whole lot of figures who can be termed villains. They shared certain features; some of which have been already discussed and identified above. Antony

Hammond gives an interesting and brief account of them, albeit with reference to perhaps the most spectacular Shakespeare's villain, Richard III:

> Of the sixty-odd characteristics of the 'formal Vice' listed by Happé, the following can be recognized in the Richard of Shakespeare's play: the use of an alias, strange appearance, use of asides, discussion of plans with the audience, disguise, long avoidance, but ultimate suffering of punishment, moral commentary, importance of name, and reluctance concerning it, self-explanation in soliloquy, satirical functions which include an attack on women, and various signs of depravity such as boasting and conceit, enjoyment of power, immoral sexuality. Of the Vice's familiar modes of expression we find impertinence, logic-chopping, use of oaths and proverbs, and the self-betraying slip of the tongue.
>
> (Hammond 2000: 100-101)

Hammond rightly stresses here the figure's theatricality: his desire to play roles, to dress up, to be taken by others as somebody else. The theatrical awareness of the villain is further accentuated in his direct addresses to the audience; these, naturally, remind one of the didactic techniques employed on medieval stage, in moralities in particular, where characters needed to be clearly defined. In order to do it, they often addressed the audience and identified themselves. Obviously, a villain needs to be depraved; he takes great pleasure in his depravity, hidden – as signalled above – behind a mask. Quite often, this depravity is linked with sexual promiscuity or treatment of the sexual partners as mere objects to satisfy sexual desire. Here, at least in the case of Richard, women are treated as trophies to be won against all odds; the higher the stake, the better. A villain enjoys challenges because in this way he is capable of showing his superiority over others and the laws and customs they represent. Moreover, he is characterised by the superb command of language which he often abuses when employing chop-logic.

The villain's depravity is also linked with his physical deformity, a visible token of the villain's differing from others. Again, the main purpose and function of the physical deformity is didactic. It thus clearly signals the villainy of the character. It seems worth considering in this context the nature of the witches' familiars – devils in the shape of animals with a physical deformity (which, actually, accompany the Weird Sisters in Shakespeare's *Macbeth*). Consequently, physical deformity points at the connection with the devil; indeed, it becomes the token of the devil. Hammond (2000: 101-102) reminds us of Bacon's view of deformity. In his essay, "Of Deformity", Bacon observes that

> Deformed persons are commonly even with nature; for as nature hath done ill by them, so do they by nature; being for the most part (as the Scripture saith) void of natural affection; and so they have their revenge of nature. ...
> Therefore it is good to consider of deformity, not as a sign, which is more deceivable; but as a cause, which seldom faileth of the effect. Whosoever hath anything fixed in his person, that doth induce contempt, hath also a perpetual spur in himself, to rescue and

deliver himself from scorn. Therefore all deformed persons, are extreme bold. First, as in their own defence, as being exposed to scorn; but in process of time, by a general habit. Also it stirreth in them industry, and especially of this kind, to watch and observe the weakness of others, that they may have somewhat to repay. Again, in their superiors, it quencheth jealousy towards them, as persons that they think they may, at pleasure, despise: and it layeth their competitors and emulators asleep; as never believing they should be in possibility of advancement, till they see them in possession. So that upon the matter, in a great wit, deformity is an advantage to rising. Kings in ancient times (and at this present in some countries) were wont to put great trust in eunuchs; because they that are envious towards all are more obnoxious and officious, towards one.[14]

Bacon notes several significant aspects of physical deformity. First, he in a typical Renaissance fashion notes that deformity must somehow compensated for, by means of its negative, as it were. Therefore, since "deformed persons" are deprived of natural qualities, they become unnatural and seek "revenge on nature", on whatever is good and natural. Second, Bacon discusses deformity and following it, the propensity of other people to scorn the deformed ones, in terms of a kind of psychological immune mechanism which makes them "extremely bold" and "stirreth in them industry" to insidiously act against others, using the latter's weaknesses. Furthermore, their cunning is deceitful: the ones who they scheme against are fooled by deformed persons and place their trust in them.[15]

As signalled above, physical malformation is a sign of devilish influence. Hammond also comments on Richard's devilish nature by emphasising

> irrational aspects of Richard's behaviour: [which are in fact] the evil that the other characters react to in varying degrees of fright and horror. Such evil is also characteristic of the devil ... His behaviour is as relentlessly anti-Christian as he can manage... he is an entirely accomplished hypocrite; he is brutal, vicious, egocentric, cruel and unnatural, conceited, blasphemous: the perfect example of the anti-Christ
>
> (Hammond 2000: 102).

Thus, Richard becomes not only an arch-villain, but also an anti-Christ. Interestingly, *Richard III* is a play which in a sense abounds in villainous figures; consequently, apart from carrying out intrigues against virtuous characters, he also rivals with other negative personae. In this respect, *Richard III* is fairly exceptional in the Shakespearean canon. This feature of the play is probably the result of in-

---

14   This quotation was taken from the following source: *The Essays of Francis Bacon*, http:// ourworld.compuserve.com/homepages/mike_donnelly/lotNINE.htm#deformity (date of access: 17th March 2007).

15   Naturally, perhaps the most notable example of such a relationship between a scheming villain and his victim who trusts the villain is that between Iago and Othello.

troducing politics into the plot; after all, *Richard III* can be read as a play about the nature of power and monarchy (as can be all the other history plays). The broader political context of *Richard III* requires that we should also consider villainy in the political dimension. In Elizabethan times, a standby political villain was associated with the figure of Machiavel. Hammond quite aptly discusses the significance of this figure in the Renaissance drama in England:

> ... the stage Machiavel was already a familiar figure in 1591. There are Machiavels in *The Spanish Tragedy*, but the most recent and stimulating example was, of course, in *The Jew of Malta*.... The essential qualities of the Machiavel coincided nicely with those of the Vice: he was ambitious, cruel, morally depraved to the point of seeing immorality as something virtuous, sinister, treacherous, guileful, anti-religious, criminal from choice. The Machiavel brings some new language (Spivack remarks that 'policy' is the new word that replaces the Vice's 'gear') and some new style: horseplay, lewd jesting and coarseness are replaced by relative gravity and political interest, while the allegorical emphasis gives way to 'the moral image of a formidable, if depraved, human nature, drawn from history and dramatized by the method of naturalistic art'. Richard identifies himself as a Machiavel in *3H6*, especially in III.ii.193, where he declares he can 'set the murtherous Machevil to school'...
>
> (Hammond 2000: 104)

The Renaissance drama thus adds another villain-figure to the repertory: a politically-derived Machiavel. Interestingly, as signalled by Hammond above, the appearance of this figure, or more likely, a reference to it, was not limited to plays whose theme was political. After all, Marlowe's *Jew of Malta* is not, strictly speaking, a political drama. Yet, it is one which shows one of the most memorable villains: the Jew Barabas. It seems worth noting at this point that the Prologue to the play delivered by Machevill was probably written by "Thomas Heywood and referred to as 'The Prologue to the Stage, at the Cock-Pit' ... [f]unctions like a good programme or playbill" (Fabiszak 1995: 196) and is in fact a meta-theatrical comment on the figure of a villain.

Another well known Shakespeare's villain, who is politically active, is naturally Macbeth. His villainy is, however, markedly different from that of Richard's (one can note here the development of conception of such a figure: from an early history play to a late tragedy). Such a development is also observed by Bernard McElroy who notes:

> In *Macbeth*, Shakespeare focuses his attention fully upon a problem he had dealt with peripherally in *Hamlet* and *Measure for Measure*: that of the criminal who is deeply aware of his own criminality, is repulsed by it, but is driven by internal and external pressures ever further into crime. What differentiates such villains as Claudius, Angelo, and Macbeth from Richard III, Iago, and Edmund is that the former fully admit the validity and worth of the moral laws they violate, while the latter dismiss the ethical standards of the world as so much folly and delusion. The latter three relish their superiority over their victims, while the former judge themselves from the same ethical perspec-

tives as their victims. The descendants of the Vice believe in what they do, while the conscience-stricken criminals are in the agonizing position of being committed by their actions to one set of values while committed by their beliefs to quite another.

(McElroy 1973: 206)

Thus, Macbeth lacks the comic qualities of the previous villains and their contempt for the values prevalent in the worlds they inhabit. As suggested by Bacon, such villains actually want to revenge themselves on their opposites, they intend to bring chaos and destruction into the "natural" world. Macbeth's idea is to commit the crime, make a one-time departure from the values he shares with others, and then return to the world where he is known as a brave and honourable general. But the logic of crime would not allow for it, of which Macbeth is perfectly aware:

> If it were done, when 'tis done, then 'twere well
> It were done quickly: if th'assasination
> Could trammel up the consequence, and catch
> With his surcease success; that but this blow
> Might be the be-all and the end-all—here,
> But here, upon this bank and shoal of time,
> We'd jump the life to come.—But in these cases,
> We still have judgment here; that we but teach
> Bloody instructions which, being taught, return
> To plague th'inventor...

(*Macbeth*, 1.7.1-10)[16]

Macbeth realises that the crime will affect the world, which will respond to it by punishing the perpetrator. Such reasoning resembles the line of argument known from Bacon's essay. The unnatural act must be compensated for by nature. Macbeth does not intend to destroy the natural world or retaliate on those who are "normal" in either physical or psychological sense. He affiliates himself with the "normal" world, which – as he well knows – does not tolerate deviations. Macbeth thus displays an intelligence that is different from that of Richard or Iago. This intelligence allows him to coldly calculate the pros and cons of committing crime, embracing the consequences and counting profits.

Eventually, Macbeth faces another choice, which he has been trying to avoid, hoping – against all odds – that he will commit "only" two crimes: killing Duncan and Banquo and Fleance and then he will be able to become again his previous self. When Banquo's ghost harasses Macbeth's imagination, Macbeth publicly loses control over himself; he is rescued (for the last time) by his wife. When he

---

16   All quotations from *Macbeth* come from the following edition: William Shakespeare. 2005. *Macbeth*. (Edited by Kenneth Muir.) (The Arden Shakespeare edition.) London: Thomson Learning. References include the title followed by act, scene and line number(s).

recovers, he braces himself to face the ultimate choice: "I am in blood / Stepp'd in so far, that, should I wade no more, / Returning were as tedious as go o'er" (*Macbeth*, 3.4.135-137). Macbeth takes yet another, this time final and irrevocable decision: either he will return to the world he previously belonged to, or he will abandon it and become a freak, a monster.

This rather sketchy description of Macbeth's villainy is naturally significant in that it affects the way in which Shakespeare conceives of Lady Macbeth, another villain in the play. However, before a discussion of Lady Macbeth's takes place, it appears only proper to provide a wider context of other female villains at least in the Shakespearean canon. I propose to group them into several categories according to the criterion of the reasons which lead them to become villainous figures. Thus, one can distinguish jealous mothers, witches, queens and shrews. Of course, the borders between these classes are fuzzy and a jealous mother may happen to be a queen at the same time. Be that as it may, the first group includes characters who turn into villains because they believe that the well-being of their children is threatened (e.g. Tamora, Queen Eleanor, Dionyza or the Queen from *Cymbeline*). The child is *always* thought of in the mother's mind as inferior to his/her peer of either royal descent or exceptional beauty and goodness, or both. The second class is comprised of figures who do have contact with the devil and declare themselves the devil's servants or companions (e.g. Joan la Pucelle, Sycorax, the Queen from *Cymbeline*). The third category refers to those she-villains who are politically oriented and who take an active part in shaping the politics of the fictional world (e.g. Goneril and Reagan, Tamora, the Queen from *Cymbeline*). The last, fourth, sort of villains contains nagging women, who – from the present-day perspective – challenge the male-dominated world (e.g. Adriana, Katherina and Beatrice). As noted already, these categories are far from fixed; Cymbeline's wife referred to as the Queen is a jealous mother (jealous of Posthumus's enjoying Imogen's love instead of her son's), a politician who makes Cymbeline challenge the Romans, and a witch experimenting with poisons. Characteristically, the figure of the Queen resembles the mixed type of villainy found in Lady Macbeth.

Lady Macbeth's complexity is also a result of the context in which this figure is presented. On the one hand, she closely collaborates with her husband and certainly is affected by the kind of villainy he is associated with. On the other, she is often linked with the Weird Sisters, or the witches, to the point of being called the "Fourth Witch". Like her husband, Lady Macbeth is an intelligent character and quite soon she realises the nature of her crime. Also, like Macbeth, she will pay for it with a symbolic loss of her soul (Macbeth's will be his utter cruelty, cynicism, inability to feel compassion, thus resembling Doctor Faustus's or Claudius's inability to pray). Finally, like Macbeth, she soon realises the committed evil; however, she will not step back.

Thus, perhaps the first signals of the realisation of the hideousness of the crime (murdering Duncan) appear when she confesses that "Had he [Duncan] not resembled / My father as he slept, I had done't" (*Macbeth*, 2.2.12-13) and faints when the news of Duncan's death reaches everybody in Macbeth's castle. Naturally, her fainting can also be treated as feigned, as part of the show she stages for the sake of her guests to remove suspicion from herself and Macbeth. Nevertheless, Shakespeare leaves this interpretation open, so one may as well consider her shock and losing consciousness genuine. The next sign is definitely more clear-cut: similarly to her husband's musing before the murder quoted above, she voices doubts as to the effectiveness of their crime:

> Nought's had, all's spent,
> Where our desire is got without content:
> 'Tis safer to be that which we destroy,
> Than by destruction dwell in doubtful joy.

(Macbeth, 3.2.4-7)

She fully comprehends the futility of the crime. The result of the deed is for her emptiness, lack of true joy which comes from an unburdened conscience. In this way, Lady Macbeth becomes a moral agent who suffers because she can no longer return to the world of nature, which prohibits such a hideous crime (cold blooded murder of king, good man, kinsman and guest, as Macbeth realises in the "If it were done, when 'tis done, then 'twere well" soliloquy). Interestingly, Lady Macbeth, her husband's accomplice in the crime, feels *equally* guilty and responsible for it. This awareness will finally lead her to madness and the allegedly suicidal death. In her madness, Lady Macbeth reveals her fear of hell and hellish pain: "Hell is murky" (*Macbeth*, 5.1.34) and she is clearly afraid of darkness keeping the lit taper by her bed.[17] The spilt blood of Duncan, which she thinks of, takes the form of a physical obsession when she keeps on rubbing and washing her hands to remove imaginary blood stains. The scene of madness illustrates, however, a fundamental difference between Lady Macbeth's and her husband's awareness: she is not fully able to reflect so deeply on the crime as Macbeth; her insanity becomes an escape from such realisation.

Lady Macbeth's madness is an abnormal state, a sign of spiritual deformity: she behaves in an *unnatural* way. However, she is also in a sense physically deformed, which brings her close to the Weird Sisters. These, when Macbeth and Banquo meet them for the first time in the heath, are physically amorphous and their sex is difficult to establish. Banquo cannot contain his amazement at seeing the witches:

---

17   This observation is now classic in Shakespeare scholarship. As Kenneth Muir notes (Shakespeare 2005: 139, footnote), it was made by A.C. Bradley in his seminal *Shakespearean Tragedy* as early as 1904.

> What are these,
> So wither'd and so wild in their attire,
> That look not like th'inhabitants o'th'earth,
> And yet are on't? Live you? or are you aught
> That man may question? You seem to understand me,
> By each at once her choppy finger laying
> Upon her skinny lips: you should be women,
> And yet your beards forbid me to interpret
> That you are so.
>
> *(Macbeth*, 1.3.39-47)

The major feature of the witches' looks is thus their physical deformity which makes Banquo even question their gender.

In the case of Lady Macbeth, it is not others but herself who questions, or attempts to question the nature of her gender. The first signal of such a stance is sent when on hearing about the witches' prophecy and afraid that her husband lacks determination, she calls on evil forces:

> Come, you Spirits
> That tend on mortal thoughts, unsex me here,
> And fill me, from the crown to the toe, top-full
> Of direst cruelty! make thick my blood,
> Stop up th'access and passage to remorse;
> That no compunctions visitings of Nature
> Shake my fell purpose, nor keep peace between
> Th'effect and it! Come to my woman's breasts,
> And take my milk for gall, you murth'ring ministers,
> Wherever in your sightless substances
> You wait on Nature's mischief! Come, thick Night,
> And pall thee in the dunnest smoke of Hell,
> That my keen knife see not the wound it makes,
> Nor Heaven peep through the blankest of the dark,
> To cry, 'Hold, hold!'
>
> *(Macbeth*, 1.5.40-54)

Lady Macbeth wants to be deprived of the tokens of her femininity: her blood is to be made thick, her milk turned to gall. Her desire to be unsexed is further voiced against in her exchange with Macbeth in 1.7, when she needs to persuade her husband to kill Duncan:

> I have given suck, and know
> How tender 'tis to love the babe that milks me:
> I would, while it was smiling in my face,
> Have pluck'd my nipple from his boneless gums,
> And dash'd the brains out, had I so sworn...
>
> *(Macbeth*, 1.7.54-59)

Lady Macbeth consequently denies her femininity when producing an even more convincing image: one in which she not only turns a woman's milk into poison but acts against the symbol of femininity: motherhood. Even Macbeth is impressed by her argument; in a way, he acknowledges at least a change in her gender when he says: "Bring forth men-children only!" (*Macbeth*, 1.7.73).

Lady Macbeth's reference to child bearing is significant as it points at another defect of her body, as it were: that although she delivered babies ("I have given suck"), she nevertheless is childless and cannot give birth to another child, which will lead to another crime (Macbeth's attempt to have both Banquo and Fleance killed) and the utter futility of their violation of the natural order. Thus, Lady Macbeth is doubly deformed: her verbal renunciation of the gender is seconded by an actual physical denial.

The "Come, you Spirits" soliloquy cited *in extenso* above also points at another affinity between Lady Macbeth and the witches, that is her desire to make contact with evil forces. In other words, she presents herself in such a way as if she were a servant of the devil, which was a typical feature of the shrew, Vice and witch in the medieval culture. Another Vice-like quality that can be identified in her soliloquy is that she is ready to utterly and whole-heartedly devote herself to the evil, dark world, which McElroy saw as characteristic of villains associated with the Vice. Interestingly, it is also here that one can observe the change that occurs in her throughout the play: in 1.5 she welcomes darkness ("Come, thick Night", "the dunnest smoke of hell"), in 5.1, shortly before her death "Hell is murky".

The soliloquy is also an example of Lady Macbeth's linguistic manipulation. One of the reasons for uttering this speech is for the character to prepare herself for the exchange with Macbeth, whom she suspects to have doubts. In other words, she must first persuade herself before she will argue with her husband. Interestingly, in both cases – the soliloquy and the talk to Macbeth – she uses the argument of "unsexing", or becoming virile. She further extends it when she questions Macbeth's masculinity, referring to precisely the same term that he has just employed, with a different sense, though:

> MACBETH. I dare do all that may become a man.
> Who dares do more, is none.
> LADY MACBETH.　　　　　What beast was't then,
> That made you break this enterprise to me?
> When you durst do it, then you were a man...

> (*Macbeth*, 1.7.46-49)

While Macbeth speaks of the limits of humanity, going beyond what is natural, she speaks of a man in terms of his virility, of his breaking the limits constraining him and bravely facing challenges. Also, she makes a reference to the generic meaning of the word "man" when she contrasts it with "beast", thus belittling her husband. Such manipulation will be later on resorted to by Macbeth himself, in his attempt to convince the Murderers to kill Banquo and Fleance in 3.1. When the First Murderer, explaining his refusal to murder Banquo, argues that "We are men, my Liege" (*Macbeth*, 3.1.90), Macbeth twists this argument and responds:

> Ay, in the catalogue ye go for men;
> As hound, and greyhounds, mongrels, spaniels, curs
> Shoughs, water-rugs, and demi-wolves, are clept
> All by then name of dogs...

(Macbeth, 3.1.91-94)

This is the lesson he learnt from his wife. Thanks to his intelligence and capability of profound and thorough analysis, he cleverly employs a trick which earlier has been used with success on him. It seems that Lady Macbeth's (and later, her husband's) linguistic manipulation can be viewed as a specific use of chop-logic so characteristic of the Vice.

Lady Macbeth is an example of one of the most complex villainous figures in the Shakespearean canon. In drawing the character, the Bard capitalised on the rich dramatic, cultural and political traditions. Consequently, the villainy of Lady Macbeth combines the features of the Vice, shrew and witch, as well as the specific type of a villain represented by her husband. Shakespeare, as was his literary habit, not only uses certain traditions but also modifies them. For this reason, self-reflexivity is rather limited in Lady Macbeth although not entirely removed from the construction of the character. Shakespeare introduces it in further stages of the psychological development of the figure, thus ultimately presenting the reader with a most complex villain hero. Lady Macbeth's complexity can also be observed in that it is difficult to classify her into one of the four groups of female villains distinguished above, even that of a jealous mother since she clearly suffers from the fact that she has no children.

References:

Bacon, Francis
   2007   *Essays of Francis Bacon*, http://ourworld.compuserve.com/homepages/ mike_donnelly/lotNINE.htm#deformity (date of access: 17th March 2007).
Bible. New International Version, The
   1973 [1989]   London – Sydney – Auckland – Toronto: Hodder & Stoughton.

Blamires, Alcuin (ed.)
  1992   *Woman defamed and women defended. An anthology of medieval texts.*
           Oxford: Clarendon Press.
Brown, Lesley (ed.)
  1993   *The new shorter Oxford English dictionary on historical principles.* 2
           vols. Oxford: Clarendon Press.
Dresen – Coenders, Lène (ed.)
  1987   *Saints and she-devils. Images of women in the 15th and 16th centuries.*
           (Translated by C.M.H. Sion and R.M.J. van der Wilden.) London: The
           Rubicon Press.
Dresen-Coenders, Lène
  1987   "Witches as devils' concubines" (translated by C.M.H. Sion), in: Lène
           Dresen-Coenders (ed.) 59-82.
Eccles, Mark (ed.)
  1969   *The Macro Plays.* London – New York – Toronto: Oxford University
           Press.
Fabiszak, Jacek
  1995   "The (inter-)theatricality of Marlovian prologues", *Studia Anglica Pos-*
           naniensia 39, 189-197.
Goldberg, P.J.P. (ed.)
  1995   *Women in England c. 1275-1525.* Manchester – New York: Manchester
           University Press.
Hammond, Antony
  1981 [2000] "Introduction", in: William Shakespeare. 2000. *King Richard III*, 1-119.
Harrison, G.B. (ed)
  1933   *Plays by Webster and Ford.* London – Toronto: J.M. Dent and Sons Ltd.
Holy Bible. Authorized King James Version, The
  [n.d]   London: Eyre - Spottisswoode Publishers.
Lester. G.A. (ed.)
  1972   *Three late medieval morality plays.* Mankind, Everyman, Mundus et In-
           fans. London: A & C Black - New York: W.W. Norton.
Lumiansky, R.M. - David Mills (eds.)
  1974   *The Chester mystery plays.* London – New York – Toronto: Oxford Uni-
           versity Press.
McElroy, Bernard
  1973   *Shakespeare's mature tragedies.* Princeton, New Jersey: Princeton Uni-
           versity Press.
Marlowe, Christopher
  1969   *The complete plays.* (Edited by J.B.) Steane. Harmondsworth: Penguin
           Books.
Mendelson, Sara – Patricia Crawford
  1998 [2003] *Women in Early Modern England 1550-1720.* Oxford: Clarendon Press.
Pegeaud, Renée
  1987   "Woman as temptress. Urban morality in the 15th century" (translated by
           R.M.J. van der Wilden), in: Lène Dresen-Coenders (ed.), 39-58.

Shakespeare, William
  1981 [2000]   *King Richard III*. (Edited by Antony Hammond.) London: Thomson
                Learning.
  1984 [2005]   *Macbeth*. (Edited by Kenneth Muir.) (The Arden Shakespeare edition.)
                London: Thomson Learning.
     2000   *The Taming of the Shrew*. (Edited by Brian Morris.) (The Arden Shake-
                speare edition.) London: Thomson Learning.
Schlauch, Margaret
     1956   *English medieval literature and its social foundations*. Warszawa: PWN.
Webster, John
     1933   "The Duchess of Malfi", in: G.B. Harrison (ed.), 95-184.
Woolf, Rosemary
     1972   *The English mystery plays*. Berkeley – Los Angeles: University of Cali-
                fornia Press.

Rewriting Arthurian legends in Soseki: "Kairoko" and Malory

Keiko Hamaguchi, Kyoto

Japanese literature has been influenced in many ways by English literature. While he was in England from 1901 to 1903, Natsume Soseki[1] (1867-1916), an outstanding Japanese novelist of the Meiji Era, was influenced by the medievalism of the Victorian Era in art and literature, but saw the medievalism not through the eyes of a Westerner but through the eyes of a non-Westerner. This essay explores how Soseki, based on Malory, rewrites Arthurian legends from the perspective of a Japanese novelist. Before discussing his rewriting of Arthurian legends in "Kairoko", I will discuss his encounter with his cultural Other, Western modernization, and Western literature, specifically medieval literature. Soseki was sent to England by the Japanese government to study English language. In the Meiji Restoration, the Japanese government embarked on modernizing Japan by bringing European systems of politics and culture into Japan.[2] As in the cases of a mimic French man in Senegal and a mimic English man in India[3] (Young 1990: 147), the Japanese government engaged in the production of "mimic Europeans" by dispatching promising young Japanese men to Europe for the modernization of Japan. Feeling a sense of otherness in England, Soseki was reluctant to be "a mimic English man". According to his "The Tower of London", Soseki is annoyed by the crowd and noise in London night and day ("The Tower of London", 8).[4] When he goes out, he is threatened by crowds of people, feeling as if he might be washed away by "waves" of people. When he stays at his lodging, he fears that a train might crash into his room ("The Tower of London", 8). Soseki identifies himself as the Other in England, comparing himself to a rabbit of gotenba that is thrown into the middle of Nihonbashi bridge ("The Tower of London", 8).[5] During his stay in England for two years, Soseki spent most of his time reading English literature,

---

1   Natsume Soseki is a pen name of Natsume Kinnosuke, who in Japan is customarily referred to as Soseki. Natsume is the family name and, in accordance with the Japanese tradition, is usually placed first.

2   According to Edward W. Said (1979: 325), "modernizing" is defined as "[giving] legitimacy and authority to ideas about modernization, progress, and culture".

3   For a mimic French man in Senegal, see Frantz Fanon (1967), for a mimic English man in India, see Homi K. Bhabha (1984), and for both, see Young (1990).

4   All the quotations from Soseki's short stories: "Londonto" ["The Tower of London"], "Maboroshi no Tate" ["The Shield of Vision"] and "Kairoko" ["A Dirge"] come from Soseki Natsume. 1952 [1980]. *Londonto, Maboroshi no Tate* [The Tower of London, The Shield of Vision]. Tokyo: Shinchosha. References include the title of the story followed by a page number.

5   For Japanese production of mimic Englishmen and Soseki's sense of otherness, see Hamaguchi (2006: 1).

including medieval English literature, rather than learning English language at school. Soseki became interested in medieval English literature when he attended a lecture on medieval English literature by William Paton Ker at University College (Eto 1991: 130). Soseki owned sixteen books on medieval literature: *Epic and Romance* and *The Dark Ages* by W.P. Ker, *The Fourteenth Century* by F. J. Snell, *Specimens of Early English Metrical Romances* by G. Ellis, *History of Reynard the Fox* translated by F.S. Ellis, works of Gower, Langland, Chaucer, Ossian, Malory, and so on (Eto 1991: 162).

Two early works of Soseki, "Maboroshi no Tate" [The Shield of Vision] and "Kairoko" [A Dirge] are inspired by medieval English literary materials, in particular, Arthurian legends.[6] However, he intentionally avoids imitating his literary authorities, Sir Thomas Malory and Alfred Lord Tennyson in his rewriting of Arthurian legends. For Soseki, Malory's work deserves admiration because of its simplicity and its plainness but, simultaneously, it is boring, seen from a perspective of a Japanese novelist ("Kairoko", 124). Soseki asks his readers of "Kairoko" not to regard his work as merely introduction of Malory's work. Referring to Tennyson's Idylls of the King, which takes up Arthurian legends, Soseki articulates that he is not going to imitate it. According to Soseki, Tennyson's *Idylls of the King* is elegant poetry ("Kairoko", 124), reflecting nineteenth-century English people in its characterization of Arthurian legends ("Kairoko", 124). When Soseki writes his "Kairoko", he, for a moment, wonders if he should reread Tennyson's poem as his literary authority in order to renew his memory. In the end, he decides not to do so, lest he will imitate Tennyson. From the perspective of a Japanese novelist, he changes the events, situations and characterization in his sources. Soseki's pride as a Japanese novelist is shown in his refusal of imitation and in his challenge to his English literary authorities.

The structure of "Kairoko" consists of five chapters: "Chapter One: Dream"; "Chapter Two: Mirror"; "Chapter Three: Sleeve"; "Chapter Four: Sin"; and "Chapter Five: Boat". Focusing on "Dream" and "Sin", this essay explores how Soseki rewrites Arthurian legends in Malory, by changing situations, events, and characterization. I will also examine symbolical signs such as roses, a snake, and a crown, which are Soseki's additions.

Focusing on "Mirror", "Sleeve", and "Boat", Jun Eto mainly compares Soseki's "Kairoko" with Arthurian legends in The Lady of Shallott, Lancelot and Elaine, and Idylls of the King by Tennyson (Eto 1991: 244-296). He also examines how Soseki is inspired by paintings by Victorian artists who painted or illustrated Arthurian legends: Aubrey Beardsley, William Morris, William Holman Hunt, John Everett Millais, and Dante Gabriel Rossetti (Eto 1991: 198-243). The

---

6   For Arthurian Legends, see Geoffrey of Monmouth (1966), *Alliterative Morte Arthure and Stanzaic Le More Authur* (1988), *La Mort le Roi Artu* [The Death of King Arthur] known as the Vulgata Cycle (1971), Chrétien de Troyes (1999) and Malory (1969, 1971, 1990).

purpose of Eto is to speculate to whom Soseki dedicated his "Kairoko" (Eto 1991: 41). According to Eto (1991: 39), Soseki took the title of "Kairoko" from a Chinese elegy, which was sung at funeral services of noble persons when their coffins were placed on boats in river. Chapter five of Eto (1991: 128-166) is titled "Malory and Soseki" but in this chapter he does not discuss "Dream" and "Sin" in detail.

How does Soseki change the characterization of Guinevere and Lancelot? "Dream" ("Kairoko", 124-129) is based on Book XVIII, Chapter 8 and 9 in Malory, but the majority of Soseki's "Dream" is, as Eto points out, Soseki's own creation. Soseki complains about the characterization of Guinevere and Lancelot in Malory, saying that in fact, Malory's Lancelot is like a rickshaw puller in some points and his Guinevere is like the mistress of a rickshaw puller. Soseki revises their characterization based on the sketchy details provided by Malory ("Kairoko", 124).

Comparing Soseki's Guinevere with Malory's, I will first argue how Soseki's revisions highlight Guinevere's complicated and ambivalent feelings about guilty and passionate love.[7] Guinevere in Malory cares only about social rumor and advises Lancelot to depart for a joust. She does not feel guilty about her love for Lancelot. After King Arthur's departure for a joust with his knights, Guinevere calls Lancelot to her chamber and says,

> Sir, ye ar gretly to blame thus to holde you behynde my lorde. What woll youre enemyes and myne sey and deme? "Se how sir Launcelot holdith hym ever behynde the kynge, and so the quene doth also, for that they wolde have their plesure togydirs." And thus woll they sey.
>
> (Malory 1971: 622; Bk. XVIII, Ch. 8)[8]

Malory does not describe the inner voice of Guinevere, which wavers between guilt and love. His Guinevere is practical, simply giving advice to Lancelot in order to prevent rumor: in King Arthur's absence, Guinevere and Lancelot will have their pleasure together. This probably reminded Soseki of vulgar heroines of

---

7   In Tennyson's "Lancelot and Elaine" in *Idylls of the King*, Guinevere condemns Lancelot for staying alone with her at her chamber after the departure of King Arthur and his knights for a joust, and she asks him to depart for a joust (1983: 170-172). In Tennyson, Guinevere's ambivalent feelings about guilty and passionate love are not described. Concerning *La Mort le Roi Artu* [The Death of King Arthur], one of medieval French Arthurian romances, James Cable writes, "The whole of *The Death of King Arthur* is in fact a sort of spiritual and psychological biography of Lancelot. In the book, Lancelot gradually climbs from the depths of sin to what is practically a form of sainthood at the end" (1971: 13). In Soseki, Lancelot is too much attracted by love to understand Guinevere's dilemma between love and sin, which I will discuss later ("Kairoko", 126).

8   All the quotations from Malory are from Sir Thomas Malory. 1971. *Complete works of Malory*. (Edited by Eugene Vinaver.) Oxford: Oxford University Press. References include book and chapter number(s).

fabliaux[9] and made him call her "the mistress of a rickshaw puller" ("Kairoko", 124). It is possible to think that Guinevere is similar to realistic lower class women of Chaucer's fabliaux. In "the Miller's Tale" Alyson makes Nicholas keep their love secret, fearing that her adultery may be suspected by her husband.[10]

Soseki's Guinevere is more complicated and ambivalent than Malory's counterpart who cares exclusively about rumor. In Soseki, on the one hand, Guinevere feels guilty about her adultery; on the other hand, she cannot give up her love for Lancelot.[11] Her ambivalent feelings are expressed in her accusation of Lancelot: "you did not go to a joust in the Northern region. What is disheveled/tousled is not only your hair" ("Kairoko", 125).[12] For the word 'disheveled/tousled', Soseki uses Japanese word, midareru which has multiple meanings. According to Kojien (Japanese Language Dictionary),[13] the word midareru (verb) is defined as 'be corrupted', 'fall into disorder or chaos', 'be dissolved', 'become rude and indecent', 'lose temper', 'feel anxiety and unhappiness', 'be disturbed', and 'be disheveled/tousled'. Guinevere anticipates that their love will throw the Arthurian kingdom into disorder and into corruption. She pretends to smile at Lancelot, trying to control her sorrow and anxiety in vain, but her lips are still trembling ("Kairoko", 126).

In order to relieve Guinevere's anxiety, Soseki's Lancelot insists that their love is eternal both in this world and in the other world after their death. He does not mind if he loses his life because of his love ("Kairoko", 126). In the counterpart scene in Malory, Lancelot lacks such passionate and romantic affection. In Malory, Lancelot's reply to Guinevere sounds mechanical:

> Have ye no doute, madame, . . . I alow youre witte. Hit ys of late com syn ye were woxen so wyse! And there[fore], madam, at thys tyme I woll be ruled by youre counceyle, and thys nyght I woll take my reste, and to-morow betyme I woll take my way towarde Wynchestir. But wytte you well, . . . at that justys I woll be ayenste the kynge and ayenst all hys felyship.
>
> (Malory 1971: 622; Bk. XVIII, Ch. 9)

His remark, "thys nyght I woll take my reste, and to-morow betyme I woll take my way towarde Wynchestir", is so practical and realistic as to remind us of characters in fabliaux. Malory's Lancelot obeys Guinevere without questioning. His

---

9   Characterization of fabliaux was kept to minimum so as not to hinder the speedy movement of action (Mascatine 1973: 63).

10   For women in Chaucer's fabliaux and "the Miller's Tale", see Hamaguchi (2005: 43-75).

11   As Eto suggests, Soseki may have got inspiration from two paintings, *Queen Guinevere* by William Morris or *Lancelot in Queen's Chamber* by Dante Gabriel Rossetti (Eto 1991: 300).

12   English citations from Soseki are my abridged translations.

13   *Kojien* (Japanese Language Dictionary). 1998. (5th edition.) Tokyo: Iwanami Shoten.

behavior may be suitable for a courtly lover,[14] but he does not express his own sentiments: he is just mechanical and simple.

In contrast to Malory's Lancelot, who, following Guinevere's advice, promises to depart, Soseki's Lancelot is so romantic as to forget his reply to Guinevere. For him, love has precedence over anything else ("Kairoko", 126-127). Judging from the doctrine of love or codes of love inscribed by Andreas Capellanus (1969), we can regard him as an ideal lover. Though Soseki's collection of books does not contain Andreas Capellanus nor Chrétien de Troyes, Soseki seems to have knowledge about the codes or doctrines of courtly love. In "Maboroshi no Tate" [The Shield of Vision], Soseki refers to thirty-one codes of love and narrates that the story of the shield happened in the time of King Arthur when this "constitution", or the code of love, was influential ("Maboroshi no Tate", 44-45). Unlike Malory's counterpart, Soseki's Lancelot does not behave conventionally like the stereotype of a courtly lover who blindly follows the advice of his lover. When Guinevere advises him to depart for a joust, he is in rapture because of his love and his joy of being left alone with Guinevere in her chamber. He says, "I am intoxicated by the scent of roses I have given you" and looks at the main road where King Arthur and his knights rode away to the Northern region in the morning ("Kairoko", 126). Eto suggests that the rose represents sensual love between Lancelot and Guinevere (1991: 301). Soseki's Lancelot is obsessed with their love and says, "What? Rendezvous of only today? " ("Kairoko", 126). Lancelot neglects the fear of Guinevere, saying that we cannot love when we care about other people. He tries to distract Guinevere's mind from her worries and says, "Life is long but love is longer than life, don't worry!" ("Kairoko", 126). However, hearing the dream Guinevere had the previous night, Lancelot accepts Guinevere's request and leaves for a joust in the Northern region. The motif of dream appears only in Soseki but not in Malory.

Let us see Guinevere's dream in Soseki ("Kairoko", 128). In the dream, Guinevere and Lancelot lie among yellow, red, and white roses. She wears a crown with a golden snake on it. As the golden crown is burned by a fire of roses, the snake on it begins to move around on her hair. Then the snake turns its head toward Lancelot and its tail toward Guinevere's breast. The snake coils around Lancelot and Guinevere so tightly that they are not able to leave each other. Even though Guinevere was bitten and stung by the snake, she wishes the fearful snake to bind her to Lancelot forever. The fire of red roses burns the snake up. The golden scales of the snake are torn off, emitting blue smoke. While Guinevere prays for her body and soul to disappear from this world, she hears someone

---

14   Courtly love is defined as "a highly conventionalized medieval system of chivalric love and etiquette first developed by the troubadours of southern France and extensively employed in European literature from the twelve century throughout the medieval period" (*Oxford English Dictionary*. CD-ROM. 2002. (2nd edition.) Oxford: Oxford University Press).

laugh. Then she wakes up from her dream but the laugh echoes in her ears. Guinevere shudders at Lancelot's laugh, taking it as the remnant of the laugh in her dream. Lancelot is so shocked by Guinevere's story of the dream that he decides to depart for a joust in the Northern region.

In the story of the dream, there are three symbols of Guinevere's love and guilty conscience: roses, a snake, and a crown. First, I will discuss the symbolical meaning of roses. As I have already noted, roses symbolize the passionate love (Eto 1991: 301) between Guinevere and Lancelot and their thorns sting Guinevere's guilty conscience. According to Soseki ("Kairoko", 128), even if her pleasure of love is guilty, Guinevere wishes her sinful pleasure to last longer. She is not able to give up her desire for passionate love even though it leads to her betrayal of King Arthur. By his usage of roses, Soseki emphasizes romantic attachment and Guinevere's suffering in his characterization of her.

Next, introducing Western myth and a Japanese legend concerning a snake, I will argue that the snake is a symbolical sign representing a passionate love and guilt. A snake reminds us of the serpent that tempts Eve in the Garden of Eden. As well, the coiled snake decorating Guinevere's crown conjures up an image of Medusa's head in Metamorphoses, "the Gorgon's snaky head" (Ovid 1990: 233). In "Maboroshi no Tate", Soseki cites Gorgon Medusa's head in his description of a relief carved on the mysterious shield ("Maboroshi no Tate", 46-47). On the relief, there is the horrible snaky head of a demon which, Soseki says, is like "Gorgon Medusa whose sight turned its gazers to a stone" ("Maboroshi no Tate", 47). Like the Gorgon, the shield also curses gazers from every direction ("Maboroshi no Tate", 46-47). Though Soseki does not refer to Gorgon Medusa in "Dream" in "Kairoko", his usage of the "snaky head" in Guinevere's dream underscores her guilty conscience and horror.

In addition to the symbolical meaning of a snake in the Western myth, Soseki probably keeps in mind a Buddhist legend of a monk and a young woman who is transformed into a snake or dragon. In the seventeenth century, the Dojoji temple (built in 701) attracted believers by picture scrolls illustrating the legend of Anchin and Kiyohime, which originated in the tenth century. Legends of Dojoji or of Anchin and Kiyohime are popular subjects of Jyoruri, Kabuki, and Noh (Koyama 1975: 234-248). Although there are several versions, I will introduce the main story. The daughter of Soji, Kiyohime, falls in love with Anchin, a priest, who stays for the night at her house on his way to make the pilgrimage to Kumano. Anchin promises to meet her on his way back from Kumano. On his return, overcoming his passion, he avoids visiting her house. Kiyohime knows that she is betrayed by him and chases after him. In order to cross the Hidaka River, she transforms herself into a snake. In the Dojoji temple, the snake/Kiyohime finds a bell under which the monks of Dojoji temple have hidden Anchin. The snake/Kiyohime suspects that Anchin is hiding under the bell because the bell is lowered. The snake/Kiyohime curls around the bell and melts the bell in the fire of her rage, killing Anchin and herself together (Koyama 1975: 244-245).

The snake curling around the bell in Dojoji can be associated with Soseki's snake, which winds around Guinevere and Lancelot, keeping them together. Both snakes represent sinful passion and destruction. In Dojoji, the snake disappears when the bell is melted. Similarly, Soseki's snake is burnt off by the fire caused by the red roses. By using a snake as a symbol of sinful and passionate love and horror, Soseki underscores Guinevere's guilty conscience about her passionate love. The snake is not found in Malory.

Finally, I will discuss the crown in "Dream" in "Kairoko" as a symbol of Guinevere's guilt. Like roses and the snake, the crown also symbolizes Guinevere's guilty conscience, which is not found in Malory. The crown suggests King Arthur and in turn, Guinevere's sin of adultery ("Kairoko", 125). Holding her bright crown with her hands, Guinevere shouts, "this crown, this crown, which burns my forehead!" ("Kairoko", 126). Furthermore, she cries, "if I got my wish, I would take off this golden crown and would throw it down outside the window!" ("Kairoko", 127). According to Soseki's narration, when Lancelot leaves for a joust, Guinevere leans forward from the window and waves white silk. Her crown slips off her hair and drops down on the paving stones. When Lancelot lifts the crown with the top of his lance and gives it back to Guinevere, she says, "this disgusting crown!" ("Kairoko", 129).

In "Dream", Soseki has depicted Guinevere's dilemma: she cannot give up her passionate love for Lancelot but she feels guilty about her adultery. In "Sin", Soseki adds Guinevere's jealousy of a beautiful girl in his description of Guinevere's complicated dilemma. Though the beautiful girl is never called "Elayne of Astolat" in "Sin", it is obvious that she is the girl who gives her sleeve to Lancelot as a token of her love in Malory. The first section of "Sin" ("Kairoko", 142-146) is based on Malory, Book XVIII, Chapter 15 (Malory 1971: 632-633), but the situation, events, and characterization are altered by Soseki. In Malory, Guinevere, being informed that Lancelot bore her red sleeve in a joust, feels jealous of Elayne of Astolat. Guinevere says to Bors, "A, sir Bors! Have ye nat herde sey how falsely sir Launcelot hath betrayed me?" (Malory 1971: 632). Malory's Guinevere worries only about Lancelot's betrayal but not her own betrayal of King Arthur. In Malory, King Arthur does not appear.

Soseki replaces Sir Bors with King Arthur and changes the situation and events so as to underscore the discomposure of Guinevere who has a guilty conscience and is at the same time jealous. Soseki begins the section of "Sin" with Guinevere's monologue: "I do not hate King Arthur but I do love Lancelot!" ("Kairoko", 142). Concerning Lancelot's delay in his return, King Arthur says, "Why is Lancelot delayed in his return? Is he bound to anywhere else? " ("Kairoko", 143). Guinevere is delighted to hear the words, "Lancelot" and "bound", but she pretends to be indifferent, saying "there is neither a day nor a month to bind him" ("Kairoko", 142). The word "bind" reminds us of the snake that bound them together in her dream. Not being suspicious of Guinevere, King Arthur attributes Lancelot's delay in his return to his love for the beautiful girl who gave her sleeve to Lancelot as a token of love. When King Arthur says, "the owner of the sleeve must be beautiful"; Guinevere is so jealous of her that she stamps her foot violently, shouting "a beautiful girl! a beautiful girl!" ("Kairoko", 143). Soseki presents Guinevere's inward agony in relation to King Arthur and Lancelot. Guinevere, following God's teaching, believes that to be a faithful wife is to lead a peaceful and comfortable life though she thinks that lifestyle is old fashioned. However, Guinevere cannot help falling in love with Lancelot. At her sigh of agony, King Arthur says in surprise, "What is the matter?" ("Kairoko", 143-144). King Arthur is shocked by the corpse-like pale cheek of Guinevere and at that moment Mordred and Aggravayne appear with twelve knights before King Arthur.

The latter part of "Sin" ("Kairoko", 146-147) including the appearance of Mordred, Aggravayne, and the twelve knights, is based on Malory, Book XX, Chapter 3 (Malory 1971: 675-677), but the situation is different. In Malory, Mordred, Aggravayne and the twelve knights burst into Guinevere's chamber when Lancelot is staying with her. King Arthur does not appear at all. Mordred and Aggravayne attack Lancelot for his love affair with Guinevere, crying "Thou traytoure, sir Launcelot, now ar thou takyn!" (Malory 1971: 676). Guinevere asks Lancelot to rescue her from this crisis, saying "I wolde nat doute but that ye wolde rescowe me in what daunger that I ever stood in" (Malory 1971: 676).

Soseki changed Guinevere's chamber into the chamber of King Arthur, where Lancelot is not found. In Malory (1971: 676), Lancelot is charged with his betrayal while in Soseki, Mordred and Aggravayne urge King Arthur to punish Guinevere for her guilt ("Kairoko", 146-147). King Arthur asks them to show proof that Guinevere is guilty. Mordred and Aggravayne say, "The charge is one. Please ask Lancelot. There is the proof of her guilt" ("Kairoko", 147). Guinevere, almost falling down, cries "Lancelot!", while King Arthur cannot understand what has happened and what he should do ("Kairoko", 147).

In "Dream" ("Kairoko", 124-129), Guinevere's complicated vacillation between love and guilt is presented by dialogues between Guinevere and Lancelot, and also the dream with its symbols of roses, snake, and crown. In "Sin", King Arthur's knights reveal her betrayal before King Arthur ("Kairoko", 146-147). In Malory (1971: 675-677), Guinevere is too selfish to feel guilty about her betrayal of King Arthur. She cares only about herself and not about King Arthur. Soseki changed Malory's Guinevere into a more complicated woman: his Guinevere, despite her guilty conscience, cannot forget Lancelot nor her love for him.

The ambivalence in Guinevere represents Soseki's own inward conflict and his suffering in his encounter with his Other in England. In his rewriting of Arthurian legends in "Kairoko", he reflects his own original ideas and interests by creating the new Guinevere. The guilty conscience he highlighted in his characterization of Guinevere continues to haunt his mind, and he pursues this topic in several novels such as Kokoro, Mon, Meian and so on. Soseki's project to rewrite Arthurian legends in his own novel can be regarded as subversive. [15]

As has already been noted, the title of "Kairoko" is derived from a Chinese elegy which is sung when the coffin of a noble person is carried on a funeral boat in a river (Eto 1991: 24-41). Eto notes that ancient China and medieval England echo each other through the medium of the world of death in "Kairoko" (1991: 24-41). West and East, first, seem in conflict, but they are finally mingled together in the novel. Soseki was successful in rewriting Arthurian legends in Eastern style and perspective. As I argued earlier, Soseki's rewriting of Arthurian legends turns out to be subversive because his "Kairoko" can be a starting point for establishing his status as an outstanding novelist.

References

Andreas Capellanus
    1969   *The Art of Courtly Love.* (Translated by John Jay Parry.) New York - London: W.W. Norton.
Bhabha, Homi K.
    1984   "Of mimicry and man: The ambivalence of colonial discourse", *October* 28: 125-133.
Chaucer, Geoffrey
    1987   *The Riverside Chaucer.* (Edited by Larry D. Benson.) Boston: Houghton Mifflin.
Chrétien de Troyes
    1999   *The complete romances of Chrétien de Troyes.* (Translated by David Staines.) Bloomington - Indianapolis: Indiana University Press.
Death of King Arthur, The
    1971   (Translated by James Cable.) Harmondsworth: Penguin Books.
Eto, Jun
    1991   *Soseki to Arthur Oh Densetsu* [Soseki and Legends of King Arthur]. (In Japanese.) Tokyo: Kodansha.
Fanon, Frantz
    1967   *Black Skin, White Masks.* (Translated by Charles Lam Markmann.) New York: Grove Press.
Geoffrey of Monmouth
    1966   *The History of the Kings of Britain.* (Translated by Lewis Thorpe.) Harmondsworth: Penguin Books.
Hamaguchi, Keiko
    2005   *Chaucer and women.* Tokyo: Eihosha.

---

15   For subversive mimicry, see Bhabha (1984: 125-133).

2006   *Non-European women in Chaucer: A postcolonial study*. Frankfurt am
            Main: Peter Lang.
King Arthur's Death: Alliterative Morte Arthure and Stanzaic Le Morte Arthur
1988   (Translated by Brian Stone.) Harmondsworth: Penguin Books.
Koyama, Hiroshi – Kikuo Sato – Kenichiro Sato (eds.)
1975   *Yokyokusyu* 2 [A Collection of Noh Songs 2]. (Nihon Kotenbungaku
            Zensyu 34 [The Complete Works of Japanese Classic Literature 34].) (In
            Japanese, translated into modern Japanese by Hiroshi Koyama – Kikuo
            Sato – Kenichiro Sato) Tokyo: Shogakukan.
Malory, Sir Thomas
1969   *Le Morte D'Arthur*. (Edited by John Lawlor.) Harmondsworth: Penguin
            Books.
1971   *Complete works of Malory*. (Edited by Eugene Vinaver.) Oxford: Oxford
            University Press.
1967 [1990] *The works of Sir Thomas Malory*. (Edited by Eugene Vinaver and revised
            by P. J. C. Field.) 3 vols. Oxford: Clarendon Press.
Mascatine, Charles
1973   *Chaucer and the French tradition*. Berkeley: University of California
            Press.
Ovid
1999   *Metamorphoses*. (Edited and revised by G. P. Goold, translated by Frank
            Justus Milller.) Vol. 3. Cambridge, Mass.: Harvard University Press.
Said, Edward W.
1979   *Orientalism*. New York: Vintage.
Soseki, Natsume
1952 [1980] *Londonto, Maboroshi no Tate*. (In Japanese.) Tokyo: Shinchosha.
Tennyson, Alfred Lord
1983   *Idylls of the King*. (Edited by M. Gray.) Harmondsworth: Penguin Books.
Young, Robert
1990   *White mythologies: Writing history and the West*. New York: Routledge.

The portrayal of (d)evil in Iris Murdoch's *The Flight from the Enchanter, A Fairly Honourable Defeat* and *The Time of the Angels*

Łukasz Hudomięt, Poznań

Iris Murdoch was a writer and moral philosopher who persistently reminded her readers of the incontestable value of simple human goodness. It was a most diffi-cult task at the time when she started to write her novels because in the post-war, post-Nietzschean world without God such words as love, compassion, or good-ness rang hollow. In the contemporary, post-modern reality the situation seems to be comparable. It is a great challenge for a present-day novelist to write or to talk about core human values without being accused of sounding trivial or démodé. It seems out of fashion to discuss the issue, and numerous attempts at such debates have proved to be either inconclusive or were quickly turned into ideological bat-tlefields. In her treatment of human morality Murdoch managed to avoid both of these dangers. Moreover, she confronts numerous ethical problems of the contem-porary world without the irritating moralising tone of a preacher who knows bet-ter. Murdoch's didacticism is not aimed at instructing but rather at demonstrating the complexity of modern morality. The notions of goodness and evil in her nov-els are not presented in the traditional manner as black-and-white oppositions. Rather, she often portrays the former as weak and tedious while the latter is pow-erful and fascinating. Her characters cannot resist the influence of the attractive evil, which in turn reveals the moral superficiality of contemporary man.

In many of Iris Murdoch's twenty-six novels the contemporary reader can de-tect, apart from the didactic tone, the continuation of numerous medieval themes, elements and patterns. However, this is by no means an attempt to reconstruct the medieval world in present-day reality. Rather, these categories enable the writer to tell new stories concerning the condition of human morality. In *The Flight from the Enchanter* (1956), *A Fairly Honourable Defeat* (1970), and *The Time of the Angels* (1966), she introduces, respectively, the figures of the trickster, the devil-tempter and the fallen angel. Murdoch borrows these elements from the medieval tradition but places them within contemporary framework in which they are read and interpreted in an altered, also contemporary, manner. What emerges eventu-ally is a complex portrait of modern (d)evil and human vices.

Iris Murdoch uses the figure of Reynard the Fox, which has its origins in the popular medieval beast fable,[1] as a model for Mischa Fox - the protagonist of her

---

1   One of the first sources in which Reynard the Fox appears is the Old French *Le Roman de Renart* written by Perrout de Saint Claude around the year 1175. The character is also present in the medieval Latin poem *Ysengrimus*, written in Flanders in 1149 by a monk Master Ni-vardus. *Reinaert I* and *Reinaert II* are the thirteenth-century Middle Dutch versions depicting

novel *The Flight from the Enchanter*. The fact that Murdoch's "true strength lies in the creation not of lovable characters but of fable-like plots" (Gordon 1995: 23) is particularly evident in the discussed novel. As his very surname indicates, Mischa's character is patterned on an animal which bears an ongoing role in culture and literature, both medieval and contemporary. Mischa in particular resembles the famous evil trickster and deceiver Reynard the Fox. This parallel provides Murdoch with a pretext and material for expressing her ideas on human selfishness and its disastrous consequences. " [F]or fable, or at least animal fable, to work we have to accept the metaphorical nature of the narrative, and the usual reason given in the Middle Ages for doing so is the worth of the moral message which is conveyed through the invented anecdote" (Davenport 2004: 81). In a broader sense, *The Flight from the Enchanter* can be perceived as such a metaphorical fable with a witty moral commentary.

The most notable feature to connect Mischa with Reynard is the former's peculiar physicality. He is often portrayed "in predatory terms" (Bove 1993: 168), has a long, gently curving mouth (*The Flight from the Enchanter*, 79, 82), [2] and white teeth that often flash (*FE* 81, 135), and he drinks like a cat (*FE*, 131). Moreover, he has "the face of a demon" (*FE*, 202) with each eye of a different colour (*FE*, 79). The animal elements are best visible in his movements. Annette sees him getting up "in the graceful loose-limbed manner of an animal rising" (*FE*, 82), and "Rainborough remarked the ... extraordinary flexibility of his feet and ankles. The human foot, which is usually a stiff and jointed object, quite unlike the smoothly bending limbs of an animal, appeared in Mischa to have lost its rigidity" (*FE*, 190). Such descriptions clearly suggest Mischa's similarity to a fox more than any other animal. Moreover, similar to foxes from numerous beast fables, he bears some resemblance to the typical medieval devil who was often portrayed as a beast and "could appear as almost any animal" (Russell 1992: 112). On numerous medieval woodcuts, paintings, frescoes and carvings the fiend is represented as a hoofed, bat-winged creature with horns, antlers or talons of prey. Mischa and Reynard possess also analogous characters and temperaments, and this fact in particular enables the author to spin her story about the condition of our morality.

In discussing the problem of goodness in the post-war and post-religious world, Murdoch – both in her novels and philosophical works – claims that one

---

the adventures of Reynard. In 1485 William Caxton printed the first English translation of the Dutch version of the fable. The analysis is based on N. F. Blake's edition of Caxton's *The History of Reynard the Fox*, published in 1970 by Oxford University Press.

2   Henceforth *The Flight from the Enchanter* will be referred to as *FE*. All the quotations from the novel come from Iris Murdoch. 2000. *The Flight from the Enchanter*. (Edited and introduced by Patricia Duncker.) London: Vintage. References include the abbreviation of the title followed by page number(s).

reason for the century's spiritual barrenness is human selfishness. "Influenced by Freud, [the novels] intensify Plato's picture of the mind as a cave of illusory images by stressing the egoism that generates illusions, making us reluctant to accept the plainness of truth" (Gordon 1995: 5). This self-centeredness, which stems from human vanity, creates a veil of shadows which makes Iris Murdoch's protagonists incapable of discerning reality from misleading appearances. "By opening our eyes we do not necessarily see what confronts us. We are anxiety-ridden animals. Our minds are continually active, fabricating an anxious, usually self-preoccupied, often falsifying *veil* which partially conceals the world" (Murdoch 1999: 369; original emphasis), she says. The state of imprisonment in the cave of illusions makes them simultaneously susceptible to the power and influence of other characters. In *The Nice and the Good*, a novel published in 1968, Murdoch uses Plato's philosophy as a background in stating:

> There are mysterious agencies of the human mind which, like roving gases, travel the world, causing the pain and mutilation, without their owners having any full awareness, or even any awareness at all, of the strength and the whereabouts of their exhalations. Possibly a saint might be known by the utter absence of such gaseous tentacles, but the ordinary person is naturally endowed with the ghostly power of appearing in other people's dreams. So it is that we can be terrors to each other, and people in lonely rooms suffer humiliation and even damage because of others in whose consciousness perhaps they scarcely figure at all. Eidola projected from the mind take on a life of their own, wandering to find their victims and maddening them with mysteries and fears which the original source of these wanderers could not be justly charged with inflicting and might be indeed very puzzled to hear of.
>
> (*The Nice and the Good*, 150)[3]

The author places the powerful agencies of evil, which prey on our souls, inside human beings. Her concept of evil takes the form of Platonic Eidola, which is a "[d]emonic influence ... typically imagined as an invisible but noxious charisma or aura ... to which others are susceptible" (Gordon 1995: 62). Mischa Fox, just like his predecessor the medieval trickster Reynard the Fox, uses his charismatic influence and intelligence to exert power and lure his victims into various traps. All this is enabled by their moral blindness and weakness.

The fox held a peculiar position among animals in medieval culture and literature, and numerous elements of his traditional portrayal have been transported into the contemporary world. It is "an animal of the periphery which is at the same time inextricably meshed in the dealings of everyday life. It is this paradox which provides the key to its significance" (Yamamoto 2000: 58). Reynard the Fox cunningly eludes other fellow animals by "neatly snaring them by means of their own weaknesses". He is "a small, malevolent master of ceremonies ... infinitely more

---

3   Iris Murdoch. 1987. *The Nice and the Good*. London: Penguin Books.

inventive ... a prolific story-spinner [who] weaves his stories out of the very elements his victims present him with, running rings around the controlling discourse
as he does so" (Yamamoto 2000: 61-63). Mischa Fox, just like Reynard, dwells
both within and outside the community. He seems to coexist with the remaining
characters but at the same time he is physically and psychologically beyond their
reach. In a physical sense he often travels and is never to be found, unless he
wishes to. Psychologically, he remains aloof, leaving other characters rarely able
to read and interpret his actions and his true nature properly. In this respect Mischa resembles the medieval devil who is "a creature dissolving the boundaries of
natural species, a monster, humanoid in appearance but grotesquely deviating
from the shape of man, or an anomaly with features both human and animal or
with the features of various animals in combination" (Gregg 1997: 34). The medieval world abounds in anomalous manticores, mantygers and other hybrids of
various forms and sizes. The devil's moral instability, which deprives him of spa-
tial stability (he belongs to more than one realm), is, consequently, reflected in his
bodily instability (Yamamoto 2000: 23). Therefore, he is often represented as the
animal-human crossbreed.

At the beginning of *The Flight from the Enchanter*, Mischa is presented as a
very amorphous figure. All the other characters in the novel cannot describe him
in any concrete terms. He first appears in the story from overseas, a fact which
his friends in London learn from newspapers because Mischa is a celebrated
person and his brief visits to the city always arouse much interest. Not much,
however, is known about the source of his fame. The only hint that Murdoch
gives is that Mischa Fox is a rich press tycoon. During his first encounter with
Annette Cockeyne, the girl mysteriously asks: "Are you the person they call
Mischa Fox? ... I believe you're famous for something or other ... but I'm
afraid I can't remember what it is ...". To this Mischa replies: "I am not surprised that you don't remember ... for in fact I am not famous for anything in
particular. I am just famous" (*FE*, 81). Apart from rumours concerning his past,
and the fact that Mischa is of East European origins, not much about him is revealed. The odd pieces of information that circulate among characters are more
enigmatic and ominous than explanatory. Rainborough and Rosa Keepe, two of
the main figures in *The Flight from the Enchanter*, describe Mischa Fox during
one of their conversations in the following way:

> No one knows Mischa's age. One can hardly even make a guess. It's uncanny. He could
> be thirty, he could be fifty-five. Have you ever met anyone who knew? ... No one
> knows his age. No one knows where he came from either. Where was he born? What
> blood is in his veins? No one knows. And if you try to imagine you are paralysed. It's
> like that thing with his eye. You can't look into his eyes. You have to look *at* his eyes.
> Heaven knows what you'd see if you looked in.
>
> (*FE*, 35; original emphasis)

The indeterminacy of his age, origins and, especially, the question of Mischa's blood, present him as a devilish character. Any contact with him might be paralysing and destructive. In fact, everyone in the novel is aware of Mischa's sinister nature, although no one can pinpoint what is so menacing about him. Even before he appears in the plot, other characters depict him in a somewhat paranoiac manner.

In spite of the terror that Mischa evokes, all his friends and acquaintances seem to be enchanted and cannot resist his influence even though they are aware that it might be destructive. He "apparently loves power and tries to keep his victims in thrall through blackmail, manipulation and the enslavement of love" (Phillips 1991: 227). Fox wants at all costs to take control of the former suffragette and now feminist magazine *Artemis*, which is edited by Rosa's brother, Hunter. Everyone is puzzled and does not comprehend why he should want to appropriate such an insignificant periodical. Most probably "the clue is there in the name. Mischa collects women. He requires their devotion. Artemis is the goddess of chastity, purity, and quite specifically, women's liberty" (Duncker 2000: ix). Mischa's attempts to take possession of the magazine symbolise his desire to restrain the freedom of the women he encounters. Although Rosa Keepe "had decided ten years earlier that any relation with Mischa could only do her harm" (*FE*, 102), she now – despite her earlier avowal and Mischa's move to take *Artemis* - does not hesitate to ask Mischa for help when she feels in danger of the menacing Lusiewicz brothers. She feels that "[w]here Mischa was concerned, ... [she] was prepared to believe anything. When she felt that she had to go to Mischa she was quite ready to acknowledge herself to be under a spell ... suddenly all the force of those years was to be felt in the pull which drew her in spite of herself towards him" (*FE*, 235-236). Moreover, just a few moments after entering Fox's apartment, they begin "exchanging long kisses like people after an exceedingly long thirst who drink at last" (*FE*, 240). Rosa feels debased and defeated and yet she yields to Mischa's charm – "[s]he felt as if she were selling herself into captivity. But to be at his mercy was at that moment her most profound desire. If there had been a fire between them she would have leapt into it" (*FE*, 241). She managed to flee from the enchanter in the past and now she is drawn into his orbit again. Rosa once again becomes Mischa's pawn, almost his slave, and she is doing it entirely of her own free will.

Murdoch's predator character recalls Reynard the Fox, who takes advantage of the flaws the animals possess and uses them for his own purposes. Reynard's success as a trickster is achieved partly due to his intelligence and partly due to greed, gluttony and sheer stupidity of the animals who cannot outwit him. Even when brought to court, his ability to manipulate other characters by means of language wins him a victory. In a deriding tone he tells his nephew Grymbert that

> ... many ben ther that be so plompe and folishe that whan they wene beste to prononce
> and shewe their matere and conclude. They falle besyde and oute thereof. And can not
> thenne helpe hem self and leue theyr mater without tayl or heed and he is a compted for
> a fool And many mocke them ther with but who can gyue to his lesynge a conclusion
> and prononce it without tatelyng lyke as it were wreton to fore hym and that he can so
> blende the peple That hid lesynge shal better be bileuid than the trouthe That is the man.
>   (*The History of Reynard the Fox*, 61)[4]

Reynard invariably wins because he definitely "is the man" who knows how to employ the art of rhetoric and flattery which, in combination with the animals' vanity, guarantees success. Therefore, just as in the case of Murdoch's character, he merely sets the machine of manipulation in motion and then, literally, observes how the situation develops. Apart from being triumphant in court, Reynard, like Mischa Fox, wins the reader's regard and admiration because we are more inclined to condemn the animals' dull-wittedness rather than the Fox's fascinating resourcefulness.

Both *The Flight from the Enchanter* and *The History of Reynard the Fox* abound in vivid examples of the characters' readiness and willingness to yield to the demands and manipulations of the two foxes, irrespective of the consequences of such blind submission. They are all, to a varying extent, vain, egoistic, deaf to other characters' needs or simply greedy. This self-centredness makes them blind and unable to detect evil. They have "interpreted ... [the enchanter] in accordance with the needs of their own imagination" (Phillips 1991: 243) and, therefore, what they see are mere illusions. According to Iris Murdoch, this state of moral blindness, which makes it impossible to perceive the difference between good and evil, is also the great error of modern man who, much like her protagonists, has to learn to resist the corrupt influence of the enchanter, just as the animals have to learn to recognise Reynard's deceits. Only then is the spell broken, the Platonic cave ceases to be a prison, and true freedom can be achieved.

The medieval individual lived in a world of clear-cut oppositions, such as body and soul, life and death, heaven and hell. The dominant dichotomy was that of good and evil, and the eternal struggle between these two forces was the main theme of morality plays, a genre which was widely popular in the later Middle Ages. Iris Murdoch's *A Fairly Honourable Defeat* draws on the vices/virtues dualism of medieval morality plays and employs psychomachia, the device probably first used by Aurelius Clemens Prudentius, as its underlying pattern. In the original *Psychomachia*,[5] the army of vices literally confronts the army of virtues in an

---

4   *The History of Reynard the Fox*. (Translated from the Dutch original by William Caxton. Edited by Norman F. Blake.) London - New York - Toronto: Oxford University Press. Reference includes the title followed by page number(s).

5   *Psychomachia*, written by Aurelius Prudentius Clemens (348 – 413?), a Christian Latin poet, is the first completely allegorical poem in European literature. It was extremely influential in the Middle Ages.

allegorical battle during which the forces of evil are invariably defeated. Murdoch's novel "as the title suggests, concerns the struggle between good and evil which takes place in everyday life" and "between several characters, but primarily between Tallis Browne, the figure of good who is one of Murdoch's rare saintly figures, and the figure of darkness, Julius King" (Bove 1993: 67-69). *A Fairly Honourable Defeat* is a work which "exemplifies the eternal struggle between the forces of light and of darkness for mastery of the human soul" (Phillips 1991: 228). The novel could therefore be seen as akin to morality play. However, the medieval elements which constitute the novel's foundations and which Murdoch borrows and transports into the twentieth-century context, have to adapt themselves to the new milieu where the concepts of good and evil have altered drastically. The former has vitiated in the popular imagination and has fallen out of literary favour, while the latter is seen as cunning and appealing. Consequently, the manner of the battle and its outcome differ from the medieval context. The novel repeats the innocence – temptation – redemption structure of morality plays but the last element has a rather contemporary resolution. The main objective of *A Fairly Honourable Defeat* is to demonstrate that the egomania, irresponsibility and indifference of the modern man are the cause of this struggle between opposites, and that therefore no one else but we have to suffer its often fatal consequences and, moreover, that salvation is in our own hands.

Moral excellence in *A Fairly Honourable Defeat* is represented by Tallis Browne, who reflects Julius's idea that "human goodness is in reality a tiny phenomenon, messy, limited, truncated, and ... dull", as opposed to evil which "is exciting and fascinating and alive. It is also very much more mysterious than good. Good can be seen through. Evil is opaque" (*A Fairly Honourable Defeat*, 214-215).[6] Goodness is predictable and tedious whereas evil is tantalising and that is the reason why individuals choose the latter, however hazardous such a choice may turn out to be. Iris Murdoch endows Julius and Tallis with bodies that strengthen the idea of dull goodness and exciting evil. Consequently, the former is described as a "terribly good-looking" (*FHD*, 17) and "awfully handsome" (*FHD*, 26) man who "has *style*" (*FHD*, 25; original emphasis), lives in a "posh" (*FHD*, 132) house furnished with works of art and, moreover, is "considerably taller than Tallis" (*FHD*, 75). The latter is, by contrast, a "sort of *runt*" (*FHD*, 17; original emphasis), who for Morgan "represented holy poverty" and was "weak and unsuccessful" (*FHD*, 212). When Hilda visited Tallis "[t]he indescribably horrible smell of the house assailed her ... The sink was piled with leaning towers of dirty dishes ... A bin, crammed to overflowing, stood open to reveal a rotting coagu-

---

6   Henceforth *A Fairly Honourable Defeat* will be referred to as *FHD*. All the quotations from the novel come from Iris Murdoch. 2001. *A Fairly Honourable Defeat*. (Edited and introduced by Philip Hensher.) London: Vintage. References include the abbreviation of the title followed by page number(s).

lated mass of organic material crawling with flies" (*FHD*, 59-60). When Julius encounters Tallis for the first time in Axel and Simon's house, he describes him as a "very strange little person" who "ought to be sitting on a toadstool" (*FHD*, 77). The figure of Tallis Browne is the embodiment of Iris Murdoch's belief that "[h]umility is a rare virtue and an *unfashionable* one and one which is often hard to discern" (Murdoch 1999: 385; my emphasis). Tallis, for both the other characters and the reader, appears as an unattractive, ordinary and slightly annoying person, as opposed to the figure of Julius who is the handsome and enigmatic incarnation of the evil tempter.

Right from the beginning of the novel, Julius gives the impression of belonging to a totally different sphere than other characters. During his conversation with his brother-in-law, Rupert Foster, he states that he has "no general respect for the human race. They are a loathsome crew and don't deserve to survive" and adds that "they are destroying themselves quite fast enough without my assistance" (*FHD*, 209). For Rupert this is a typical remark of his sarcastic friend but Julius replies: "It isn't cynicism. These little games will end civilization and probably end human life on this paltry planet in the not too distant future" (*FHD*, 209-210). He makes a point of declaring to Rupert that people "*are* puppets ... [a]nd we didn't need modern psychology to tell us that" (*FHD*, 216; original emphasis). The position he assumes clearly demonstrates that he excludes himself from common humanity. Rather than speculating, he assumes the tone of one who knows that even without his sordid schemes, the miserable puppets would annihilate themselves. Nevertheless, he physically lives within the community, in London, among the victims of his machinations.

In order to prove that his words are not mere pretensions, Julius plans to demonstrate the omnipresence of egoism by snaring his friends into what can be seen as a contemporary morality play, devised and directed by him. Julius's actions resemble the wickedness of the medieval agencies of evil from such morality plays as *Mankind* or *Wisdom*. He destroys the initial state of innocence by tempting Morgan to be the devil's accomplice and offering her a wager:

> There is no relationship, dear Morgan, which cannot quite easily be broken and there is none the breaking of which is a matter of any genuine seriousness ... All human beings have staggeringly great faults which can easily be exploited by a clever observer ... I could divide anybody from anybody. Even you could. Play sufficiently on a person's vanity, sow a little mistrust, hint at the contempt which every human being deeply, secretly feels for every other one. Every man loves himself so astronomically more than he loves his neighbour. Anyone can be made to drop anyone.
>
> (*FHD*, 224-225)

Morgan, unaware that Julius's experiment includes also her as an object of examination, is delighted with the prospect of this trickery and bets ten guineas that Julius will loose. They choose the homosexual couple, Simon Foster and Axel

Nilsson, to be the devil's first victims. Julius tempts, lures, and instigates jealousy and doubt in the life of the couple. Their stable love helps them, eventually, to survive this ordeal but Simon and Axel are only an appetiser and they are not the main objects of his test.

Unbeknown to Morgan, Julius lures Simon into collaboration in a similar "puppet show" (*FHD*, 252) whose aim is the destruction of Hilda and Rupert's marriage. Julius is in possession of Hilda's love letters to Rupert and he also has Morgan's love letters addressed to the plotter himself. The plan is to make Rupert and Morgan fall in love with each other. Julius sends fake letters, prepared from pieces of the original correspondence, to both of them and, thus sets a "midsummer enchantment" (*FHD*, 253) in motion. Rupert and Morgan meet clandestinely for the first time in a museum where they are being observed by Simon and Julius. When the boy says that it is "a *demon* thing to do" (*FHD*, 256; original emphasis), Julius replies: "But they deceive themselves! They are having an absolutely wonderful time" (*FHD*, 257) and adds: "[h]uman loves don't last, Simon, they are far too egoistic" (*FHD*, 259). Indeed, it turns out he is right in this case – "Egoism moves them, fear moves them, and off they go" (*FHD*, 396) without much further intervention on Julius's part. He only finishes his experiment by craftily suggesting to Hilda that her husband is having an affair with her sister. However, the plan gets out of control because Rupert, "flawed as a result of the – usually unconscious – illusions he has about himself and others" (Phillips 1991: 18), is unable to bear this plight and commits suicide. He is the most spectacular but not the only pawn whose foolhardiness the devilish game reveals.

In fact, Murdoch makes Morgan a more appalling character than Julius – not only is she egoistic and vain, but she is also presented as a heartless mother. She confesses to Julius that she was pregnant but had an abortion. When he asks about the sex of their unborn child, Morgan says: "I didn't think of it as having a sex. As far as I was concerned it was a disease" (*FHD*, 96). Even the devilish character Julius is shocked by this crude declaration and the indifferent manner in which Morgan makes it. Moreover, he himself gives the woman the following warning: "I merely wish you to recognize that you are a person endowed with free will and reason … I told you clearly that I could not offer love. I made it plain to you what I could offer. You seemed to agree … You are an intelligent woman. Try to see this …". To which Morgan replies: "I see it. And it's *hell* … I know you never deceived me, never, never, never. I deceived myself" (*FHD*, 93-94; original emphasis). Ironically, Morgan does not see that it's hell because her egoisms make her blind and unable to comprehend Julius's true nature: "How can you so misconceive my character?" - he asks - "I thought then that you knew me" (*FHD*, 94). Paradoxically, Julius seems surprised that Morgan is so blind to what is so evident. To her declaration: "Julius, I could be your slave", the man replies frigidly: "I don't want a slave" (*FHD*, 134), nor does he want her to kiss his feet.

Julius strives to warn Morgan against worshipping the wrong god but he fails. She is the prisoner of Plato's cave who mistakes fire for sun and shadows for reality.

Julius's experiments give him the desired results because egoism and the blinding veils of illusion it creates make human beings susceptible to his temptations. As a consequence, the characters perfectly fit into his concept of a modern man and act out the roles he devised for them:

> Human beings set each other off so. Put three emotional fairly clever people in a fix and instead of trying quietly to communicate with each other they'll dream up some piece of communal violence … It's all egoism of course. They will do the most dreadful things to each other rather than seem to be made a fool of or seem not to be in control of the situation.
>
> *(FHD, 419)*

The reader tends to despise the self-centred Morgan and not Julius, who only divulges her moral repulsiveness. In *A Fairly Honourable Defeat* "the reader cannot help admiring this demonic character's talent for assessing people and for devising the scheme that destroyed so much" (Phillips 1991: 259). Owing to his charm and intelligence Julius attracts the reader and even, in certain scenes, wins his approbation.

Quite astonishingly, the battle for human souls between good and evil, represented by Tallis Browne and Julius King, is in fact hardly a battle at all. "It is only in concrete situations where abstaining from interference would be synonymous with approval of Evil that the good man, Murdoch's saint, will attempt to and occasionally manage to curb Evil" (Phillips 1991: 237). This happens because Tallis represents the position which for Iris Murdoch was the closest to the ideal. He is the only humble man in the novel and for the writer "[h]umility is not a peculiar habit of self-effacement, rather like having an inaudible voice, it is selfless respect for reality and one of the most difficult and central of all virtues" (Murdoch 1999: 378). Tallis, free from the veils of illusion produced by human egoism, is capable of comprehending and accepting the surrounding reality together with its evil element, Julius. No combat is required because, in fact, no combat could win a victory over the fiend owing to the fact that the agencies of evil are no longer external forces. Rather, they are located inside human beings and they develop out of our own inherent flaws. Consequently, Julius cannot be regarded according to the medieval tradition as absolute evil responsible for human tragedies and miseries. He only "occasionally takes delight in unveiling people's weaknesses to themselves and to their entourage by exposing their true selves and their driving forces of egotism and vanity" (Phillips 1991: 227-228). Paradoxically, Julius to some extent helps the characters to comprehend the real source and nature of evil. If it is located inside us, evil cannot be eradicated by any external action but only by our own striving to become good.

The novel ends in a defeat which is fairly honourable "in that, of the five persons tested by Julius, two fail (Rupert and Morgan), one disappoints (Hilda), and two manage to defend our human honor (Simon and Axel)" (Gordon 1995: 35). Iris Murdoch uses the *psychomachia* pattern but there is no ultimate victory of good over evil, as usually happens in medieval morality plays, because Murdoch's moral and philosophical standpoint would not allow such a solution. The final meeting of the two forces in Tallis's kitchen, where " [f]aced with an opponent of equal or even greater strength Julius becomes strangely ordinary" and where, and nowhere else in the novel, "Julius displays human qualities" (Phillips 1991: 234-235), reveals the complementary nature of the two characters, of good and evil which, in the contemporary world, have to coexist:

> 'I'm sorry', said Tallis. 'But there it is.'
> 'I quite understand. Well, what am I to do?'
> 'What do you mean?'
> 'You know what I mean.'
> 'Oh just go away', said Tallis. 'I don't think you should live in the Boltons or Priory Grove. Go right away.'
> 'Yes, yes, of course. I didn't really intend to settle here. I was only playing with the idea. I'll go abroad. I may take on another big assignment quite soon. This was just an interim' ... 'Goodbye. I suppose in the nature of things we shall meet again.' He still lingered. 'You concede that I am an instrument of justice?'
> Tallis smiled.
>
> (*FHD*, 422)

The "nature of things" in *A Fairly Honourable Defeat* is similar to the nature of things in the real world. Tallis and Julius "shall meet again" and the (d)evil Julius is likely to get involved in another task "quite soon". Actually, they will be confronting each other forever because the struggle is perpetual owing to the fact that human characters are inherently tainted with selfishness. *A Fairly Honourable Defeat* presents the struggle between good and evil in and among humans but neither side wins. There is no clear-cut medieval resolution of this psychomachia and there is also no possibility of redemption, at least not in the medieval sense. Evil cannot be annihilated but whether we foster it by our egoism or strive to combat it by selflessness depends wholly upon us. This conclusion of the battle clearly suggests that no one else but human beings can be the source of their own deliverance.

In *The Time of the Angels* Iris Murdoch uses the motif of the fallen angel to engage in a debate on morality in the post-Nietzschean world devoid of God. As was the case with *The Flight from the Enchanter* and *A Fairly Honourable Defeat*, the writer employs a medieval theme but, once again, it functions in the modern context. *The Time of the Angels* suggests parallels between Lucifer and Carel Fisher. In both cases their major sins are the abuse of free will and pride. The difference between these two characters is that the fall of the former is the consequence of his challenge to God. Lucifer's first sin is *superbia* - pride. Later he crosses the threshold of the garden without permission and causes Adam and Eve to act against God's law. His "crimes are specifically against God, and Lucifer is guilty of treason against God, the lord of all things" (Marx 1995: 108).[7] Carel Fisher is a desperate existential loner who falls victim to an alternative system of values which he himself constructs in order to fill the void created by the extinction of God. His fall is the consequence of losing faith, not of a rebel against God. Moreover, it is a tragedy which takes place on human, not on superhuman, level.

Almost all the scenes in *The Time of the Angels* take place in an old rectory in St. Eustace Watergate, London. Despite its urban location, the building resembles an island of red bricks in the middle of an abandoned building site. In the neighbourhood "[t]here were no houses, only a completely flat surface of frozen mud" (*The Time of the Angels*, 22).[8] Apart from the ominous Wren tower, not much is left of the church, which was seriously damaged during the war. Moreover, the building is, throughout almost the whole novel, enshrouded in thick fog and the rectory gives the impression of being a Gothic, self-contained universe. In this modern wasteland dwells Carel Fisher, "[a]n atheistic Anglican priest ... the fisher king gone astray, the estranged "saver" of souls" (Bove 1993: 179). Fisher used to be God's servant but having moved to the new parish he starts losing faith and, thus, his catastrophe begins. Murdoch's descriptions of the fallen priest resemble those of Lucifer from Dante's *Divine Comedy* where: "... [i]n the center of the earth was hell, and at the very center of hell, imprisoned in darkness and ice, was Satan" (Russell 1992: 142). The old rectory, which "seemed rather to have no exterior and, like the unimaginable circular universes ... to have absorbed all other space into its substance" (*TA*, 21), where sometimes "[i]t was dark even at noon, and ... exceedingly cold" (*TA*, 33), with no surrounding buildings, resembles this "center of earth" with its hell. Carel's room, with the curtains forever drawn, a place "both cold and stuffy" (*TA*, 128), is like a cube of ice. Finally, the priest, "a dark figure" (*TA*, 10), in his "black cassock" (*TA*, 8), with his bodily and emotional coldness, becomes the epitome of the fallen angel - Lucifer.

Carel's previous parish was somewhere in the Midlands, where the priest lived with his wife, Clara, and two girls, Muriel and Elizabeth, the former being his daughter and the latter being the daughter of his late brother, Julian. His younger brother, Marcus, "was more deeply disturbed than he had yet admitted ... by his brother's unexpected return to London. The parish in the Midlands had been sufficiently far off to seem inaccessible. There had been rumours of eccentricities" (*TA*, 14). The first pieces of information concerning Carel's past that are available to the reader concern his odd behaviour. A few pages further, one of the

---

7   C. William Marx in his analysis of the figure and role of Lucifer in Langland's *Piers Plowman*.
8   Henceforth *The Time of Angels* will be referred to as *TA*. All the quotations from the novel come from Iris Murdoch. 1968. London. Penguin Books. References include the title followed by page number(s).

characters, Norah, asks Marcus if he "heard that odious rumour about Carel," according to which "he was having a love affair with that coloured servant" (*TA*, 20). According to the narrator, the "coloured servant" is a half Irish, half Jamaican Pattie O'Driscoll, a girl who, prior to entering Carel's family, "had no shape" (*TA*, 24), no home, no love and even "no nationality except to be coloured" (*TA*, 25). After becoming the priest's servant in the parish in the Midlands, "Carel took her into his possession with a beautiful naturalness and tamed her by touch and kindness as one might tame an animal". His "divine hands created her in her turn a goddess" (*TA*, 27) and soon an emotional and sexual slave. While recounting Pattie's story, Murdoch reveals more facts about the unconventional behaviour of the priest:

> Carel, who had been hitherto a minimally correct though unenthusiastic parson, began ... to develop those small but unnerving eccentricities which contributed to the reputation which had preceded him to town. He became a recluse, refused to see callers or to answer letters, leaving it to Elizabeth ... He introduced curious variations of his own into the ceremonial of his services and even into the liturgy. He began a sermon by saying, 'And what if I tell you that there is no God?' and then left his congregation to fidget uneasily during a long silence. He once conducted a service from behind the altar. He was given to laughing in church.
>
> (*TA*, 30-31)

Carel's rectory in London is inaccessible to anyone, including Marcus, who desperately wishes to visit his niece. He feels that his eccentric brother deliberately deprives him of any contact with Elizabeth, for whom Marcus feels responsible. "Carel Fisher is ... closely associated with labyrinthine passages. Although his room is on the second floor of the rectory, other characters must approach him by means of tunnels" (Bove 1993: 180). Therefore, when Marcus finally manages to enter the building, it is done through the cellar; there is no electricity in the rectory and Marcus cannot see Carel's face.

This brief visit is significant because during the brothers' argument Carel explains in detail what has happened to his faith:

> You cannot imagine how often I have been tempted to announce from the pulpit that there is no God. It would be the most religious statement that could be conceived of ... There is only power and the marvel of power, there is only chance and the terror of chance. And if there is only this there is no God, and the single Good of the philosophers is an illusion and a fake ... People will endlessly conceal from themselves that good is only good if one is good for nothing ... goodness is impossible for us human beings. It is not only impossible, it is not even imaginable, we cannot really name it, in our realm it is non-existent. The concept is empty. This has been said of the concept of God. It is even more true of the concept of Good ... We have been made too low in the order of things. God made it impossible that there should be true saints. But now he is gone we are set free for sanctity. We are the prey of the angels.
>
> (*TA*, 171-174)

Since there is no God and, consequently, no Good in the modern world, the fallen priest fills the existential void with his own philosophical system, based on the only thing left - "power and the marvel of power" (*TA*, 172). This, in turn, connects him with Julius King and Mischa Fox, who abuse the power they possess over other characters. Carel Fisher is, in particular, similar to Mischa in that he also "… represents those who adulterate power; by dominating those surrounding him and forcing compliance with his own will … " (Bove 1993: 181). He is aware of the sexual control he has over Pattie and uses her in one of his travesties of the black mass:

> 'Pattie, my dark angel, I want to bind you in chains you can never break.'
> 'I am bound.'
> 'I meant to deify you. I wasn't able to. I meant to make you my black goddess, my counter-virgin, my Anti-maria.'
> …
> Carel's hands descended to her shoulders and he pressed lightly upon her as he leaned forward out of his chair and came down to the floor, blocking the light. Pattie groaned, relaxing her hold and falling back, wrapped in darkness. She felt his hands fumbling now to undo the front of her blouse.
> 'Hail, Pattie, full of grace, the Lord is with thee, blessed art thou among women'.
>
> (*TA*, 158)

It is not only Pattie who is the victim of Carel's sexual tyranny. Soon, much to her astonishment and terror, Muriel discovers that Elizabeth is having an affair with the priest. When later Pattie reveals to Muriel that, in fact, Elizabeth is not Julian's daughter, as everybody believed, but Carel's, this relationship turns out to be incestuous.

Domestic tyranny is another form of power exercised by the fallen priest. Muriel describes the situation in the rectory as a "régime" (*TA*, 100) and wonders whether it was " not time that something was done in the house which had not been minutely scrutinized and authorized in the slow darkness of Carel's mind" (*TA*, 105). The girl finally decides that she "must just be firm with Carel" (*TA*, 142) but it very soon turns out that she is too weak and she simply accepts the fact that "[h]er misery was waiting for her in the house. Here was the machine in which she belonged. Here was the stuff she was made of and running away could make no difference" (*TA*, 214). Carel enslaves all the most significant characters in the novel, Pattie, Marcus, Elizabeth, and Muriel, who are aware of his destructive powers and yet they are incapable of becoming immune to his influence. Carel is for them the substitute who fills the void left after God's death. Just like other characters from *The Flight from the Enchanter* and *A Fairly Honourable Defeat*, they suffer but cannot free themselves from the destructive bonds.

Satisfying the lust for power, which is, in turn, Carel's substitute for God, proves, however, to be insufficient. "Really imagining the consequences of a world without God brings horror and despair to Carel … His threadbare carpet and constant pacing are symbolic of his desire to escape his unsettled spirituality"

(Bove 1993: 182). Gradually, he becomes a desperate figure and the whole novel "could be said to centre on Miss Murdoch's critique of Carel as a Nietzschean sage, like his prototype maddened and destroyed by the power he evokes" (Byatt 1994: 256). He was so proud that he dared to declare the absence of God and Goodness, but when his own surrogate system fails to provide him with comfort and consolation Carel Fisher commits suicide by taking Muriel's sleeping pills.

Together with Carel "the house has fallen down" as well (*TA*, 210, 211), both symbolically and literally – Fisher's Nietzschean philosophy has gone bankrupt and caved in just like the roof of the cold and depressing rectory which is abandoned by its inhabitants and, eventually, pulled down. In *The Time of the Angels* Iris Murdoch uses the motif of the fallen angel in order to demonstrate that in the world of non-believers substitute philosophies, based on power and egoism, cannot fill the void the annulment of God has created. Nevertheless, despite Carel Fisher's tragic fall and the collapse of the rectory, the novel offers some hope for the post-Nietzschean world. It turns out that, contrary to what the priest claimed, it is perhaps possible to be good for nothing. At the very end of the novel the reader learns that Pattie O'Driscoll works in a refugee camp in Africa and that Norah has been supporting financially the rectory's old caretaker, Eugene Peshkov, and his son, Leo. Norah is "good for nothing" because the two men are unaware that the money comes from her.

Iris Murdoch's moral philosophy revolves around the anxious and desolate modern man who, deprived of God, seeks desperately for any system of values that would restore stability in his futile life. The writer examines in particular the yearning to find substitution for what has been lost. It is a most difficult endeavour because, as Iris Murdoch believed, human beings are inherently selfish, and this feature makes us incapable of discerning good from evil, especially when we find the former dull and burdensome and the latter alluring and effortless. Moreover, our innate egoism keeps us in the Platonic cave of illusions – we cannot perceive the surrounding world as it really is, but only its paltry shadows. Therefore, we often replace the void with "false suns, easier to gaze upon and far more comforting than the true one" (Murdoch 1999: 382). We are susceptible to the corrupt influence of the devil who knows how to use his power over morally weak humans. In the *The Flight from the Enchanter*, *A Fairly Honourable Defeat* and *The Time of the Angels* Iris Murdoch tells her stories concerning the search of new gods and values. These are stories which, in the broader sense, reflect the quest of modern man. In the three novels, most of the characters fail but there are also those who succeed in their pursuit. The winners learn that one is truly good only when one has unconditional goodness to offer, goodness for nothing. In order to demonstrate all this, the novels draw on medieval elements and patterns recognizable by the modern reader. There is, however, contrast between how they functioned and were read in medieval literature and culture and how they operate in Iris Murdoch's contemporary works.

References

Bove, Cheryl K.
    1993   *Understanding Iris Murdoch*. Columbia: University of South Carolina Press.
Byatt, A.S.
    1994   *Degrees of freedom*. The early novels of Iris Murdoch. London: Vintage.
Davenport, Tony
    2004   *Medieval narrative: an introduction*. Oxford – New York: Oxford University Press.
Duncker, Patricia
    2000   Introduction to *The Flight from the Enchanter*, in: Iris Murdoch (2000), vii–xiv.
Gordon, David J.
    1995   *Iris Murdoch's fables of unselfing*. Columbia – London: University of Missouri Press.
Gregg Young, Joan
    1997   *Devils, women, and Jews. Reflections of the other in medieval sermon stories*. Albany: State University of New York Press.
History of Reynard the Fox, The
    1970   (Translated from the Dutch original by William Caxton. Edited by Norman F. Blake.) London – New York – Toronto: Oxford University Press.
Marx, C.William
    1995   *The devil's rights and the redemption in the literature of medieval England*. Cambridge: D.S. Brewer.
Murdoch, Iris
    1968   *The Time of the Angels*. London: Penguin Books.
    1987   *The Nice and the Good*. London: Penguin Books.
    1999   *Existentialists and mystics. Writings on philosophy and literature*. (Edited and introduced by Peter Conradi.) London: Penguin Books.
    2000   *The Flight from the Enchanter*. (Edited and introduced by Patricia Duncker.) London: Vintage.
    2001   *A Fairly Honourable Defeat*. (Edited and introduced by Philip Hensher.) London: Vintage.
Phillips, Diana
    1991   *Agencies of the good in the work of Iris Murdoch*. Frankfurt am Main – Bern – New York – Paris: Peter Lang.
Russell Burton, Jeffrey
    1992   *The prince of darkness. Radical evil and the power of good in history*. Ithaca – London: Cornell University Press.
Yamamoto, Dorothy
    2000   *The boundaries of the human in medieval English literature*. Oxford: Oxford University Press.

Medieval dramatic tradition revisited in Peter Barnes' *Red noses*

Dagmara Krzyżaniak, Poznań

> *Literature is a palimpsest in the sense of having the cultural content written hidden behind the layers of meaning that each and every epoch inscribes upon it. The morality play is still one of the most potent configuration of contemporary literature*
>
> Liliana Sikorska[1]

Reviving any literary genre many centuries after its original time of flourishing of the given form seems an extremely challenging task. The importance of historical contexts in the reception of a literary work cannot be diminished; however, the contextual disparity of a given literary work cannot be considered as an essential determining factor that should hinder or considerably change the nature of the impact that literature has upon its recipients, either. The constant set of prerequisites of what it means to be a human being, the universality of human experience, makes the task less impossible and the idea may seem intriguing enough to tempt modern writers to test the way old forms of literature have exerted their influence on readership/audience across space and time. Peter Barnes, in his dramatic piece entitled *Red noses* (1985) has taken up the challenge and decided not only to set his play in medieval times, in the midst of the Black Plague, but also to bring the morality play back into (theatrical) life. The morality play idea is used in a travesty of the form in the play-within-the-play motif, but, what is particularly worth noticing here, it also stands the firm basis underlying the whole concept of the contemporary dramatic piece. Barnes' play can be read as a rewritten morality play and its message acquires a new, more current and actual connotations in his drama.

A social semiotic approach to reading literary texts proposed by Hodge (1990) assumes that the social meaning of text is the prime objective that goes beyond assumptions of an isolated text. From the perspective that sees literature as discourse, the rules governing literary production are social. The line of analysis here is mainly concerned with what the text does to its reader: it explores the ways in which literary works are able to moralize and teach the contemporary recipient. Roger D. Sell points out the fact that

---

1   Liliana Sikorska. 2002. In a manner of morall playe: social ideologies in English moralities and interludes (1350-1517). Frankfurt am Main: Peter Lang, 277.

> Expressed in binarisms of sender/receiver, speaker/hearer, writer/reader, narrator/narratee and so on, it could easily tend to prioritize the first terms in such pairings as agentive, and to associate the second terms with a kind of passivity after the event. Yet if communication is really to take place at all, the binarisms' second terms are clearly just as important as their first ones.
>
> (Sell 2000: 3)

In spite of the fact that the context of "receiving" is unavoidably different from that of "sending", literature may be treated as a communicative situation, as many interdisciplinary studies from the field of literary linguistics prove (Austin 1975, Petrey 1990, Herman 1995, Sell 2000). Hence, the drama analysed here will be treated from the perspective of the social effect it has upon the receiver according to the above mentioned theoretical approaches.

Peter Barnes' *Red noses* is a play about the Middle Ages, it is placed in the medieval context (setting), and, what is most important for the present considerations, it uses the morality play tradition to show the everlasting fight between good and evil. Although the moral of the play is disclosed with the use of a particular story, which is clearly a contemporary literary stratagem (medieval moralities did not incorporate plots of such kind), however the play becomes the modern version of a morality through the world-view presented in its general overtone as well as its resolution. In spite of the fact that the author does not employ all the basic morality play conventions (Barnes resigns from the use of allegory for instance), the essence of the morality play clearly does not reside only in the particular literary codes, but in the prevailing message the drama communicates to its recipients.

The moral and ethical content of medieval moralities may seem too dated for contemporary readers. However, some basic considerations of the Christian doctrines behind it can be translated into the language that should be able to appeal to readers/audiences of varied religious beliefs or cultural backgrounds. The idea of the transience of worldly joys or the considerations on the nature of death and the after-life are universal enough to deserve literary treatment without balancing on the verge of an ideological persistence on the exclusive proper world-view.[2] The central character of the morality – a mankind figure, torn between his sensual and spiritual drives, his fall and spiritual rebirth, his search for an ethical system he could rely on, is certainly worth rewriting, as it is done in Barnes' play.

Medieval morality plays were first of all theatrical projections of moral consciousness; in their drastic simplification of life, they used to bring the knowledge of good and evil to the focus of attention. Secondly, the moral allegory in its dramatic form had one predominant didactic intention, as Feldman phrases it: "to lead the members of the audience to eschew vice, repent their sins, and embrace

---

2   For ideology and the study of medieval drama, see Sikorska (2002).

virtue so that they may achieve salvation of their souls" (Feldman 1970: 43). Other distinguishing features of the genre were manifestations of the cult of death expressed in the *memento mori* as well as *danse macabre* motifs.

Peter Barnes' play proves that the contemporary version of the battle between good and evil inside the human soul in all the universality of the subject can be presented with the use of a medieval setting and with the help of the form of the medieval morality play. What is more, the entirety of the performance/drama seems to be evidently capable of moving its audiences in a similar way the medieval moral teaching used to work, and the task can be completed without the extensive didacticism typical of the ecclesiastical institutions of the time. The core of the premises on which Christian faith is based and the very nature of medieval theatrical moral teaching is transformed by Barnes in order to reach the contemporary recipient's perception.

Peter Barnes was described by Charles Marowitz as "the playwright who laughed at death (Marowitz 2004: 302). Innes describes his drama as "ferocious and its choice of subjects for humorous treatment deliberately outrageous" (Innes 2002: 251). Rabey remarks that the playwright "has forged a distinctive dramatic style which draws upon apparent disparates – Brechtian/Artaudian, literary/popular, historical/contemporary, sympathy/cruelty – in unique fusions which demonstrate exclusive dichotomies to be further means of repression and exclusion" (Rabey 2003: 100). Indeed, Barnes chooses for his play a mood that can be best described using Styan's term "the dark comedy". The mixture of the tragic and the comic, the seemingly contradictory spirits that permeate *Red noses* was something very typical for medieval popular drama in England. As Styan notes:

> The medieval Christian life was one of optimism, which invited a certain necessary contempt for the sufferings of common existence. For the devout Christian, happiness lay in the next world. Thus poverty, bad weather, bad crops, bad wives, or hate, cruelty, murder and crucifixion were part of the divine comedy. In a divine order of things the incongruity of man's baseness and stupidity was part of the sacred pattern.
>
> (Styan 1968: 11)

It is precisely that very medieval atmosphere that is presented by Barnes' drama. A profound sense of incongruity is felt, one that provokes laughter, but also seems to aim at performing a deeper, didactic function by making people think. The juxtaposition of the world conquered by ever-present death (the plague) and a group of red-nosed clowns that by their subversive performances of a morality play persist in their strong faith in God and essential human goodness is striking enough. By the use of humour and laughter they prove that humans are never thoroughly helpless or alone, provided they are able to distinguish between what is right and wrong and to make the best of their lives in a given situation.

The comic element was present in all forms of medieval art, not only literature. The interlacing of the "sublime" and the "low" was one of the most characteristic features of gothic art (Janicka 1962: 23). The grotesque, caricature, bur-
lesque and wit are enumerated as chief elements of the comic in the English mystery cycles (Janicka 1962: 50). The comic is also present in the moralities, for
instance in the presentation of the Vices, and Feldman even claims that "the basic
morality structure is in essence a comic structure, for it moves from turbulence to
tranquility and it always ends happily" (Feldman 1970: 15). It is through laughter,
not only through fear that medieval moralities taught people how to deal with reality performing their didactic intention to turn men to virtuous living.

The "Introduction" to the play informs the reader that the playwright's previous play, *The Bewitched,* was welcomed reluctantly and that it took seven years
for *Red noses* to be produced. What is much more significant, however, the "Introduction" makes the moral objective of the play explicit. Barnes writes:

> Men and women can still be overcome by a sudden wave of compassion for the poor
> and sick but they quickly get over it, while the majority, it seems, find something deeply
> offensive about any transaction in which money does not change hands. *Red Noses* is a
> letter from a transfigured world, much like ours, where statues come to life and human
> beings turn to stone. It's a letter wishing you good thoughts, but chiefly, good feelings.
>
> (Barnes 1985: 6)

Indeed, the thorough message of the play teaches the audience how to survive in a
world of turmoil, in the most difficult circumstances, in the face of death and human wickedness. Barnes completes his task by resorting to all the most significant
motifs known from medieval moralities, transforming them, at times, into more
modern terms, but still retaining their original deep sense.

In Barnes' play the bubonic plague of the fourteenth century[3] becomes a subject for comedy. A wondering monk, Marcel Flote, decides to form a particular
religious brotherhood of joy and to make people laugh against all odds. The formation of a fraternity of this kind was something very natural in medieval terms,
as Lindenbaum states:

> From the late fourteenth century, when fraternities sprang up in great numbers all over
> England, the majority of people, perhaps most people, belonged to a religious fraternity
> of some kind. Because of the spiritual benefits offered by these groups, many people as-
> sociated salvation more closely with their parish fraternity than with the parish church
> itself. In fact, religious fraternities employed more ordained priests than any other kind
> of organization.
>
> (Lindenbaum 1996: 55)

---

3   According to Lerner: "the Black Death of 1347 to 1350 falls two tenths of a point short of
     being the worst disaster in history: on the Foster scale, World War II (11. 1) ranks first, the
     Black Death (10. 9) second, and World War I (10. 5) third" (Lerner 1982: 77).

The Floties' opponents are the Black Ravens who take care of the corpses of the plague victims and make business on the infected pus extracted from the dead bodies. From the perspective of the history of theatre, two interesting endeavours emerge in Barnes' play: the brave travesty of *Everyman*,[4] and the parody of the nativity play in the second part of the drama. In spite of the fact that the Red Noses' *Everyman* is to perform one main function: to relieve people from suffering through laughter, yet, as it appears, the new frame the original drama is given does not distort its didactic meaning but enriches it with some new, social and political innuendoes just like the whole of Barnes' play does in all its multivocality. It is immensely intriguing to see the medieval morality structure mechanisms at work in this new dramatic entourage.

In the eternal battle between good and evil forces, medieval allegorical *psychomachia* personifies the Vices and Virtues and such duality is clearly visible in Barnes' play. People, shown in a moment of harsh crisis, the time of the plague are all faced with a similar choice: either to join the Black Ravens in their scavenging on others' death, to stick to their worldly attempts to rescue themselves, or to do something to help others to alleviate their pain and to join Father Flote and his Red Noses. In spite of the fact that *psychomachia* is not shown on stage in a traditional medieval way, using the well-known figures of Good and Bad Angels, like, for instance, the Bonus Angelus and the Malus Angelus from *The Castle of Perserverance*, Scarron, the leader of the Black Ravens, and Father Flote act as contraries similar to the Vices and Virtues of a morality play. Such a distribution of roles in the play is tangible as early as at the very beginning of it (Act I, Scene1): "FLOTE: I'll pray for you. SCARRON: Don't. We are the darkness" (*Red noses*, 17).[5]

Other quasi-allegorical figures that appear in *Red noses* include Lefranc and Pelico – wealthy gold merchants, equivalents of Goods in *Everyman*, believing that pleasure and excess will cure the plague. The futility of sticking to worldly means of changing the fate decided upon by God is illustrated with the use of figures like Vasques, who believes that if he does not move the plague will pass him by, and Bigod, convinced that dressing as a woman will save him. The equality of all people in the face of death is underscored by Doctor Antrechau, a scholar and a physician (the figure that asks for comparison with *Everyman*'s Doctor) who says:

> DR ANTRECHAU: I prescribe wine and they die, no wine and they die, exercise and
> they die, abstinence and they die, debauchery and they die, cold meat and they die, hot

---

4   In Barnes' version of *Everyman*, the title hero plays dice with Death and wins, Death wears hairpants instead of hairshirt (*Red noses*, 63); the play is so humorous that the plague-stricken people who watch it die laughing.

5   Peter Barnes. 1985. *Red noses*. London: Faber and Faber. All the quotations from the play are from this edition. References include the title and page number(s).

meat and they die, no meat and they die, sleep on the right side and they die, left side, ditto. I've a hundred per cent record of failure. All turn black and stinking.

(Red noses, 12)

The *memento mori* motif is juxtaposed here with the futility and helplessness of earthly knowledge. The Doctor in the medieval *Everyman* provides his epilogue to the play not only as a physician, but predominantly as a scholar whose expertise underscores the fact that salvation can be obtained by no other means than those professed by the Catholic Church and proposed by the morality play. Similarly, Dr Antrechau's powerlessness despite all his knowledge hints to the fact that if a rescue can be found, it should come from a spiritual regeneration in people.

The existence of conflict between the two forces of good and evil in Barnes' play is accompanied by the very belief that everyone can join the virtuous, the ones who bring light to the darkness of the world permeated by evil. Just as in the medieval religious belief expressed in the drama of the epoch no sin is too great to be forgiven, in Barnes' play no physical or seemingly "objective" obstacle can stop people from joining in the path of bringing hope to others. The best examples here are Le Grue – the blind juggler, the Boutros Brothers – a pair of one-legged dancers, and the symbolic stutter of Frapper who does not stop telling jokes in spite of his defect. The Floties do not give up to resignation nor despair, they rather perform the function of Good Deeds in *Everyman*: they accompany people on their way to death, if they do not help them to obtain salvation (as it will appear in the epilogue, they themselves will go to heaven), then they certainly make the last moments on earth of the dying much happier.

Humour and laughter have been known for long as fear-reducing processes and that is what Father Flote and his actors are aiming at during the time of crisis. One has to remember that laughter is an exclusive possession of *homo sapiens*, thus, by resorting to it Marcel Flote and his company underlie what is most human and incorruptible in people. As Bergler points out: "Men can be bought and their allegiances swayed; men can be drugged (even without money and promises) through the use of slogans, lies, prejudices, and what not. ... But no dictator in the world can successfully interdict personal laughter" (Bergler 1956: xii). The pleasure coming from a play with words and nonsense is not the most important benefit laughter can bring. According to Grotjahn humour and laughter enable anxiety-free communication with our unconscious and only in such a state can we become essentially human (Grotjahn 1957: 264). In their celebration of humanity then, the Floties defy death and give others a strength that will not allow any repressive authorities, represented by the Pope in the play, to subjugate them easily.

As Salingar noted: "Symbolic disguising with a ... dramatic purpose was a stock convention of the Moralities" (Salingar 1938: 409). The red noses the Floties put on serve an important function, they partly conceal their wearers' identities in the time of turmoil, and are symbolically discarded when the world is supposed to return back to normal when the plague ends. However, in Barnes' play the plague becomes a force that transcends history, just like in Camus' metaphysical vision (Lewis 1961: 57-108). The Black Death, medieval Europe's greatest disaster, serves here as an emblem of the loss of values and turmoil pervading the contemporary world and the idea of sticking to the Christian rules of serving others by giving comfort remains actual across time and space. Original medieval ways of dealing mentally with the disaster were, as Lerner states "perseverance in faith, hope, and penance, but they were not otherwise meant as calls to action" (Lerner 1982: 94).

The traditional religious approach, understood as the theory that suffering and deprivation bring salvation, is ridiculed in Barnes' play by featuring flagellants obsessed with blood and pain: "GREZ: Blood, ravished by blood! My blood their blood, our blood, God's blood. It's the salvation of blood. CAMILLE: Who's this loon? Somebody must be giving away free tickets" (*Red Noses*, 32).[6] The clergy together with the Pope himself are shown as no better than ordinary sinners, if not worse than them. The Pope is seen as a disbeliever (*Red noses*, 52), a capitalist ("To give everything you possess to a beggar is to kill a consumer and put a hundred men out of work"; *Red noses*, 49) and sharing the vices of politicians ("I'm only a Pope .... It's why I must have men about me who ... know ... when to make promises and when to break'em. No action too vile, no task too bloody"; *Red noses*, 49-50). Pope Clement VI in Barnes' play is like the medieval Devil: both funny and frightening. Father Flote together with his followers, although initially favoured by the Pope, finally turn out to be perceived as a threat to his authority, as laughter represents freedom.[7] Hence, the critique of the clergy in Barnes' play is rather a critique of the social system and the authorities who persist in imposing ideological tools to achieve power. As Sikorska notes, English medieval moralities and interludes also reflected a number of social ideologies of their time and enumerated various social vices (Sikorska 2002: 14), so what Barnes does in his play has had its precedents in the original drama of the epoch.

The boundary between a heretic and a saint has been proved by history to be extremely thin.[8] As Peter Barnes' play unfolds towards its resolution, it becomes more and more visible that Father Flote becomes even more than a saint, in his ultimate sacrifice, death and resurrection, he performs the role of a Christ-figure. He had become the fool of God, transformed himself into a sacred clown[9] only to

---

6   As Sikorska writes, the Flagellants was a movement that passed through Europe during the time of the Black Death and the group finally turned against themselves (Sikorska 2002: 277).

7   Bergler invokes the "sin-theory" of laughter and cites John Chrysostom (ca. 345-407) who claimed: "Laughter does not seem to be a sin, but it leads to sin" (Bergler 1956: 12).

8   Compare with the (literary) story of Joan of Arc, see Krzyżaniak (2005).

9   Sikorska describes the position of being the fool of God as a concept coined by the Franciscans who used to call themselves so. Sikorska remarks: "the fool of God suffered humiliation for Christ's sake, endured them patiently and thus mirrored the humiliations suffered by Christ which made him closer to God" (Sikorska 2006: 276).

suffer, die and be rewarded after death together with those who decided to follow him to death, just like the allegorical Good Deeds in the medieval *Everyman*. Flote is betrayed by a Judas-figure – Rochfort, he accepts his fate, and united with his fellow comedians is shown to continue a mutual support of hope after death when they together reach the ideal realm of Heaven.

L. G. Salingar said in 1938 that "with Jonson and *The Revenger's Tragedy*, the influence of the mediaeval tradition virtually came to an end" (Salingar 1938: 424). Some contemporary writers may indeed think the modern readership is not prepared to understand the essence of medieval morality with its ethical message and the peculiar nature of medieval mingling of the profoundly serious with the comic element (like the laughable depicting of Vices and the Devil as a comic figure).[10] Peter Barnes, however, evidently succeeds in bringing the medieval dramatic spirit back to life in his play and makes one consider the rewriting of moralities in contemporary fiction and drama something certainly worth further research. Crossing the ideological boundaries of religion and politics and resorting to the core of what is human in people is an extremely demanding task and the medieval morality with its allegorical patterns serves as an ideal starting point in the conceptualisation of the forces that govern human behaviour in the times of crisis and beyond.

References:

Austin, J. L.
    1975   *How to do things with words*. Oxford: Oxford University Press.
Barnes, Peter
    1985   *Red noses*. London: Faber and Faber.
Bergler, Edmund
    1956   *Laughter and the sense of humor*. New York: Intercontinental Medical Book Corporation.
Bevington, David
    1975   *Medieval drama*. Boston: Houghton Mifflin Company.
Brockett, Oscar G.
    1979   *The theatre. An introduction*. New York: Holt, Rinehart and Winston.
Castle of Perserverance, The
    1975   in: David Bevington (ed.), 799-900.

---

10   Such stance is represented by Barry Unsworth who does not use the occasion in his novel *Morality play* to do much beyond providing the reader with still another crime story set in medieval times.

Dziubalska-Kołaczyk, Katarzyna (ed.)
    2006   *IFAtuation: a life at IFA. A festschrift for Professor Jacek Fisiak on the occasion of his 70th birthday*. Poznań: Wydawnictwo Naukowe UAM.

Everyman
    1975   in: David Bevington (ed.), 939-963.

Feldman, Sylvia D.
    1970   *The morality-patterned comedy of the Renaissance*. The Hague: Mouton.

Grotjahn, Martin
    1957   *Beyond laughter*. New York: McGraw-Hill.

Hodge, Robert
    1990   *Literature as discourse*. Baltimore: The John Hopkins University Press.

Herman, Vimala
    1995   *Dramatic discourse. Dialogue as interaction in plays*. London: Routledge.

Innes, Christopher
    2002   *Modern British drama: the twentieth century*. Cambridge: Cambridge University Press.

Janicka, Irena
    1962   *The comic elements in the English mystery plays against the cultural background (particularly art)*. Poznań: Państwowe Wydawnictwo Naukowe.

Krzyżaniak, Dagmara
    2005   "From heresy to sainthood. Joan of Arc's quest for identity in Bernard Shaw's *Saint Joan*", *Studia Anglica Posnaniensia* 41, 289-296.

Lerner, Robert E.
    1982   "The Black Death and western European eschatological mentalities", in: Daniel Williman (ed.), 77-106.

Lewis, R. W. B.
    1958   *The picaresque saint. A critical study*. Philadelphia: J. B. Lippincott Company.

Lindenbaum, Sheila
    1996   "Rituals of exclusion: feasts and plays of the English religious fraternities", in: Meg Twycross (ed.), 54-65.

Marowitz, Charles
    2004   "A memorial tribute: Peter Barnes: the playwright who laughed at death", *New Theatre Quarterly* 20: 302-303.

Petrey, Sandy
    1990   *Speech acts and literary theory*. London: Routledge.

Rabey, David Ian
    2003   *English drama since 1940*. London: Longman.

Salingar, L. G.
    1938   "The revenger's tragedy and the morality tradition", *Scrutiny* VI: 402-424.

Sell, Roger D.
    2000   *Literature as communication*. Amsterdam: John Benjamins Publishing Company.

Sikorska, Liliana
    2002   *In a manner of morall playe: social ideologies in English moralities and
                interludes (1350-1517)*. Frankfurt am Main: Peter Lang.
    2006   "The chastising of a bad king: the interplay of the didactic and the adven-
                turous in *Robert of Cisyle*", in: Katarzyna Dziubalska-Kołaczyk (ed.),
                625-642.
Styan, J. L.
    1968   *The dark comedy*. Cambridge: Cambridge University Press.
Unsworth, Barry
    1995   *Morality play*. London: Penguin Books.
Williman, Daniel (ed.)
    1982   *The Black Death. The impact of the fourteenth-century plague*. (Medieval
                and Renaissance Texts and Studies 13.) New York: State University of
                New York at Binghampton.

Translations and imitations of medieval texts in Neoclassicism: Chaucer as a "rough diamond" that "must first be polished ere he shines"

Joanna Maciulewicz, Poznań

For the enthusiasts of postmodernist theories of transtextuality, neoclassical literature is a fascinating field of study since it is, to use Gerard Genette's terminology, so wonderfully hypertextual. John Dryden's writing career alone may serve as a perfect illustration of the indebtedness of neoclassical authors to their predecessors. In Saintsbury's words, the "one thing which to all appearance he [Dryden] could not do was to originate a theme", it seemed that "his strong and powerful mind could grind the corn supplied to it into the finest flour, but the corn must always be supplied" (Saintsbury 1915: 135, 136). Dryden seems to be emblematic for his own period since Neoclassicism is particularly wont to re-write earlier texts: neoclassical literature abounds in translations, paraphrases, metaphrases, imitations, parodies, stylisations and other forms derivative in nature. The Antiquity is an obvious but not the only source of inspiration. Next to the myriad translations and adaptations of classical literature, the neoclassical authors, most notably John Dryden and Alexander Pope, begin to take interest in Geoffrey Chaucer, who himself was a transformer rather than an inventor of stories. The medieval poet was described as a "translator" by his own contemporaries and he himself liked to be associated with classical authors like Ovid or Virgil (Saunders 2001: 5).

The study of the eighteenth-century adaptations of Chaucer reveals a similarly ambiguous attitude towards the Middle Ages that neoclassicists demonstrated towards the Antiquity. The discussion about the medieval scholarship, understood as the serious discipline intending to reconstruct the medieval world with the highest possible accuracy, and medievalism, defined as the appropriation of medieval tradition with a view to make it subservient to the uses of modernity, seems to reflect the debate about the Antiquity, dubbed by Jonathan Swift as The Battle of the Books.[1] The translations and imitations of Chaucer's texts

---

1   As George Levine explains The Battle of the Books derived from the fact that "from the very beginning, Renaissance humanism and the revival of antiquity concealed a paradox. On the one hand, the humanists had resurrected the classics for immediate use and set about imitating them for the practical purposes of their own time and place. ... On the other hand, the recovery of the ancient authors seemed to require, in order to make sense of them, the recovery of the whole world in which they lived and worked and wrote". They wanted to make them "universal and modern" but at the same time they could not overlook their "anomalies" and "strangeness" and thus "a fissure opened between imitation and scholarship" (Levine 1994: 3).

produced at the beginning of the eighteenth century reveal the same paradox in the reception of the medieval poet. On the one hand, he is recognised as the father of English poetry, a vernacular genius surpassing even Ovid himself, who needs to be rescued from oblivion in which he had fallen due to the incomprehensibility of the idiom he used. On the other, the far-reaching alterations introduced to the modernised versions of Chaucer's texts, be it translations or imitations, show the liberality with which medieval tradition is treated. The adjustment of the language as well as contemporary allusions placed in the revised poems prove that neoclassical writers searched in Chaucer what was timeless rather than what was distinct and peculiar to the Middle Ages. As Glenn Wright argues, what is evident in Dryden's adaptations of medieval poetry is the "patriotic" and "earnest" attempt to "restore Chaucer's reputation" side by side with the conviction that "Chaucer's language and versification – but also his themes, his choice of subjects, and certain aspects of his style—far from recording his genius, are ... historically contingent factors obscuring it"[2] (Wright 2001: 198). Alexander Pope's alterations, in turn, indicate the fascination with those aspects of Chaucer's works that are alien to the neoclassical decorum and the urge to polish their language.

The author who initiated the "early strand of modernization" of Chaucer (Machan 1994: 41) was John Dryden who included translations and an imitation of fragments from *The Canterbury Tales* in his *Fables Ancient and Modern* (1700), next to the translations of fragments of Homer's, Ovid's and Boccaccio's poetry. The translated tales were "Palamon and Arcite: or The Knight's Tale", "The Cock and the Fox, or The Tale of the Nun's Priest", "The Wife of Bath's Tale", and the "enlarged" imitation of a fragment from the General Prologue "The Character of a Good Parson". A poet who perpetuated interest in Chaucer was Alexander Pope. Inspired by Dryden's *Fables*, Pope tried his hand in the translations: "January and May; or the Merchant's Tale: from Chaucer", written as early as in 1704, published in Tonson's *Miscellanies* in 1709, as well as *The Wife of Bath her Prologue, from Chaucer*, written in 1704, published in Steele's *Miscellanies* in 1709. In 1715 he finished the imitation of *The House of Fame* entitled *The Temple of Fame*. John Gay's dramatisation of Chaucer in his play *Wife of Bath* performed for the first time in 1712 in Drury Lane, while Pope was working on his *Temple of Fame*, as well as Matthew Prior's *Erle Robert's Mice: a Tale in Imitation of Chaucer* (1712), are seen as the further "contribution to the revival of interest in Chaucer and his works which the young poets Pope, Gay and Prior,

---

2   Glenn Wright describes the neoclassical modernisations of Chaucer as examples of "antime-dievalism" and "de-medievalizings of Chaucer" (Wright 2001: 198) but the loose adaptation of medieval stories for the needs of modern poetics, although it has little to do with medieval scholarship proper, seems to fit some of the definitions of medievalism understood in distinction from the more "serious" undertaking of the faithful resuscitation of the medieval culture.

following Dryden's lead, were helping to bring about during the reign of Queen Anne" (Winton 1993: x). The aim of this paper is to analyse selected examples of John Dryden's and Alexander Pope's texts inspired by Chaucer: Dryden's translations of selected stories from *The Canterbury Tales*, an imitation of the character of the Parson from the General Prologue and Pope's translation of stories from *The Canterbury Tales*, his imitation *The Temple of Fame* as well as the stylisation *Chaucer*, to demonstrate the ambiguous approach neoclassicists had towards the English Middle Ages.

The approach of neoclassical writers to Middle English texts was characterised by what A.S.G. Edwards dubbed as the "history of two contending claims", that is by the simultaneous "need to make Middle English texts accessible to audiences with little or no knowledge of their grammar, orthography or syntax" and "to retrieve and preserve the text" (quoted in: Machan 1994: 41). The first edition of *The Canterbury Tales*, "typically regarded as the first truly scholarly edition of the poem", was published by Thomas Tyrwhitt in 1775 (Machan 1994: 91). Dryden's and Pope's modernisations of Chaucer's poetry are tainted by the ambiguity between the elevation of Chaucer as the national genius and the dissatisfaction with its archaic quaintness and crudeness, which gave rise to the liberal alterations of original text, on the one hand, and parodic stylisations on the other. Thus, despite repeated assertions that Chaucer was introduced and modernised to acquaint the reading public with medieval poetry which initiated the history of vernacular poetry, early eighteenth-century modernisations had little to do with the proper study of the medieval culture and what Clare A. Simmons calls the quest for the "Real" Middle Ages. Even the translations of Chaucer's texts were loose enough to claim that the reconstruction of the medieval culture was not their primary objective. Thus, it is not unjustified to claim that the modernisations of Chaucer's poetry created in the eighteenth century, be they translations, imitations or stylisations, regardless of their degree of fidelity to the original, reveal as much about the time in which they were created as about Chaucer's own period. The medieval poems were oftentimes used to shed light on cultural, political or any other aspects of the contemporary world, which makes the eighteenth-century versions of Chaucer poems true examples of medievalism, understood as the use of medieval tradition for the purposes other than its faithful reconstruction (Simmons 2001: 1).

The professed aim of the eighteenth-century translators and imitators was to rescue Chaucer from the oblivion caused by the incomprehensibility of his language. By the seventeenth century the Middle English had become difficult to comprehend, as is attested by Addison in 1694: "... Chaucer, a merry bard arose; / and many a Story told in Rhime and Prose. / But Age has rusted what the Poet writ, / Worn out his Language and obscured his Wit" (quoted in: Brewer 1978: 159). The medieval poet was known mainly from Thomas Speght's black-letter edition of *Works*, published in 1598, revised in 1602 and reissued in 1687

(Machan 1994: 42), which was, in Winton's words, "a most forbidding example of the "art of the book"" (1993: 28). Speght's text, daunting though it seemed, was provided with a glossary, which as Tim Machan points out, "can be seen as an effort to make the work as intelligible as possible to a larger audience of nonantiquarians who otherwise would not have beeen (sic!) able to read Middle English language" (Machan 1994: 41). However, the glossary was just an awkward attempt to reconcile two extreme views on how to edit Middle English literature: to preserve and introduce it, as Edwards says, "in all is quaintness and obscurity, as an emblem of the cultural change separating the modern era from the *medium avum*" (quoted in: Machan 1994: 41) and at the same time to make them comprehensible.

That the language of archaic poetry did not seem particularly appealing is evident in the critical writings of both Dryden and Pope. Dryden opts for an action to remedy the situation in which a good poet falls into an oblivion due to the obsoleteness of language: "[i]f the first end of a writer be to be understood, then as his language grows obscure, his thoughts must grow obscure" (Dryden 1987: 565), therefore it stands to reason that the language needs to be modernised. The true value of Chaucer's art can thus be made evident only by "turning some of the *Canterbury Tales* into our language, as it is now refined" (Dryden 1987: 553). In his *Essay on Criticism* (written in 1709, published in 1711) Alexander Pope laments the rapidity of the development of vernacular languages, which dooms poets to oblivion:

> Short is the Date, alas, of *Modern Rhymes*;
> And 'tis but just to let 'em live *betimes*.
> No longer now that Golden Age appears,
> When Patriarch-Wits surviv'd a *thousand Years*;
> Now Length of *Fame* (our *second* Life) is lost,
> And bare Threescore is all ev'n That can boast:
> our Sons their Father's *failing Language* see,
> And as *Chaucer* is, shall Dryden be.

(Pope 1963: 156)

Pope follows in Dryden's footsteps offering his own translations and imitations. In this way the language of medieval poetry is sacrificed in order to rescue its meaning.

In the Preface to *Fables Ancient and Modern* (1700), which is considered as Dryden's finest achievement in literary criticism, Dryden explains that he put the value of Chaucer's poetry to a test by placing translations of fragments of his *Canterbury Tales* next to the English versions of Ovid's *Metamorphoses*, Homer's *Iliad* and Boccaccio's *Decameron*. The comparison, however, was possible only if the differences in languages had been evened out.

> Having done with Ovid for this time, it came to my mind that our old English poet in many things resembled him, and that with no disadvantage on the side of the modern author, as I shall endeavour to prove when I compare them. And as I am, and have always been studious to promote the honour of my native country, so I soon resolved to put their merits to the trial by turning some of the *Canterbury Tales* into our language, as it is now refined; for by this means both the poets being set in the same light and dressed in the same English habit, story to be compared with story, a certain judgement may be made betwixt them by the reader, without obtruding my opinion on him.
>
> (Dryden 1987: 553)

In Dryden's opinion Chaucer surpassed Ovid himself in the presentation of manners, that is "the passions and, in a larger sense, the descriptions of persons and their very habits" (Dryden 1987: 558). Dryden is unreserved in singing praises about Chaucer's characterisation: "I see ... all the pilgrims in the *Canterbury Tales*, their humours, their features, and the very dress, as distinctly as if I have supped with them at the Tabard in Southwark", and thus the conclusion is clear: "the figures of Chaucer are much more lively and set in a better light" (Dryden 1987: 558). Chaucer is also better than Ovid in the expression of thoughts. The English poet's style is more restrained, devoid of witticisms abundant in Ovid's language and which Dryden considers as "glittering trifles" winning the admiration of "vulgar judges", whereas more refined critics see that "so far from being witty ... in a serious poem they are nauseous, because they are unnatural" (Dryden 1987: 558).

The only aspect of Chaucer's poetry inferior to that of Ovid is language but the disadvantage is easily accountable by "owning that Ovid lived when the Roman tongue was in its meridian; Chaucer in dawning of our language" (Dryden 1987: 558). It is for this reason that Dryden believes, despite voices to the contrary, that the benefits of modernisation of Chaucer's poetry outweigh the losses. Not only does the new translation make Chaucer more comprehensible for the general reader unaccustomed with Middle English, but also it provides an excellent opportunity for considerable improvements on the original. "If the first end of a writer is to be understood, then as his language grows obsolete, his thoughts must be obsolete" (Dryden 1987: 565). Words, according to Dryden, are of secondary importance to meaning. It is Chaucer's comprehensibility that needs to be revived. "Words are not like landmarks, so sacred as never to be removed. Customs are changed, and even statues are silently repealed, when the reason ceases for which they were enacted" (Dryden 1987: 566). The beauty of the original language malformed due to the "innovation of words" is not to be regretted for "in the first place, not only their beauty but their being is lost where they are no longer understood" (Dryden 1987: 566). The target audience of Dryden's modernised Chaucer is the general reading public among whom the medieval poet fell into oblivion, and not scholars careful about the accuracy of his text, which has to be compromised if Chaucer is to enter the consciousness of the moderns.

> How few are there who can read Chaucer so as not to understand him perfectly! And if imperfectly, then with less profit pleasure. 'Tis not for the use of some old Saxon friends that I have taken these pains with him. Let them neglect my version, because they have no need of it. I made it for their sakes who understand sense and poetry as well as they; when that poetry and sense is put into words which they understand. ... Yet I think I have just occasion to complain of them, who because they understand Chaucer, would deprive the greater part of their countrymen of the same advantage, and hoard him up, as misers do their grandam gold, only to look on it themselves and hinder others from making use of it.
>
> (Dryden 1987: 566)

Dryden thus steers the middle course between those who consider Chaucer's tales as "unworthy of their pains, and look on Chaucer as a dry old-fashioned wit, not worth receiving" (Dryden 1987: 564) and the guardians of Chaucer's medieval charm, who "suppose there is a certain veneration due to his old language; and that it is less than a profanation and sacrilege to alter it ... [and] are further of opinion, that somewhat of his good sense will suffer in this transfusion, and much beauty of his thoughts will infallibly be lost, which appear with more grace in their old habit" (Dryden 1987: 565).

There is no denying that the modernisation of Chaucer's language was a way to bring medieval poetry closer to the neoclassical reader. Yet, it is also true that some of its medieval character was lost with the alteration of its language. The preservation of the medieval quintessence of Chaucer's poetry was further compromised by the fact that translations in the eighteenth century were barely faithful. The translators customarily tried to improve the originals or, better still, to point to parallels between the past and now, and by doing so they encroached on the realm of imitations, which by definition entailed the reinterpretation of the material borrowed from a traditional source. The demarcation of a boundary between the neoclassical genres of translation and imitation is, therefore, no easy task, chiefly due to the very fact of the infidelity of translations in Neoclassicism. As Ian Fraser Gordon argues, the origin of the imitation is to be found in the verse translation popular in the seventeenth century, which was first characterised by high faithfulness to the original text only to become looser with the progress of the age. "It became more important for a translator", says Gordon, "to catch the spirit of a work rather than give a word for word rendition" (Gordon 1970: 54). The new ideas concerning rendition which after Restoration were imported from France to England stipulated that translation should be "an independent work of art in the new language". Gordon argues that the invention of the imitation is the outcome of growth of the liberalisation in translation, but at some point the imitation developed its distinctive characteristics and "became completely independent of the various levels of translation" (Gordon

1970: 55, 56). The dividing line between the new genres is determined by the different assumptions made by the authors about the target audience of their texts: "where translation was primarily intended to help those readers who could not understand the original, imitation assumed that the reader would be sufficiently familiar with the original to appreciate the author's wit in adapting it" (Gordon 1970: 56). Admittedly, there is a difference between the two genres but it is exactly the liberties allowed for in translations, liberties taken to make the translated texts more suitable and more applicable to contemporaneity, that makes the distinction drawn by Gordon arbitrary.

Translations, just like imitations, not infrequently were meant as improvements of the originals and commentaries on contemporary times, which were achieved by means of emphasis, allusions, additions or omissions. Translators customarily availed themselves of earlier translations borrowing certain lines and thus chose those which they considered more appealing or which highlighted parallels between the past presented in the original and the presence. John Dryden's rendition of Virgil's *Aeneid* for instance, as Howard Erskine-Hill argues, "implied a comparison between contemporary England and Augustan Rome". However, if the classical *Aeneid* was created to legitimise the reign of Augustus, the English one was written to express Jacobite sympathies and cast shadow on William III's right to the throne. Erskine-Hill explains:

> Virgil is woven into the fabric of English history at this time; the dead Charles and the exiled James were inextricably involved with the Augustan Myth for Dryden. Thus, far from working for a parallel between Aeneas and William, he was at pains to make his English *Aeneid* express what for him was the truth; those punished in the underworld include men 'who Brother's better Claim disown, / Expel their Parents, and usurp the Throne.' Dryden changed the sense of his text (Ruaeus's edition of 1675) to make this pointed reference to William and Mary.
>
> (Erskine – Hill 1993: 29-30)

Thus, if Dryden's primary goal was to introduce Virgil to readers who did not understand Latin, he also employed the text to shed light on certain aspects of his own age. The two genres, also in relation to the use of medieval texts, are not radically distinct. The avowed translations of Chaucer presented by John Dryden and Alexander are loose enough to share characteristics of imitations, and thus are not only the revival of Chaucer's tradition in the consciousness of their readers but also the commentary upon Neoclassicism.

Dryden himself treated imitation as a variety of translation. In his Preface to *Ovid's Epistles* (1680) he laid down his own theory of translation. For the poet there are three ways of translating: metaphrase, paraphrase and imitation. Metaphrase is defined by Dryden as a literal translation or "turning an author word by word, and line by line, from one language into another", which is fraught with numerous difficulties. "He [the translator] is to consider at the same time the thought of his author, and his words, and to find a counterpart to each in another language: and besides this he is to confine himself to the compass of numbers, and the slavery of rhymes". Dryden considers this type of translation as most difficult and least poetic:"'[t]is much like dancing on ropes with fettered legs. A man may shun a fall by using caution, but the gracefulness of motion is not to be expected, and when we have said the best of it, 'tis but a foolish task; for no sober man would put himself into danger for the applause of escaping without breaking his neck" (Dryden 1987: 160, 161).

The condemnation of the literal, or "servile", translation does not mean that Dryden unreservedly advocates the employment of imitation, which allows for much greater liberty in the rendition of one text into another. He describes an imitation as a "libertine way of rendering authors", or "an endeavour of a later poet to write like one who has written before him on the same subject: that is, not to translate his words, or to be confined to his sense, but only to set him as a pattern, and to write as he supposes that author would have done had he lived in our age, and in our country" (Dryden 1987: 162). The liberty granted to the translator in the genre of imitation precludes doing justice to the original text: "[t]o state it fairly, imitation of an author", argues Dryden, "is the most advantageous way for a translator to show himself, but the greatest wrong which can be done to the memory and reputation of the dead". Thus, the creation of the new, even if the improved version of the text still incurs the loss of the old. "By this way 'tis true, somewhat that is excellent may be invented, perhaps more excellent than the first design ... Yet he who is inquisitive to know an author's thoughts will be disappointed in his expectation. And 'tis not always that a man will be contented to have a present made him, when he expects the payment of the debt" (Dryden 1987: 162-163). In view of the argument, this kind of translation, which takes too great liberties with the source text, and thus in the attempt to surpass its excellence casts the original in shadow, seems to Dryden to do as poor service to the translated work, as a literal rendition, which allows for too little freedom, and thus does justice to the sense of the source but obliterates its artistry and grace. "Imitation and verbal version", says the poet, "are in my opinion the two extremes, which ought to be avoided" (Dryden 1987: 163).

The form of translation which Dryden recommends is a paraphrase, or "the mean betwixt them", in which a translator should truly comprehend the language, turn of thoughts and of expression and to try "conform our genius" to the author's. It is advisable to retain the beauty of the language of the original, but if it is not plausible given the too radical a difference between languages, the idea is "to vary but the dress, not to alter or destroy the substance". The most important principle of the medium model of translation is simple: "The sense of an author, generally speaking is to be sacred and inviolable" but "he may stretch his chain to such a latitude" as to alter the expression, neither is it necessary that words and lines should be confined to the measure of the original. However, this rule also has its exceptions. There are two cases in which Dryden allows for the interfering with the original sense of the text and thus for the bending of the meaning of the text: either when the "thought ... [is] notoriously trivial or dishonest" (Dryden 1987: 164). And thus he decides to omit from *The Canterbury Tales* the indecent material. He translates "The Wife of Bath's Tale" but omits its prologue, which Pope, however, in his fascination with what was indecorous in medieval culture, will later eagerly select for his own project.

Dryden argues that the alterations he introduces into Chaucer's tales, both in language and in meaning, are only to the advantage of the medieval text. Just like Chaucer refined Boccacio in reworking his tales, Dryden believes to have improved Chaucer by rendering him in modern English: "what beauties I lose in some places, I give to others which they had them not originally", he declares (Dryden 1987: 566). The alterations, however, do not stop at the level of language. The changes interfere also in the content. Despite the admiration for "the father of English poetry" (Dryden 1987: 559) Dryden points out his imperfections, explaining that "Chaucer ... is a rough diamond, and must first be polished ere he shines" (Dryden 1987: 564). Thus, Dryden endeavours to rectify what was wrong by omissions, additions and corrections using the criteria of his own times, improved manners or language, to measure the standards of Chaucerian poetry.

> I have not tied myself to a literal translation; but have often *omitted what I judged unnecessary* or *not of dignity* enough to appear in the company of better thoughts. I have presumed further in some places, and *added somewhat of my own where I thought my author was deficient*, and had not given his thoughts their true lustre for want of words in the beginning of our language. And to this I was more emboldened, because (if I may be permitted to say it myself) I found I had a soul congenial to his ... Another poet in another age may take the same liberty with my writings; if at least they live long enough to deserve correction.
>
> (Dryden 1987: 565; emphasis mine)

Dryden, thus, sees the development of literature as progressive, in which each text is an improvement upon the preceding one. The explanation is simple. Literature is to reflect nature and "mankind is ever the same, and nothing lost out of nature, though everything is altered" (Dryden 1987: 563). The poets whom he selected for his collection of translations were not great inventors themselves. "Ovid only copied the Grecian tales, and most of Chaucer's stories were taken from his Italian contemporaries, or their predecessors ... but much amplified by our English translator, as well as beautified" (Dryden 1987: 557). Translation, thus, is understood by Dryden as an enhancement of the original which becomes necessary with the progress and refinement of the language and literary conventions.

The neoclassical translations and imitations of Chaucer indicate the urge to improve the poetry of the "father of English poetry" (Dryden 1987: 559). Dryden might well have admired the realism, simplicity and adherence to nature in the works of the medieval poet but he also believed that, noteworthy though they were, they derived from "the infancy of our poetry" (Dryden 1987: 560) and therefore needed reformation. Thus, Dryden, and Pope afterwards, were freely improving Chaucer adjusting him to the contemporary conventions. This none too reverential attitude towards the medieval texts did not necessarily had to prove the low esteem in which the two neoclassicists held medieval culture. It seems closer to the truth to claim that they both believed in the progress of poetry, each stage being the improvement on the previous one. Thus, if attractions of Chaucer's poetry were to be brought to light it had to be purified of the obvious imperfections: incomprehensible language, prolix descriptions, too loose a structure or indecent content. Chaucer's texts did not receive a very different treatment from that which classical poems received, and classical literature, was obviously held in high esteem. As Pamela Poynter Schwandt argues:

> Pope translated the Iliad for an educated but unscholarly audience who were of two minds about Homer. They acknowledged that he was a supreme poetic genius, the first and best of poets, and that a worthy translation would enhance their own language and literature. But to many of these readers, who knew little about ancient Greek language and customs, Homer's poems seemed crude in technique as well as gross and immoral in subjects. If a translator were to do well by Homer, these difficulties would have to be confronted and overcome.
>
> (Schwandt 1979: 387)

Pope was the next poet-translator in a line of poets who purified Homer of his obvious deficiencies resulting from the archaism of the text and a true successor of Virgil who was confronted with the same task and was so successful in its execution that Virgil's "poem came to be the standard by which Homer's poems were judged and found wanting" (Schwandt 1979: 387). Pope thus presented a new version of Homer's *Iliad*, "an English Augustan England", which was "entire and unmutilated" but "corrected" (Schwandt 1979: 388). Chaucer's poetry had to be subjected to the same process.

Both the translations and imitations of the medieval poet showed an endeavour to reconcile the will to retain most of the original story and to conform to neoclassical conventions, with occasional allusions to contemporary world. The comparison of the tales selected by Dryden and Pope for translation is strikingly different as far as the question of decorum is taken into account. "I have confined my choice to such tales of Chaucer", Dryden explains, "as savour nothing of immodesty". Chaucer himself, as Dryden points out, apologised his readers for "the ribaldry, which is very gross, in many of his novels" but "if a man should have enquired of Boccace or of Chaucer what need they had at introducing such characters, where obscene words were proper in their mouths, but very improper to be heard; I know not what answers they could have made" (Dryden 1987: 563, 564). Dryden favours "The Knight's Tale" over the ribald tales, since "the manners [therein are] as perfect, the diction as poetical, the learning as deep and various" as in the *Iliad* or *Aeneid* (Dryden 1987: 568). "The Wife of Bath's Tale" and "The Knight's Tale" chosen by Dryden show two veins in Chaucer's poetry: the satirical and the sublime, with all the obscenities carefully omitted.

Pope's selection of the tales for translation seems to be guided by the exactly opposite criteria. He translated the "Prologue to the Wife of Bath's Tale", which Dryden rejected as "too licentious" (Dryden 1987: 567) as well as "The Merchant's Tale", regarded as the most sexually explicit out of Chaucer's stories, as if he wanted to draw attention to the indecorous nature of medieval poetry. Pope's stylisation of Chaucer (entitled "Chaucer") seems to reveal how young Pope viewed the poetry by Chaucer. The tale is about a boy who hid a duck in his "Trowzes", which tickled his "Erse Roote" and made "Buttons all-too-brest", thrusting its "white neck and red Crest" forward. This amazed a girl, who asked her mother whether "Be thilke same Thing Maids longen a'ter", which provoked the mother to respond with a moral that "Bette is to pyne on Coals and Chalke, / Then trust on Mon, whose yerde can talke" (Pope 1963: 10). This stylisation seems to directly point to the antiquated language of medieval poetry as well as to the coarseness of its subject matter and morals.

If the choice of tales made by Dryden and Pope is so radically different, the manner of translation is comparable. Both translators feel free to amplify some descriptions heightening the drama of the situation or cutting down what they consider as redundancies. Pope shortens Chaucer's Wife of Bath's tirades so radically that his version of The Prologue dwindles to 439 lines from the original 862. The number of lines in Dryden's "Wife of Bath's Tale", in turn, increases by over 140 lines in comparison to Chaucer's original since the neoclassical poet elaborates on what the medieval renders in few lines. The beginning of the story may serve as an illustration:

> In th'olde dayes of the King Arthour
> Of which that Britons speken greet honour
> All was this land fulfilled of fairye:
> The elf queen with hir jolly compaignye
> Daunced full oft in many a green mede—
> This was the old opinioun as I rede—
>
> (Chaucer 1996: 229)

Dryden not only introduces alterations, magnifying for one example Arthur's fame, but also develops the elf theme, stressing the fabulous nature of the tale and the king's glory, presumably spread by fairies.

> In days of old, when Arthur filled the throne
> Whose acts and fame to foreign lands were blown
> The king of elves, and little fairy queen,
> Gambolled on heaths, and danced on every green;
> And where the jolly troop had led the round,
> The grass unbidden rose, and marked the ground.
> Nor darkling did they dance; the silver light
> Of Phoebe served to guide their steps aright,
> And with their tripping, prolonged the night.
> Her beams they followed, where at full she played,
> Nor longer than she shed her horns they stayed,
> From thence with airy flight to foreign lands conveyed.
>
> (Dryden 1987: 802)

Nor is Dryden satisfied with the brevity of Chaucer's information about the demise of fairy times.

> I speke of many hundred years ago.
> But now can no man see none elves mo...
>
> (Chaucer 1996: 229)

Dryden's version is much more mournful and dramatic in tone:

> I speak of ancient times; for now the swain,
> Returning late, may pass the woods in vain,
> And never hope to see a nightly train;
> In vain the dairy now with mints is dressed,
> The dairy now with mints is dressed,
> The dairy-maid expects no fairy guest
> To skim the bowls and after pay the feast.
> She sighs and shakes her empty shoes in vain,
> No silver penny to reward her pain...
>
> (Dryden 1987: 802)

If general tendencies were to be found in the manner Dryden and Pope enhance Chaucer's text, it seems that Dryden looks upon the medieval poet as too crude and thus amplifies the original text, whereas Pope cuts short its prolixity.

The alterations made in the modern versions do not aim merely to heighten the artistic value of the medieval poetry. Occasionally, after the fashion of true imitations, they provide an opportunity to introduce social comment on various aspects of modernity, most notably court, art and church. The description of the reaction towards the knight's rape of a virgin in "Wife of Bath's Tale" provokes Dryden to insert an implicit criticism of the modern courtly and artistic world, which suffers in comparison to the courts of yore.

> Then courts of kings were held in high renown,
> Ere made the common brothels of the town;
> There virgins honourable vows received,
> But chaste as maids in monasteries lived;
> The king himself, to nuptial ties a slave,
> No bad example to his poets gave,
> And they, not bad but in a vicious age,
> Had not, to please the prince, debauched the stage.

(Dryden 1987: 804-805)

The most extensive insertions Dryden's introduced in the modernisation of a fragment of the General Prologue entitled "The Character of a Good Parson, Imitated from Chaucer and Enlarged". Although Dryden himself classifies the piece as an imitation it seems to be a hybrid of translation and imitation. The beginning is quite a faithful repetition of the character of the Parson, with Dryden's usual embellishments to the image. It is only the last part, some forty lines, that refers to the situation of the clergy who refused to take the oaths to Wiliam and Mary after the Glorious Revolution, known as Nonjurors. The medieval succession after Richard I paralleled the events from Dryden's England after the Glorious Revolution. Chaucerian Parson stood for Nonjurors, who refused to take allegiance to William and Mary.

> Conquest an odious name, was laid aside;
> Where all submitted, none the battle tried.
> The senseless plea of right by providence
> Was by a flattering priest invented since;
> And lasts no longer than the present sway,
> But justifies the next who come to play.
> The people's right remains; let those who dare
> Dispute their power, when they the judges are.
> He joined not in their choice, because he knew
> Worse might, and often did, from change ensue.
> Much to himself he thought, but little spoke;
> And, undeprived, his benefice forsook.

(Dryden 1987: 836)

Dryden's parson not only refuses to conform to the common wordliness of the values of clergy but also withstands political pressures exerted on his conscience.

Alexander Pope's imitation of the Third Book of Chaucer's allegory *The House of Fame* in his own *Temple of Fame* (1715) is an example of a text regarded as a true imitation. As Bonamy Dobrée explains, "Pope is no longer translating; he is imitating, that is producing an original poem as a variation upon an older theme" (Dobrée 1959: 202). Pope himself in the advertisement emphasises the great degree of his originality in the composition. "*The Design is in a manner entirely alter'd, the Descriptions and most of the particular Thoughts my own*", he

                                    J. Maciulewicz

asserts. Yet, for the sake of clarity he points to the source of inspiration to which he refers as no more than a "hint". *"Yet I could not suffer it to be printed without this Acknowledgement, or think a Concealment of this Nature the less unfair for being common* (Pope 1963: 172; italics original). Warton, however, in his very detailed notes to the poem, is sceptical about Pope's attestations of creative independence: "Pope seems unwilling to confess *all* he owes to Chaucer. What is most *poetical* in the whole composition belongs to Chaucer; but from the account here given of the mere hint, and the tame ending of Chaucer, one might be led to conclude that the chief merit of the arrangement and *imagination* belonged to Pope" (included in notes in: Pope 1806: 107). It is true that Pope's version of *The House of Fame* does not follow the phrasing of the original poem and the degree of liberty in the process of modernisation is considerably greater than in translations. Pope omits certain fragments, replaces some of the descriptions with those of his creation, adds certain fragments. However, his poem scarcely meets the criteria of imitations. The medieval story retold by Pope is not a pretext to comment on the modern world. Rather, it is a medieval story but adjusted to the neoclassical literary taste.

Both the arrangement of the incidents and the expressions employed to describe them, modernized though they are, are recognisably borrowed from Chaucer. Some phrases are, after orthographic and syntactic modernisation, directly repeated – some are refined stylistically, with a view to eliminate the uncouthness of the Middle English language. Most descriptions are summarised since Pope's poem is briefer by half in comparison to the original. The fragment where Pope's Dreamer arrives in the Temple of Fame may well serve as an illustration of Pope's practices:

> *High on a Rock* of Ice the Structure lay,
> *Steep its Ascent*, and slipp'ry was the Way ;
> The wondrous Rock like *Parian* marble shone,
> And seemed to distant Sight of Solid stone.
>
> (*The Temple of Fame*, ll.27-30; emphasis mine)[3]

Chaucer's poet arrives at the House of Fame,

> That stood *upon* so *high a roche*,
> Hier stant ther non in Spayne.
> *But up I clomb with alle payne*,
> And though to clymbe it greved me
> Yit I ententyf was to see,
> And for to powren wonder lowe,

---

3   All the quotations from *Temple of Fame* come from Alexander Pope. 1963. *The poems of Aleksander Pope*. (Edited by John Butt.) London – New York: Routledge.

> Yf I koude any weyes knowe
> What maner stoon this roche was
> For that hyt shoon ful more clere;
> But of what congeled matere
> Hyt was, I nyste redely.
> But at the laste aspied I,
> And found that hit was every del
> A roche of yse, and not of stel.
>
> (*The House of Fame*, ll. 1116-1130, emphasis mine)[4]

Pope squeezes Chaucer's 14 lines of description into four and retains basic images: a structure situated on a high rock, which he renders by the same phrase, the steepness of the location, which he condenses into a simple "steep in ascent", whereas Chaucer's poet "clomb with alle payne" and the ice as the shining material of the rock is in Pope revealed at once while Chaucer's poet ponders the matter for some time before he makes the discovery. Pope's description may well be a refinement, but he leaves out its concluding lines to the detriment of the clarity of the allegorical meaning of the poem. Chaucer makes the significance of the ice rock upon which the House of Fame is founded quite explicit

> Thoughte I, "By seynt Thomas of Kent!
> This were a feble fundament
> To bilden on a place hye.
> He ought him lytel glorifye
> That hereon bilt, God so me save!
>
> (*The House of Fame*, ll. 1131-1135)

If by the device of condensation Pope made the piece more elegant, by the renunciation of the final lines, he diluted their meaning. It seems, thus, that what he gained in style, he lost in the clarity of meaning. Not all the alterations are unequivocally the improvements of the of the poem.

If most modifications introduced by Pope tend to make *The Temple of Fame* more concise, there are also examples of amplifications of descriptions or additions of the altogether new ones. The modern version of the poem is, for one instance, enriched by an elaborate depiction of the exterior whereas Chaucer's poet is lost for words to describe its beauty:

> [I] fond upon the cop a woon,
> That al the men that ben on lyve
> No han the kunnynge to descrive

---

4   All the quotations from *The House of Fame* come from Geoffrey Chaucer. [n.d.] The complete worts of Goffrey Chaucer. (Edited by F.N. Robinson.) London: Oxford University Press.

> The beaute of that ylke place
> …
> That hyt astonyeth yit my thought,
> And maketh al my wyt to swynke,
> On this castel to bethynke,
> So that the grete craft, beaute,
> The cast, the curosite
> Ne kan I not to yow devyse;
> My wit ne may me not suffise.

(The House of Fame, ll. 1166-1169, ll. 1174-1181)

Chaucer's Poet repeatedly indicates that he purposefully omits details "What should I make lenger tale / Of alle pepil y ther say, / Fro hennes into domes day?" (*The House of Fame*, 1282-1284), he asks. "But hit were al to longe to rede / The names; and therefore I pace" (*The House of Fame*, ll. 1354-1355), he explains on another occasion. Where Chaucerian Dreamer's skill fails or the superfluity of details overwhelms him, Pope's Dreamer elegantly describes. Chaucer's House of Fame is "of ston of beryl … / Withouten peces or joynynges" with "sondry habi-tacles, In which stoden, al withoute", which the Poet hurriedly enumerates. This description is replaced in *The Temple of Fame* with an orderly description of four "faces" of the symmetrical and harmonious "Dome" –

> … and ev'ry Face
> Of various Structure, but of equal Grace:
> Four brazen Gates, on Column lifted high,
> Four brazen Gates, on Columns lifted high,
> Salute the diff'rent Quarters of the Sky.

(The Temple of Fame, ll. 65-68)

Each of the sides of the temple faces a different side of the world, "*as an Intimation that all Nations of the Earth may alike be receiv'd into it*" (Pope 1963: 175; italics original), as Pope explains in a footnote, which is none too subtle a way to assist the decoding of the allegorical meaning, and each face is constructed in a different architectural style corresponding to the part of the world to which it is directed. An example of an entirely new description may be one of "miraculously evocative little insets" (Dobrée 1959: 202) of a winter landscape, which according to the author satisfies readers need for verisimilitude, which they experience even in dream poems, which by definition allow for greatest liberties of fancy. Thus, Pope justifies his inset description, arguing that it "*renders it not wholly unlikely that a* Rock *of* Ice *should remain for ever, by mentioning something like it in the Northern Regions, agreeing with the Accounts of our modern Travellers*" (Pope 1963: 174; italics original)

The incidents in the plot of Pope's poem, with few variations, closely follow Chaucer's storyline in *The House of Fame*. A Poet sees a Temple of Fame, enters it, sees "pompous columns" with famous writers on them, they see the Fame with "A Thousand busy Tongues ... / And Thousand open Eyes, and Thousand list'ning Ears" (*The Temple of Fame*; ll. 268-269), sees her arbitrarily grant and thwart the pleas for glory or its absence from people learned, just, valorous, modest, wanton or villainous, and eventually visits the House of Rumour. There are variations in the plot; to name but a few: Pope's vision opens with a depiction of the spring while Chaucer's Poet dreams in December, the quite famous winter image and the most conspicuous addition of a moral, which Chaucer failed to provide. The medieval author cuts his poem short: his Poet sees a stranger, who seems to be a man of great authority; Pope smoothly rounds his composition off with a moral about the strange ways of Fame and an invocation

> if the Purchase costs so dear a Price,
> As soothing Folly, or exalting Vice
> ...
> or if no Basis bear my rising Name,
> But the fall'n Ruins of Another's Fame:
> Then teach me, Heaven! To scorn the guilty Bays;
> Drive from my Breast that wretched Lust of Praise;
> Unblemished let me live, or die unknown,
> Oh grant an honest Fame, or grant me none!
>
> (*The Temple of Fate*, ll. 515-516, 519-524)

Thanks to the moral the plot of *The Temple of Fame* seems to be much better constructed than that of the original. The polished descriptions seem to be an improvement on the original, which seemed to be tainted by the haste of the narrator in the way he was relating his vision.

The obvious looseness in Pope's rendition of Chaucer's story automatically classifies it as an imitation. Critics, however, vary in the opinions whether the imitation is successful. A proper imitation should use an earlier text to comment upon modernity, whereas Pope basically retells the same story enhancing Chaucer's version to suit the taste of neoclassical readers. *The House of Fame* seems to be like a raw text for his own polished version of the story. Thomas Warton in his *History of English Poetry* argues that the attempt was doomed to fail since for Neoclassicism the irregularities of medieval poetry had to be seen as design flaws to be rectified. "When I read Pope's elegant imitation of this piece", says Warton, "I think I'm walking among modern monuments unsuitably placed in Westminster Abbey". He explains the experience by the incongruity of "order and exactness of imagery" and "a subject formed on principles so professedly romantic and anomalous" (quoted in: Pope 1806: 112). However, what some critics see as a weakness, others see as a forte. Bonamy Dobrée, Wilson Knight and Professor Tillotson see in *The Temple of Fame* the poem which "combines two kinds of poetry", revealing Pope to be "both as a romantic poet and as a moralist" (Dobrée 1959: 203). If *The Temple of Fame* is an imitation (rather than translation) in the sense of a reworking of an earlier text with a view to point to some aspects of modernity, the modernisation of Chaucer's *The House of Fame* does not lie in making the medieval text an implicit comment on contemporary political or social life. Rather, it is a comment upon the aesthetic duality in the poetic discourse of Neoclassicism – its endeavour to reconcile the classical and the romantic.

The resolution of the problem of how the deployment of medieval poetry in Neoclassicism relates to the distinction between medieval scholarship proper and medievalism is none too easy. Dryden and Pope both declare they took interest in Chaucer to promote national literature and thus to make their audiences acquainted with a poet whom they pronounced as the "father of English literature". In this self-professed aim they become the allies of antiquarians. On the other hand, no matter how fond of their father neoclassicical poets claim to be, they approach his works in a conspicuously patronising manner. Their modernisation of Chaucer's poetry, in terms of language, style and content, deprives it of its quintessentially medieval character. The alterations, however, are quite timid, and not sufficiently creative as to make Chaucer just a pretext for the modern social commentary. Therefore, the medieval poet seems to be suspended between the Middle Ages and neoclassicism, translation and imitation and thus between medieval scholarship and medievalism.

References

Brewer, Derek (ed.)
>   1978   Geoffrey *Chaucer: The critical heritage*. London – New York: Routledge.

Chaucer, Geoffrey
>   [n.d.]   *The complete works of Geoffrey Chaucer*. (Edited by F.N. Robinson.) London: Oxford University Press.
>   1969   *The Canterbury Tales. A selection*. London: Penguin Books.

Dobrée, Bonamy
>   1959   *English literature in the early eighteenth century 1700-1740*. Oxford: Clarendon Press.

Dryden, John
>   1962   *Of dramatic poesy and other critical essays. In two volumes*. London: J.M. Dent and Sons Ltd – New York: E.P. Dutton and Co Inc.
>   1987   *The major works*. (Edited by Keith Walker.) Oxford: Oxford University Press.

Erskine-Hill, Howard
>   1993   "John Dryden: the poet and critic", in: Roger Lonsdale (ed.), 7-39.

Genette, Gerard
    1997   *Literature in the second degree.* (Translated by Channa Newman and Claude Doubinsky.) Lincoln – London: University of Nebraska Press.
Gordon, Jan Robert Fraser
    1970   The Public – Sprited Poet: a study of Alexander Pope's *Imitations of Horace.* [Unpublished Ph.D. dissertation, University of California.]
Lonsdale, Roger (ed.).
    1993   *Dryden to Johnson.* London: Penguin Books.
Levine, Joseph M.
    1994   *The battle of the books. History and literature in Augustan Age.* Ithaca - London: Cornell University Press.
Machan, Tim William
    1994   *Textual criticism and Middle English texts.* Charlottesville – London: University Press of Virginia.
Miner, Earl – Jennifer Brady
    1993   *Literary transmission and authority.* Cambridge: Cambridge University Press.
Pope, Alexander
    1806   *The works of Alexander Pope, Esq. in verse and prose containing prinicipal notes of Drs Warburton and Warton...* London: [n.d.]
Pope, Alexander
    1963   *The poems of Alexander Pope.* (Edited by John Butt.) London – New York: Routledge.
Saintsbury, G.
    1915   *English Men of Letters. Dryden.* London: Macmillan and Co.
Saunders, J. Corinne (ed.)
    2001   *Chaucer.* Oxford: Blackwell Publishing.
Saunders, Corinne
    2001   "The development of Chaucer criticism", in: Corinne J. Saunders (ed.), 5-21.
Schwandt, Pamela Poynter
    1979   "Pope's transformation of Homer's similes", *Studies in Philology* 4, 387-417.
Simmons, Clare A. (ed.)
    2001   *Medievalism and the quest for the "real" Middle Ages.* London: Routledge.
Simmons, Clare A.
    2001   "Introduction", in: Clare A. Simmons (ed.), 2-28.
Winton, Calhoun
    1993   *John Gay and London theatre.* Lexington: University of Kentucky Press.
Wright, Glenn
    2001   "Geoffrey the unbarbarous: Chaucerian 'genius" and eighteenth-century antimedievalism", *English studies* 3: 193-202.

The witch in English literature: negotiation of power and gender politics

Małgorzata Milczarek, Poznań

In European culture, the image of the witch revolves around her gender. It was created in the Middle Ages and developed in the early modern period. The witchcraft motif revives in contemporary literature in the context of feminist ideas. This paper will discuss texts written both in the times of the witch-hunt and in recent times. *The Witch of Edmonton* (1621), a play by Thomas Dekker, John Ford and William Rowley, and *The Visitation* (1983), a novel by Michèle Roberts, present women defined through witchcraft. The characters in both texts resist the internalisation of patriarchal values and gain consciousness of how imposed stereotypes immobilize them. In the process, they transform their role from that of the powerless to the powerful. Paradoxically, their status of being condemned relegates them to a liminal realm where they are no longer under the control of the patriarchal order.

The witch-hunt phenomenon took place roughly between 1450 and 1750. It was mostly women that were tried for witchcraft (Levack 1995: 1). The phenomenon represented the first instance of a massive attack on women. "[W]itchcraft was a sex-related but not a sex-specific crime. Women, in other words, were more readily suspected and prosecuted for witchcraft by virtue of their sex" (Levack 1995: 133). In Europe, females constituted 75, but sometimes even 90 per cent of the accused of witchcraft. The statistics show that witchcraft came to be considered as gender specific. Levack presents the process of transformation from a male magician to a female witch and stresses the fact that although both magicians and witches were believed to make pacts with the Devil, magicians were able to gain control over the Devil, whereas witches became Satan's victims (Levack 1995: 38). The medieval belief in the Devil's presence and influence on people's lives can be explained by social circumstances. "Satan was drawing nearer. Ever more robustly he stalked a world subject to increasing change and dislocation: rapid population growth, immigration to the cities, changes in economic patterns, shifts in politics, and disturbing movements of reform and counterreform in the Church" (Russel 1972: 101). The witch, being a victim of the Devil, came to be treated as the other who could be blamed for the effects of the instability of the changing world. Since women were considered to be morally deficient and, in consequence, more susceptible to the Devil's deception, a stereotypical witch was female.

The Witch of Edmonton, written in the period of the witch-hunt, reflects its social and ideological background and it presents the process of making a woman the other by labelling her a witch. One of the sources of *The Witch of Edmonton* is a pamphlet by Henry Goodcole, *The Wonderfull Discoverie of Elizabeth Sawyer, a Witch* (1621). The two writings differ in the approach to the witch they take. Goodcole's pamphlet is an account of a witch trial and its tone reflects its didactic purpose, whereas the play approaches the witch as a human being and explains how she is driven to resort to witchcraft, how society victimizes her, and how she seeks power to take revenge. Therefore, the analysis of both texts shows how the idea of a witch presented in *The Witch of Edmonton* differs from the simplistic image of a condemned woman described in court records. Elizabeth Sawyer, the accused in *The Wonderfull Discoverie of Elizabeth Sawyer, a Witch*, is denied the opportunity to express her experience. Rushton acknowledges the significance of the fact that our knowledge about witchcraft comes from written accounts:

> 'Bewitchment' is constituted in the depositions themselves: we cannot go behind the testimonies to find another source. ... If accusations took an appropriately legalistic form, were framed within a convincing narrative structure, and were supported in court by testimony from authoritative witnesses, contemporary criticism could be disabled, the accused left only with blank denials. Words were therefore still powerful.
>
> (Rushton 2001: 35)

Rushton approaches trial records as narratives to which historians have limited access as the accounts could be manipulated to fit the belief system in which they were composed (Rushton 2001: 21-35). The testimonies, mediated by males who created the legal discourse and transcribed the confessions, became more or less disengaged from women's lives. Women remain subject to the power of the masculine language. Since the use of language involves certain interpretation, it may disauthenticate women's experience. "Language is used to interpret and define experience and to give meaning to it. When I use the term 'experience' I am referring to physical and psychic events, how women reacted to them, and how women remembered them" (Jackson 2001: 264). Rushton's and Jackson's attitudes to trials demonstrate how women can actually be left mute. Limitations imposed by the pattern of a judicial examination renders testimonies into collections of questions and accused women's replies rather than delineating of how a woman became perceived as a witch.

The Witch of Edmonton adds the dimension that trial accounts lack: it investigates how the society defines the witch as the other, since the other is what it needs to structure itself. Finding a scapegoat to be blamed for the evil the society has to face is one of the means to explain the reality it confronts.

> The witch may have been responding to social or economic pressures when she cursed at her enemies or used sorcery against them, but her neighbours, by denouncing the witch and testifying against her, were being no less responsive to the social conditions in which they lived. Witchcraft accusations allowed members of early modern European communities to resolve conflicts between themselves and their neighbours and to explain misfortunes that had occurred in their daily lives.
>
> (Levack 1995: 125)

Jackson argues that the sheer fact of calling a woman a witch makes her one, since "[j]ust as she had, with a strong input from others, constructed what ultimately became a written testimony, so that ... text would end up constructing her, both in terms of her identity within the community and of self-identity" (Jackson 2001: 264). *The Witch of Edmonton* is different from its source as well as from other witch-plays in that it presents and explains the process of becoming a witch.

Returning to Goodcole's pamphlet, it states by way of introduction:

> This triall, though it was slight and ridiculous, yet it setled a resolution in those whom it concerned, to finde out by all means they could endeavour, her long and close carried Witchery, to explaine it to the world; and being descried, to pay in the ende such a worker of Iniquity, her wages, and that which she had deserved (namely, *shame* and *Death*) from which the Divell, that had so long deluded her, did not come as shee said, to shew the least helpe of his unto her to deliver her; but being descried in his waies and workes, immediately he fled, leaving her to shift and answere for her selfe, with publike and private marks on her body.
>
> (Goodcole 2000: 303-304; original emphasis)

The didactic purpose decides the tone of the pamphlet. Hence, Elizabeth Sawyer is introduced as deserving condemnation from the very beginning. There is no questioning of the reasons for the accusation. Her experience is reduced to the question and answer format concerning the details of her alleged encounter with the devil. By contrast, the emphasis of the playwrights is on the accused Mother Sawyer's initial innocence (Comensoli 1989: 43).

> And why on me? Why should the envious world
> Throw all their scandalous malice upon me?
> 'Cause I am poor, deformed and ignorant,
> And like a bow buckled and bent together
> By some more strong in mischiefs than myself,
> Must I for that be made a common sink
> For all the filth and rubbish of men's tongues
> To fall and run into? Some call me witch,
> And, being ignorant of myself, they go
> About to teach me how to be one.
>
> (*The Witch of Edmonton*, 2.1.1-10)[1]

Unlike Elizabeth from the pamphlet, Mother Sawyer does not remain a passive recipient of the accusations. She reacts to the power of words which define her as a witch by giving a very conscious analysis of her position. Comensoli uses the

---

1   *The Witch of Edmonton*, in: Peter Corbin – Douglas Sedge (eds.). 1986. *Three Jacobean Witchcraft Plays: The Tragedy of Sophonisba, The Witch, The Witch of Edmonton*. Manchester: Manchester University Press. All the quotations from the play are from this edition. References include the number of act, scene and line(s).

above passage to argue that Mother Sawyer "is endowed with a powerful eloquence that deflects the accusations of her enemies ... In breaking the theatrical decorum by having a poor, uneducated female describe with considerable rhetorical acumen her status as a social outcast, the dramatists elevate and dignify the character, enhancing the audience's sympathy for her" (Comensoli 1989: 43-44). Thus, the audience is faced with a character whose only blame is her low social status that puts her in a disadvantaged position, a character who is given voice and expresses her own experience and victimized feelings. That is Mother Sawyer's power – her eloquence – an advantage she gains over Elizabeth Sawyer in Goodcole's pamphlet.

In the same soliloquy Mother Sawyer claims that it is the people from her village who, by the sheer fact of calling her a witch, make her one: "'Tis all one / To be a witch as to be counted one" (*The Witch of Edmonton*, 2.1.118-119). Mother Sawyer is a victim of the society and she is perfectly aware of that. Comensoli puts emphasis on the fact that it was "inassimilable women" that became the objects of the accusations of witchcraft (1989: 45). Mother Sawyer recognizes herself as an outcast and, just like in the soliloquy above, she is capable of describing and analysing her case.

> Why then on me
> Or any lean old beldame? Reverence once
> Had wont to wait on age. Now an old woman
> Ill-favored grown with years, if she be poor
> Must be called bawd or witch. Such so abused
> Are the coarse witches: t'other are the fine,
> Spun for the devil's own wearing.

> (*The Witch of Edmonton*, 4.1.120-126)

Being an old, lonely and impoverished woman, she is contrasted with Sir Arthur, who is male and in the position of power as lord of the manor. Sir Arthur, by his plotting, is one of the reasons for Frank Thorney's crime. Secretly married to Winnifride, Frank commits bigamy with Susan, a daughter of a rich farmer, to fulfil his father's will. Sir Arthur pretends to help Frank, but he only uses Thorney to avoid responsibility for Winnifride, whom he seduced. Sir Arthur's scheming results in Frank killing Susan. "It is a splendid double irony that Mother Sawyer should be the dramatist's spokesman in voicing contempt for Sir Arthur's seduction of Winnifride, and that Sir Arthur, who in the end escapes with only the payment of fines, should be the one who seems finally to convince the Justice that Mother Sawyer is a witch" (Onat 1980: 77). Mother Sawyer, who is an outsider, is a character who, through contrast, reveals the hypocrisy of the society. Being in a handicapped position, as a woman devoid of the protection of males, Mother Sawyer's only way to defend herself against the violence of the society is to resort to witchcraft. She chooses to sign the pact with the devil only after the accusations and as a form of revenge. In fact, revenge with the help of the supernatural seems to be the only power she can gain.

Sawyer is juxtaposed not only with men, but also with other women who, in order to avoid condemnation, perpetuate the patriarchal order. She is the only woman in the play who turns the status of the other into a source of power. That is due to the fact that she defies the image of the passive woman imposed on females by the society, even if in consequence she becomes a scapegoat labelled a witch. When pushed into the liminal, rather than trying to restore the image of innocence, like Winnifride and Susan, she chooses to accept the role of the one who transgresses and claims her right to do that. The other two become frustrated by the fact that they do not obey patriarchal rules and that is what prevents them from gaining power. Winnifride feels responsible for the fact that she was sexually harassed by her master: "Then were my happiness / That I in heart repent I did not bring him / The dower of a virginity. Sir, forgive me, / I have been much to blame. Had not my lewdness / Given way to your immoderate waste of virtue, / You had not with such eagerness pursued / The error of your goodness" (*The Witch of Edmonton*, 1.1.160-165). Feeling guilty and afraid of being stigmatised, she decides to "change [her] life / from a loose whore to a repentant wife" (*The Witch of Edmonton*, 1.1.190-191). Immobilised by the feeling of guilt, Winnifride is unable to distance herself form the masculine definition of her position and assumes the role of a victim. The same holds true for Susan. She has to die, since, in the words of Frank, being his second wife, she is his whore (*The Witch of Edmonton*, 3.3.30) and so, she has "dogged [her] own death" (*The Witch of Edmonton*, 3.3.39). Susan's response is that of a woman who has internalised the patriarchal order: "I deserve it: / I'm glad my fate was so intelligent. / 'Twas some good spirit's motion. Die? O, 'twas time! / How many years might I have slept in sin? / Sin of my most hatred, too, adultery!" (*The Witch of Edmonton*, 3.3.40-43). Mother Sawyer, Winnifride and Susan all have to pay for the fact they do not conform to the patriarchal idea of a submissive woman. However, Winnifride and Susan, as opposed to Mother Sawyer, blame themselves for the transgressions of men and finally perpetuate the patriarchal order. Mother Sawyer is the only one who remains a rebel and does not feel remorse. Unlike the others, she feels strong enough to transform her disadvantaged position into independence.

Turning to witchcraft, Mother Sawyer tries to gain power out of her inferior position using the same power that was used against her – the power of language.

> Would some power, good or bad,
> Instruct me which way I might be revenged
> Upon this churl, I'd go out of myself
> And give this fury leave to dwell within
> This ruined cottage ready to fall with age,
> Abjure all goodness, be at hate with prayer,
> And study curses, imprecations,

> Blasphemous speeches, oaths, detested oaths,
> Or anything that's ill; so I might work
> Revenge …
>
> *(The Witch of Edmonton*, 2.1.107-116)

Mother Sawyer uses cursing as a threat to the society. Her power results from the belief that word can affect reality. Levack shows how cursing allowed women to manipulate the power whose source is, paradoxically, a negative stereotype of femininity.

> The power to bring about harm by magical means was one of the few forms of power that were available to women in early modern Europe. Even if women did not actually have recourse to the magical arts for such purposes, they were naturally suspected of doing so. This popular view of the witch as a powerful woman reminds us that although the witch was often a scapegoat for the ills of society and a victim, many of her neighbours viewed her as both powerful and threatening.
>
> (Levack 1995: 141)

In the early modern period, resorting to the power of speech was considered to be typical of women. "With the witch's capacity to do harm through speech … we are encountering one facet of what contemporaries would have seen as a much more complex zone of female power" (Sharpe 2001: 160). The way women could make words powerful was through cursing. "Cursing was one of the most important methods supposedly employed by witches to injure their victims" (Macfarlane 1970: 93). The transgression was one of the sins of the tongue, "regarded as an offshoot of blasphemy" (Bardsley 2003: 149). Larner compares cursing and bewitching women to violent men (Larner 1984: 87). Lacking in physical power, the power of language was the means for women to protect themselves against victimization. Mother Sawyer accepts the role of the witch imposed on her by society. However, she rejects the role of a scapegoat as a natural consequence of the accusation. Instead, she explores the freedom the label of witch gives her. She resists the internalisation of the patriarchal view that her sex and low social status justify her victimization. Having realised that proving her innocence is impossible, Sawyer becomes a witch and uses the threatening power of language that witchcraft offers her.

Mother Sawyer is a scapegoat of the community that needs to find the explanation for the evil that affects them. Resorting to witchcraft is an act of revenge on the society. Moving to a recent novel about contemporary times, *The Visitation* presents the idea of witchcraft as more complex in relation to the issue of feminine power. In the novel, the notion of the woman as witch is both a means to immobilize her as well as a source of power. The ambiguity of witchcraft results from the fact that the image of witch imposed on a woman consigns her to the realm of negative views on females, who are considered to be driven by their sexuality, but at he same time, a redefinition of witchcraft leads to the revival of femininity. The process of such a redefinition is what takes place in the case of Helen, the main character of *The Visitation.*

Whereas Mother Sawyer is faced with direct and explicit accusations, Helen is confronted with a negative stereotype created by Western culture, in which "W is certainly for Woman and Witch" (*The Visitation*, 97).[2] Helen wants to become a writer, but she suffers from a writer's block. This is due to the fact that faced with views about femininity in patriarchal discourse and writing, she is not capable of expressing herself as a writer. In a scene in a bookshop Helen opens a book in which

> [t]he male author's entries for W rivet her: warts; weevils; whites, woman's whites ... witches, ... wolfbane; womb: women's weeping therefrom; women in childbed; women's complaints, ... women's curses, ... women's diseases; women's longings; women's pains; worms in the ears. When she turns the leaves of the index, she finds no corresponding entry for Man.
>
> (*The Visitation*, 97-98)

Femininity equals body, and female body is problematic. "To write, Helen always feels she has to cancel her body out, become pure mind. Genderless, transcendent, like a man" (*The Visitation*, 99). In order to create, Helen must fight the negative image of woman as reduced to her body which is the foundation of the patriarchal culture.

Mother Sawyer is defined as the other due to her social status, though her sex made her prone to the accusations. In the case of Helen, it is her sexuality that makes her the other. Helen's self-definition relies on the historically grounded notion of woman. Female sexuality was condemned by the Church Fathers' interpretations of the Bible. The misogynist potential of the Bible reveals itself most clearly in Paul's statement on women:

> A woman should learn in silence with full submission. I do not allow a woman to teach or to have authority over a man; instead, she is to be silent. For Adam was created first, then Eve. And Adam was not deceived, but the woman was deceived and transgressed. But she will be saved through childbearing, if she continues in faith, love, and holiness, with good sense.
>
> (I Timothy, 2:11-15)[3]

Paul's words show how the Fall narrative was the most formative for the foundation of misogyny. Using the Old Testament motif, similarly to Paul, Tertulian (c.160 – c.225) reduced women to materiality and criticised any aspect of women's sexuality:

---

2   Michèle Roberts. 1983. *The Visitation.* London: The Women's Press. All the quotations from the novel are from this edition. References include the title and page number(s).

3   *Holman Christian standard Bible.* 2004. Nashville: Holman Bible Publishers.

> Do you not know that you are Eve? The judgement of God upon this sex lives on in this age; therefore, necessarily the guilt should live on also. You are the gateway of the devil; you are the one who unseals the curse of that tree, and you are the first one to turn your back on the divine law; you are the one who persuaded him whom the devil was not capable of corrupting; you easily destroyed the image of God, Adam. Because of what you deserve, that is, death, even the Son of God had to die.
>
> (Tertullian quoted in: Blamires 1992: 51)

St Augustine (354-430) also stressed the need of woman to be subjected to the will of man: "[I]t is not by her nature but rather by her sin that a woman deserved to have her husband for a master. But if this order is not maintained, nature will be corrupted still more, and sin will be increased" (Augustine quoted in: Blamires 1992: 80). The original sin was, according to Augustine, caused by the fact that woman, as opposed to man's rationalism, was driven by her body:

> If Adam was a spiritual man, in mind though not in body, how could he have believed what was said through the serpent, namely, that God forbade them to eat of the fruit of that one tree ... Was it because the man would not have been able to believe this that the woman was employed on the supposition that she had limited understanding, and also perhaps that she was living according to the spirit of the flesh and not according to the spirit of the mind?
>
> (Augustine quoted in: Blamires 1992: 80)

The Middle Ages created the image of woman as corrupted due to her bodily functions. Purity was demanded of women, but it was problematised by the female body. Brain argues that in the time of the witch-hunt menstruation, liquids produced when giving birth to a child and lactation were the reasons why women were perceived as unclean (Brain 1989: 18). Thus, the risk that a woman could be accused of witchcraft was always present in early modern Europe, since her nature as such made her more vulnerable to the accusation.

Helen needs to face the heritage of the Middle Ages present in the Christian ideology. As an adolescent, she begins to experience her femininity. That is also the time of her first attempts to write. Becoming aware of sexuality coincides with the need to express herself through writing.

> She can't sleep. You're whores, nothing but whores. She's too hot, clammy between the sheets. If she dared, she'd take off her nylon nightdress and sleep naked. The nuns teach her how to compose herself for sleep: lie on your back, arms folded across your breast, and think of the four last things. Death, judgement, heaven and hell. She sits up, switches on the light beside her bed, grabs her notebook and begins to write. The dictates of the male saints will keep interrupting her, will intervene, cancelling her apocryphal words. O felix culpa, says St Augustine, O happy fault of Adam's, necessitating the advent of the Christ, O happy fault from which the world was then so gloriously redeemed. Helen's pencil trembles between her fingers.
>
> (*The Visitation*, 33)

The above passage shows that Helen had internalised the patriarchal ideology, which accounts for her rash that appears every time she tries to write (Palmer 1989: 25). The rash is a symptom of the frustration which results from the discrepancy between Helen's needs and what is expected of her. She represses her femininity and that is what precludes her writing.

> I must write a good novel. Only I am frightened, because what I need to write about will tear the seamless garment of goodness and sexlessness I have worn so long. To mark. To brand and to burn. To burn at the stake. It is dangerous, what we are doing, practising witchcraft, and we will be punished for it. Marks on my skin. The Word is made flesh. Each red bump a little red mouth shrieking with longing and rage, each red bump a little female hill, swollen, pulsating and hot with desire.
>
> (*The Visitation*, 101-102)

Just like Mother Sawyer, Helen craves for the power of language. Expressing her femininity in writing would give her access to authority denied to women in Paul's statement. However, whereas Mother Sawyer used cursing as a form of defence, Helen is afraid of disrupting the masculine discourse. She realises she is a contemporary witch and that immobilises her whenever she attempts to express her experience: "The groans and howls of the new feminist fiction, one woman reviewer called it, the kind of book that she writes: humourless, whining, strident. Language laid on like whips, words with the hiss and punch of arrows, the armoury of the new witches" (*The Visitation*, 97). The protagonist in *The Witch of Edmonton* is very conscious of the fact that the only way to oppose the accusation of witchcraft is to take revenge verbally. Helen, on the contrary, does not feel the need to take revenge on the society, especially as it is not particular people but an ideology that she has to confront. What is more, the ideology is what she also perpetuates.

> I just know there's *something* there that wants to come out. I know I'm looking for *something*. I don't know exactly what it is. ... It's as though there's a block ... which I can't see through. I'm beginning to think it's inside me. I've got to deal with it, before I go on to whatever the next stage is.
>
> (*The Visitation*, 91; original emphasis)

Helen fears the threat of the feminine power she can possess. When she succeeds, "[s]he's done it: the thing she's most frightened of: asserted her own needs" (*The Visitation*, 153). That is the point at which she achieves internal unity.

The unity is gained thanks to the support of another woman. In *The Witch of Edmonton* the idea of the community of women fighting the patriarchy was impossible to accomplish. Mother Sawyer was an outcast rejected by the society, a scapegoat. Helen, on the other hand, in one of her visions, asks her grandmother's ghost to heal her.

> Old Mrs Home obeys … changes herself into a witch. She is young and beautiful… The witch is full of mystery, and tremendously old, despite her look of youth. Her wisdom goes back years, beyond the day of Helen's birth, beyond the nine months in the womb, to the generations and centuries beyond. Her ears can hear the echo of old voices, ancient griefs, and far-off battle cries; her eyes can pierce the soul, see ghosts, glimpse distant lands that Helen has not yet visited. … I want to be healed … I'm scared … and I don't know why.
>
> (*The Visitation*, 101-102)

It is the grandmother's ghost, representing the history of suppressed and condemned femininity, that heals Helen. Her grandmother is not simply a frightening witch, but a woman healer, one of those who in the past were referred to as "wise women" (Levack 1995: 138). She is the one who has the forbidden power and uses it to support Helen in redefining her conception of femininity.

> She [Helen] must travel down inside herself, pull the earth over her head, explore her twisting passages, her narrow tunnels, her connecting caverns underground. No idea what she will find. … Creatures from her buried mind will creep back into her, surge along her veins, burst from her mouth. She will give birth to a rain of lizards and snakes. She will speak, and there will pour forth a stream of serpents and monkeys.
>
> (*The Visitation*, 103)

The woman into which Helen is transformed resembles that of Lilith, "both the first woman *and* the first monster", the symbol of women who "have been told they must pay for attempting to define themselves", "cursed both because she is a character who 'got away' and because she dared to usurp the essentially literary authority implied by the act of naming" (Gilbert – Gubar 1984: 35; original emphasis). Lilith is the archetype of a woman rebel in patriarchal culture. Her defiance was aimed at the male's superiority, with access to language as its particular component. Being the first monster, the other, she is like a witch who transgresses patriarchal rules. Accepting her otherness, Helen allows her repressed femininity to emerge. This makes it possible for her to become a writer, to claim the right to the feminine way of expression.

Femininity, then, ceases to be equated with potentially sinful sexuality. Redefined, it escapes the simplistic patriarchal definition and embraces various aspects of being a woman. Like in the novel, "[t]here are a lot of witches now, meeting in groups. … They expose their lives to one another, they talk of their contradictory needs, … the drives that pull them apart, in different directions, within themselves, and that make them disagree with one another" (*The Visitation*, 157). Helen's successful transformation allows her to accept all forms of femininity. She understands that femininity is not a unified idea, that there is no ideal woman that would address the patriarchal image of the feminine. That is what allows her to find support in the community of women.

The Visitation discusses the issue of how the traditional idea of femininity as a passive and powerless state can be transformed into power. The revalorisation of femininity relies, to a large extent, on the redefinition of witchcraft from destructive to creative. The witch becomes a powerful woman who uses her power to change reality around her not as a form of revenge, but in order to fulfil her own needs. This can be done only if femininity stops being a problematic issue and becomes accepted by women themselves. In the novel, the history of witchcraft is presented as the history of women. If it is revised, witchcraft gives the strength that can be used to question the phallocratic culture.

Regardless of historical data which show that male witches also existed, witchcraft goes along with the concept of femininity. *The Witch of Edmonton* and *The Visitation* demonstrate how Western patriarchal culture relies on the phallocentric definition of woman and how the image of a woman transgressing the rules of the dominant ideology has always been a threat to the patriarchal order. Woman, always potentially dangerous, is denied power, but she deconstructs the order which defines her as inferior. She challenges her subordinate position and, through valorization of what has been condemned, she tries to transform the position of victim into that of one who is able to affect and transform reality around her. What is suppressed/repressed by the dominant ideology finally reappears and becomes a source of power.

References

Bardsley, Sandy
    2003   "Sin, speech, and scolding in late medieval England", in: Thelma Fenster – Daniel Lord Smail (eds.), 145-164.
Bible, The
    2004   *Holman Christian standard Bible*. Nashville: Holman Bible Publishers.
Blamires, Alcuin (ed.)
    1992   *Woman defamed and woman defended: an anthology of medieval texts*. Oxford: Clarendon Press.
Brain, James L.
    1989   "Anthropological perspective on witchcraze", in: Jean R. Brink – Allison P. Coudert – Maryanne C. Horowitz (eds.), 15-27.
Brink, Jean R. – Allison P. Coudert – Maryanne C. Horowitz (eds.)
    1989   *The politics of gender in early modern Europe*. Kirksville, MO: Sixteenth Century Journal Publishers.
Clark, Stuart (ed.)
    2001   *Languages of witchcraft: narrative, ideology and meaning in early modern culture*. Houndmills – Basingstoke – Hampshire – London: Macmillan Press.

Comepnsoli, Viviana
1989   "Witchcraft and domestic tragedy in *The Witch of Edmonton*", in: Jean R. Brink – Allison P. Coudert – Maryanne C. Horowitz (eds.), 43-59.
Corbin, Peter – Douglas Sedge (eds.)
1986   *Three Jacobean witchcraft plays:* The tragedy of Sophonisba, The witch, The Witch of Edmonton. Manchester: Manchester University Press.
Dekker, Thomas – John Ford – William Rowley
1986   *The Witch of Edmonton*, in: Peter Corbin – Douglas Sedge (eds.), 143-209.
Douglas, Mary (ed.)
1970   *Witchcraft confessions and accusations.* London: Tavistock Publications.
Fenster, Thelma – Daniel Lord Smail (eds.)
           Fama: The politics of talk and reputation in medieval Europe. New York: Cornell University Press.
Gibson, Marion (ed.)
2000   *Early modern witches: witchcraft cases in contemporary writings.* London – New York: Routledge.
Gilbert, Sandra M. – Susan Gubar
1984   *The madwoman in the attic.* New Haven – London: Yale University Press.
Goodcole, Henry
2000   "The Wonderfull Discoverie of Elizabeth Sawyer, a Witch", in: Marion Gibson (ed.), 299-315.
Jackson, Louise
2001   "Witches, wives and mothers: witchcraft, persecution and women's confessions in seventeenth-century England", in: Brian P. Levack (ed.), 257-277.
Larner, Christina
1984   *Witchcraft and religion: The politics of popular belief.* Oxford: Basil Blackwell.
Levack, Brian P.
1995   *The witch-hunt in early modern Europe.* Harlow: Longman Group Limited.
Levack, Brian P. (ed.)
2001   *Gender and witchcraft.* (New perspectives on witchcraft, magic and demonology 4.). New York – London: Routledge.
Macfarlane, Alan
1970   "Witchcraft in Tudor and Stuart Essex", in: Mary Douglas (ed.), 81-99.
Onat, Etta Soiref
1980   "Introduction", in: *The Witch of Edmonton*: a critical edition, 1-160.
Onat, Etta Soiref (ed.)
1980   *The Witch of Edmonton*: a critical edition. New York – London: Garland Publishing.
Roberts, Michèle
1983   *The Visitation.* London: The Women's Press.

Rushton, Peter
2001   "Witchcraft accusations and the demonstration of truth", in: Stuart Clark (ed.), 21-35.
Russel, Jeffrey Burton
1972   *Witchcraft in the Middle Ages.* Ithaca – London: Cornell University Press.
Sharpe, J.A.
2001   "Witchcraft and women in seventeenth-century England", in: Brian P. Levack (ed.), 153-173.

Teaching the English Middle Ages on film – possibilities, problems, perspectives

Hans Sauer, Munich

Introduction

This paper is basically a report about a seminar with the title "The English Middle Ages on Film", which I conducted together with Ursula Lenker a few semesters ago at the English Department of the University of Munich. In the following chapters I present a brief outline of its structure, aims and results; I discuss some of the general results of our analyses and also look at one specific motif and its relevance, that is the motif of the Holy Grail, its importance in Medieval literature as well as its adaptation in some modern films.[1]

Films about the Middle Ages have been popular and also commercially successful for a long time, almost as long as films have existed. Classics that come to mind almost immediately include silent movies such as Fritz Lang's *Nibelungen* (1923/24) and Carl Theodor Dreyer's *La passion de Jeanne d'Arc* (1928), talkies such as Sergej Eisenstein's *Alexandr Newski* (1938), Michael Curtiz's *The Adventures of Robin Hood* (1938) and Ingmar Bergman's *The Seventh Seal* (1956), as well as more recent films such as John Boorman's *Excalibur* (1981), Antoine Fuqua's *King Arthur* (2004), Ridley Scott's *Kingdom of Heaven* (2005) etc. As the list shows, specifically English topics occupy a prominent place in this tradition, in particular films about King Arthur and about Robin Hood, but also about Chaucer's *Canterbury Tales*. Even people who have never read a medieval text have a more or less clear image of the Middle Ages in their minds, and this image is largely due to films about the Middle Ages they have seen.[2] Since most of our students would be familiar with at least some of the "medieval" films, the basic idea of our seminar was to use this knowledge to deepen their understanding of the Middle Ages, especially of medieval literature and culture, but also to enhance their critical awareness of the "medieval" films.

---

[1]   The present paper is a revised, condensed, and English version of the German report given in Sauer – Lenker (2005). For critical comments, my thanks are due to Ursula Lenker as well as to Judith Götzelmann and Julia Hartmann.

[2]   The Middle Ages or at least a popular image of the Middle Ages seem to be generally fairly attractive to the general public: for example there are "medieval" games and computer games, medieval markets and tournaments, and most theme parks such as Disney World, Legoland etc. have a medieval castle with knights, dragons and so on. A recent German sequence of the printed version of the comic *Futurama* (no. 27, May 2007) features the *Futurama* heroes Leela, Fry, Bender and others in a parody of the Robin Hood story.

1. The seminar

We conducted a seminar on "The English Middle Ages on Film" at Munich University during the winter semester 2001/2002. It was for advanced students in their third, fourth or fifth year. The main aim was to make these films and their images of the Middle Ages useful for students of English with an interest in medieval literature and culture; more specific aims were to relate the films back to their medieval literary sources, and to introduce the students to some basic techniques of film analysis. About twenty students and junior colleagues took part in the seminar, and six of the students subsequently expanded their seminar papers into M.A. (or equivalent) theses. From this point of view the seminar was quite successful, although the demands on the students' time and energy were higher than in a normal seminar. Whereas a normal seminar just has one weekly session of two academic hours (i.e. 1 ½ real hours), the students who attended our seminar in addition to the regular seminar sessions (which took place on Wednesdays 17.15-18.45) also had to watch the films, which were shown on the preceding evenings (i.e. on Tuesdays from 19.00 to c. 21.00, of course depending on the length of the films).[3] One principle of the seminar was that all the films that were to be discussed should be shown previously in their entirety and students should have the opportunity to watch them – during the seminar sessions obviously only brief excerpts could be shown, but students could also borrow the films (or rather videos) and watch them at home. Incidentally the seminar also showed the rapid technical progress in this area: for the seminar, all the films discussed were available and shown on video – now, of course, videos have been more or less replaced by DVDs.

2. The films shown

The selection of films was determined by three factors:

(a) Length of the semester: The semester comprised fourteen weeks; therefore fourteen films could be shown.

(b) Availability of the films: Not all of the films we would have liked to show and to discuss were available on video. This apparently does not necessarily depend on the age of the films: thus the Robin Hood film of 1938 with Erroll Flynn (*The Adventures of Robin Hood*) could still be bought without any

---

3   In order to enhance the popularity of medieval studies at our department, the Tuesday film-evenings were publicly announced and open to all students, not just to the participants in the seminar.

problem, whereas, for example, George Romero's *Knightriders* from 1981 was unavailable.[4]

(c) Thematic emphasis: We concentrated on films about King Arthur, Robin Hood, and Chaucer; we did not take into account films about *Beowulf*, about Anglo-Saxon topics (e.g. King Alfred) and about the Vikings, nor about Mark Twain's *A Connecticut Yankee in King Arthur's Court* nor *Seven* (1995), a modern account of the seven deadly sins. Some films were too recent at the time to be shown on video, e.g. *A Knight's Tale* (2001). Of course all these films as well as the films produced after 2001/2002 could provide material for a future seminar on the (English) Middle Ages on film.

(d) On the other hand we showed and discussed not only films set in the Middle Ages, but also films set in the twentieth century which use medieval motifs (such as the Holy Grail). The films also reflected the dominance of the US film industry: nine of the films were produced in the USA, two in Britain (*Monty Python, Lion in Winter*), two in Italy (Pasolini), and one in France (*L'Éternel Retour*).

Thus the following films were shown in the sequence indicated below; they can be grouped into four thematic units:

(1) Pier Paolo Pasolini's adaptations of Boccaccio's *Decamerone* (1970) and of Chaucer's *Canterbury Tales* (*I racconti di Canterbury;* 1972) – these films have not only the same director and share the Middle Ages as their background, but the *Decamerone* probably also served as the inspiration for Chaucer's *Canterbury Tales*.

(2) Three of the numerous Robin Hood films, namely *The Adventures of Robin Hood* (1938) by Michael Curtiz with Errol Flynn and Olivia de Havilland, which is still a classic; furthermore *Robin Hood: Prince of Thieves* (1991) by Kevin Reynolds with Kevin Kostner (see below), and the parody *Robin Hood: Men in Tights* (1993), directed by Mel Brooks.

(3) Selection of the numerous films about King Arthur, in particular: *Excalibur* (1981) by John Boorman; *The First Knight* (1995) by Jerry Zucker and with Sean Connery, Richard Gere and Julia Ormond; the parody *Monty Python and the Holy Grail* (1975) by Terry Gilliam and Terry Jones, which still has many fans and enjoys a cult-status. Furthermore the adaptation of Marion

---

4   Some of the well-known French films, e.g. Robert Bresson's *Lancelot du Lac* (1974) and Eric Rohmer's *Perceval le Gallois* (1978), also proved difficult to obtain.

Zimmer Bradley's *The Mists of Avalon* by Uli Edel and with Anjelica Huston
and Julianna Margulies (2001), and two films which transpose the Grail story
into the twentieth century, i.e. *Indiana Jones and the Last Crusade* (1989) by
Steven Spielberg and with Sean Connery and Harrison Ford, and *The Fisher
King* (1991) by Terry Gilliam and with Jeff Bridges and Robin Williams.

(4) Finally, a somewhat mixed group: two films based on historical events, *The
Lion in Winter* (1968) directed by Anthony Harvey and with Katharine Hep-
burn and Peter O'Toole, about the quarrels of the aging Henry II (1133-1189)
with his wife and his sons, and *Braveheart* (1995) by and with Mel Gibson
about the Scottish freedom fighter William Wallace (c. 1270-1305), who was
eventually captured, tortured and executed by the English. Last but not least,
the French film *L'Éternel Retour* (1943) by Jean Delannoy with Jean Marais,
a version of the Tristan and Isolde theme transposed into the 1940s.[5]

3. Themes, aims, and problems of the seminar

The seminar had several aims: one obviously was to analyse the films from a film-
and mediatheoretical perspective, and to introduce the students to film analysis;
another, to compare the films with their medieval sources, in order to find out how
far the image of the Middle Ages which the films convey accords with (or differs
from) the image which the medieval sources themselves present. Many of the
seminar papers were thus concerned with a comparison of the films and their literary sources, especially Chaucer's *Canterbury Tales* for Pasolini's film;
Malory's *Morte Darthur* for the Arthurian films, the Grail motif etc.; the Robin
Hood ballads for the Robin Hood films.
      Starting from these premises many of the seminar papers (and later MA the-
ses) also showed a binary structure: first they presented and analysed the medieval
sources (e.g. Malory or the Robin Hood ballads) and the historical and cultural
background; then they described and analysed the corresponding films. Topics
were, e.g. "The structure and the genres of the *Canterbury Tales* and of Pasolini's
film", "The relation of the Robin Hood films to the late medieval Robin Hood
ballads", "The figure of Maid Marian in the Robin Hood films of 1938 and 1991",
"The reality of the medieval knight and his image in the films", "The Holy Grail
and the quest as a motif in medieval literature and in contemporary films", "King
Arthur's Round Table in medieval literature and in the Arthurian films", "The

---

5   During the second session we presented some electronic versions (CD-ROM) of important
     texts, manuscripts, catalogues and dictionaries, in particular *The Electronic Beowulf, The
     Canterbury Tales* (Hengwrt Manuscript), *The Bayeux Tapestry, Scientific Writings in Old
     and Middle English, The Oxford English Dictionary.*

Arthurian women Morgaine and Guinevere in Marion Zimmer Bradley's *The Mists of Avalon* and in the film by Uli Edel", "The figure of Merlin in the sources and in the films", "The presentation of weapons and clothes in the films", "Parodies, e.g. *Monty Python and the Holy Grail* and *Men in Tights*", "Archaizing language in the film about the Middle Ages", etc.

A major problem was the following: on the whole the students found it easier to deal with the texts and the literary analysis, which is probably due to their mainly philological training – they found it much more difficult to deal properly with the details of film analysis and to describe the function of elements such as music and sound effects, dialogue, insertion of writing or graphics, visual effects such as composition of a picture, *mise-en-scene*, camera movement, perspective, kinds of shots, montage and cutting techniques, rhythm, etc. This is not surprising, however, because they had had no previous training in this area and had to learn as they went along. We recommended some basic literature on film analysis (especially James Monaco's *How to read a film*), but even this did not really help to solve the problem.

Nevertheless the students (and the teachers) enjoyed the seminar and they also learnt a lot; so we found the seminar very rewarding on the whole. It was an enrichment to our medieval curriculum and helped students to find out more about the Middle Ages, but it also provided a good opportunity for looking critically at films and discovering their more or less hidden ideology and contemporary relevance.

4. General results: the Middle Ages as a pretence, as a platform for contemporary issues

Only few of the films follow their sources relatively closely, e.g. John Boorman's *Excalibur*, which is largely based on Malory, but even Boorman takes some liberties with his source (see below).

The majority of the films, however, deal with the Middle Ages fairly freely; often they use them as a platform, a pretence, a mythological stage or a projection screen for discussing contemporary issues, for launching modern ideologies, or for showing Hollywood-type love stories in medieval costume. Sometimes this is done fairly discreetly and subtly, as in the Robin Hood film of 1938 with Errol Flynn: on the surface this is predominantly a still entertaining and even exciting adventure and love story with good and evil characters, set in the Middle Ages; but on a deeper level it can also be interpreted as the (finally successful) struggle of a small band of freedom-fighters against the oppressive Nazis.

Sometimes the contemporary relevance is much more obtrusive and crude as in Kevin Kostner's Robin Hood film of 1991; Kostner wants to be politically correct and to do justice to feminist tendencies as well as to the blacks (Robin Hood brings along a very learned and technologically advanced, dark-skinned Arab friend, but

Arabs or blacks probably hardly existed in thirteenth and fourteenth century England), but fails conspicuously on the whole. Whereas Maid Marian starts out as a fighting knight defending her castle against attackers, her character degenerates in the course of the film: during the final fight between Robin Hood and the evil sheriff she is just a helplessly weeping bystander – thus the feminist stance is given up or even perverted, and the figure of Maid Marian assumes the traditional cliché of the weak woman who depends entirely on her man to defend her.

An example of the Hollywood-type love story in medieval (or pseudo-medieval) costume is *The First Knight*, where the love-triangle between King Arthur (played by Sean Connery), his foremost knight Lancelot (played by Richard Gere) and his queen Guinevere (played by Julia Ormond) occupies the main interest, whereas the political implications of the rise and fall of King Arthur are hardly touched upon. In the end King Arthur dies, but against all the literary sources only in order that Lancelot and Guinevere can be united and can take over the government. And the costumes are very reminiscent of those worn in *Star Trek*.

Some films (or rather their makers) even turn the perspective around and claim that certain aspects of the Middle Ages are still alive in the present time; thus there are several films set in the twentieth century which pretend that the Holy Grail still exists and can be discovered, notably *Indiana Jones and the Last Crusade* and *The Fisher King* (see below). Most of these films are not really interested in showing or exploring the reality or the alterity of the Middle Ages; they present modern stories in medieval (or pseudo-medieval) costume or transpose medieval myths into the present and adapt them for use in a contemporary context.

On the other hand, we should probably not be too strict with producers and directors who take a lot of liberties with the medieval stories and characters, who use them partly or even mainly as a pretext for their own agenda and ideological message, who twist the traditional stories or tell new stories about the characters, because the main British or English heroes, namely King Arthur and Robin Hood, are mythical figures with little if any base in historical reality anyway. Thus, there is no reason not to develop and to transform the mythology even further. King Arthur and Robin Hood at best go back to historical figures originally – Arthur would have lived in the second half of the fifth century, and Robin Hood in the early thirteenth century – but the popular stories about them are mythical and not historical, and therefore filmmakers cannot be blamed for not being authentic: they cannot be authentic, even if they wanted to, because neither Arthur nor Robin Hood are authentic in any historical sense.

Although the historical Arthur (if he existed at all) must have lived in the later fifth century in Britain, the early Middle Ages hardly know him; he only appears prominently in literature from the twelfth century onwards, at first in Geoffrey of Monmouth's *Historia regum Britanniae* of c. 1138, and then around 1200 in France (Chrétien de Troyes) and Germany (Gottfried of Strassburg, Wolfram of

Eschenbach). The great English collection of Arthurian stories, Malory's *Morte Darthur*, even dates only from the very end of the Middle Ages (c. 1469).

And although there lived people called Robin Hood around 1200, it is rather doubtful whether they have anything to do with the legendary archer. The legend of Robin Hood is first alluded to in Willam Langland's *Piers Plowman* (c. 1370),[6] texts about Robin Hood, especially ballads, however, are only attested from after 1400.

It is interesting to see that in the collective memory of the English and the English-speaking people precisely such stories are most popular that do not really have a historical basis and that are mainly transmitted in popular genres, e.g. the ballads in the case of the Robin Hood stories.

5. Specific results: The Holy Grail as a motif in medieval literature and in films of the late twentieth century

To illustrate the binary structure of many of the seminar papers and MA theses which were written in connection with our seminar with the help of one example, we briefly present the thesis by Maria Schmid on "The Holy Grail as a motif in medieval literature and in twentieth century films". In the first main part of her thesis, she discusses the development of the Grail motif in medieval literature; in the second main part, she analyses a number of films in which the Grail motif is used, either as the main plot or as an important subplot.

In her first part Schmid shows that even in the Middle Ages there was no canonical or uniform version of the Grail legend. There were different descriptions of the Grail and its effects; sometimes Perceval is the Grail knight, and sometimes Galahad. The connection to King Arthur and his Round Table is sometimes close and sometimes fairly loose. Thus, it is not surprising that twentieth-century scriptwriters and directors use the Grail motif freely and put it into new contexts. Due to its vagueness and openness, this can be done fairly easily.

In her second part Schmid analyses five films that deal with the Grail motif in quite different contexts. In addition to three of the films shown and discussed in the seminar, i.e. *Excalibur, Indiana Jones and the Last Crusade, The Fisher King*, she also includes *Knights of the Round Table* (1953) and *The Natural* (1984, after a novel by Bernard Malamud).

The most "medieval" of those five films is certainly John Boorman's *Excalibur* (1981), which is relatively closely based on Malory's *Morte Darthur*. In *Excalibur* the Grail is a pagan object without Christian references. Boorman, how-

---

6   "I kan noght parfitly my Paternoster as the preest it syngeth, / But I kan rymes of Robyn Hood and Randolf Erl of Chestre" (*Piers Plowman*, B-Version, Passus V, 395-396; quoted from William Langland. 1978. *Piers Plowman*. London: Dent.)

ever, evokes a religious aura in different ways. Contrary to Malory, Perceval is the Grail knight; even more strikingly Arthur himself becomes the ailing Fisher King (maimed king) who can only be healed by the Grail. The quest for the Grail takes up a considerable part of the film and Boorman creates impressive images. Thus, Perceval takes off his armour under water, which evokes several associations such as the renunciation of knightly ideals, but also purification, forgiveness and even baptism. Due to its striking imagery Boorman's film is still worth seeing today (even if some might find it a bit bombastic).

In *Knights of the Round Table* the Grail becomes prominent only towards the end; it can be interpreted as a symbol of hope for America in the early 1950s, when the second world war had just finished but there was a widespread fear of communism.

The remaining three films are all set in the twentieth century, which shows the permanent fascination and also flexibility and adaptability of the Grail motif. In Spielberg's *Indiana Jones and the Last Crusade* (1989) the quest for the Grail is integrated into an adventure story that is set in the 1930s and takes its main hero Indiana Jones (Indy) and his father from the United States of (North) America to Europe and then to the Orient. The Grail appears as one of the highlights of the film in a test scene: The "genuine" Grail is a vessel hidden among numerous cups and chalices and the protagonists must find it. The evil characters, who are connected to the Nazis, in their greed choose the wrong vessel, a splendid and obviously very valuable chalice; they are accordingly punished and must die on the spot. Indy, the hero, on the other hand, chooses the "right" vessel, a very simple and unobtrusive wooden cup. With its help he can heal his wounded father – Indy here personifies the figure of Perceval and his father represents the Fisher King. Indy also achieves spiritual perfection and is reconciled with his father. At another level, Indiana Jones is the American hero who delivers the world from evil as embodied by the Nazis. Although the film is set in the 1930s, implicitly it also refers to the 1990s and thus has a twofold agenda. The medieval motif is twice made use of for twentieth century issues.

In *The Fisher King* (1991) already the title alludes to the Grail legend, i.e. to the maimed king who can be healed by the Grail; the legend has, however, been detached from its Arthurian context and has been transferred into a contemporary New York. But still the Grail retains its main function: eventually it heals bodily as well as spiritual wounds. The main characters are Perry and Jack, who combine features of Perceval and the Fisher King. Jack inadvertently causes the death of Perry's wife; Perry subsequently turns into a destitute beggar. Eventually, however, Jack heals Perry by stealing the Grail from a millionaire who resides in Fifth Avenue, and taking it to Perry. In the film the vessel is a silver goblet which is just a trophy for the millionaire; for Perry, however, it represents the Holy Grail.

The Grail motif occurs only very implicitly in *The Natural* (1984). This is the story of the talented baseball player Roy Hobbs, who at first fails in the game, but sixteen years later leads his team to victory. It is easy to recognize the motif of the double quest (double cursus) here, but otherwise the parallels to the Grail story (and the equation of Roy Hobbs with Perceval) are not very obvious; they are rather the result of intense interpretation, or perhaps overinterpretation.

Maria Schmid shows in her selection of films as well as in her interpretations that the Grail motif is not only important in films about the Middle Ages, especially about King Arthur and his knights; it can moreover also be transferred fairly easily into the present time. In one aspect the modern Grail versions, however, differ fundamentally from the medieval story: In the modern versions the heroes seek self-fulfilment and their own identity; the discovery of the Grail gives them inner peace, satisfaction, and happiness. The quest for self-fulfilment is often taken to be a modern phenomenon. In Malory's novel as well as in the relatively literal Arthurian films (such as *Excalibur*), however, not even the discovery of the Holy Grail can prevent the fall of Arthur's kingdom and Arthur's death as well as that of most of his knights. Thus, many of the modern Grail films are basically ahistoric: in their centre they have the self-discovery of the subject, which is usually seen as one of the main characteristics of the Modern Period as opposed to the Middle Ages; and whereas Malory's story ends tragic, all the modern versions have a happy ending.

Conclusion

Other characters, motifs and groups of films could be analysed along similar lines, e.g. the figure of Merlin, the concept of the Round Table, the character of Maid Marian, etc. Most of the films purporting to show the Middle Ages also have modern ideological implications and transport or discuss contemporary issues and concerns. To give just another very brief example: Pasolini's version of Chaucer's *Canterbury Tales* (as well as his film versions of the *Decamerone* and the *Thousand and One Nights*) shows the concerns of a director who grappled with the sexual morale of the 1970s: Pasolini selected mainly the fabliaux from the *Canterbury Tales* and ignored most of the tales representing other genres (the romances, saints' lives, fables, tragedies are missing, for example).[7] Parts of Pasolini's film are sexually explicit and come close to a soft-porn; interestingly, many of the students were uncomfortable with this aspect and were quite critical of the film.

---

7   Pasolini's *Canterbury Tales* (*I racconti di Canterbury*) contain a frame (the writing author) and eight tales (or elements from them): "The Merchant's Tale" (January and May); "The Miller's Tale" (Nicholas and Alysoun); "The Friar's Tale" (the summoner and the devil); "The Cook's Tale" (Perkyn; a homage to Charlie Chaplin); "The Reeve's Tale" (the miller and the two students from Cambridge); "The Pardoner's Tale" (the three rioters and death); "The Wife of Bath's Prologue" (the Wife of Bath and her husbands); "The Summoner's Tale" (a friar and a vision of hell).

Nevertheless the seminar was stimulating to both teachers and students; they could enjoy the films as well as learn something about critical film analysis, about important medieval texts, and about aspects of medieval culture. Therefore, we recommend it to colleagues to teach such a seminar and we shall probably also teach it again some time.

Select bibliography

Aberth, John
   2003   *A Knight at the movies: medieval history on film*. London – New York: Routledge.
Attolini, Vito
   1993   *Immagini del Medioevo nel cinema* [Images of the Middle Ages in the cinema]. Bari: Dedalo.
Barta, Tony (ed.)
   1998   *Screening the past: Film and the representation of history*. Westport, CT: Praeger.
Bretèque, Francois Ami de la (ed.)
   1985   "Le Moyen Age au Cinéma" [The Middle Ages on film], *Les Cahiers de la Cinémathèque* 42/43: 3-182.
   2004   *L'imaginaire médiéval dans le cinema occidental* [The imagined Middle Ages in Western cinema]. (Nouvelle bibliothèque du moyen age 70.) Paris: Honoré Champion.
Carpenter, Kevin (ed.)
   1995   *Robin Hood: Die vielen Gesichter des edlen Räubers* [The many faces of that celebrated English outlaw.] Oldenburg: Bibliotheks – und Informationssystem der Universität Oldenburg.
Driver, Martha W. – Sid Ray (eds.)
   2004   The medieval hero on screen: Representations from Beowulf to Buffy. Jefferson, NC: McFarland.
Johnston, Andrew James
   2004   "Filming the Seven Deadly Sins: Chaucer, Hollywood and the postmodern Middle Ages," in: Thomas Honegger (ed.), 1-32.
Harty, Kevin J.
   1999a   *The Reel Middle Ages*. Jefferson, NC: McFarland.
   1999b   *King Arthur on Film*. Jefferson, NC: McFarland.
Honegger, Thomas (ed.)
   2004   *Riddles, Knights and Cross-dressing Saints: Essays on Medieval English Language and Literature*. (Collection Variation 5.) Frankfurt am Main: Peter Lang.
Kanzog, Klaus
   1997   *Einführung in die Filmphilologie* [Introduction to film philology]. (2nd edition.) (Diskurs Film 4.) München: Schaudig und Ledig.

2001　　*Grundkurs Filmrhetorik* [Introduction to the rhetoric of film]. (Diskurs Film 9.) München: Schaudig und Ledig.

Kiening Christian – Heinrich Adolf (eds.)
2006　　*Mittelalter im Film* [The Middle Ages on film]. (Trends in medieval philology 6.) Berlin: Mouton de Gruyter.

Knappe, Gabriele (ed.)
2005　　*Englische Sprachwissenschaft und Mediävistik: Standpunkte – Perspektiven – Neue Wege* [English linguistics and medieval studies: positions – perspectives – new approaches]. Frankfurt am Main: Peter Lang.

Langland, William
1978　　*Piers Plowman.* (Edited by A.V.C. Schmidt.) London: Dent.

Monaco, James
2000　　*How to read a film.* (3rd edition.) New York: Oxford University Press
[2000]　　[German version: *Film verstehen.* (2nd edition.) Reinbek: Rowohl.]

Nollen, Scott A.
1999　　*Robin Hood: A cinematic history of the English outlaw and his Scottish counterparts.* Jefferson, NC: McFarland.

Olton, Bert
2000　　*Arthurian legends on film and television.* Jefferson, NC: McFarland.

Roberts, Adam
1998　　*Silk and potatoes: Contemporary Arthurian fantasy.* Amsterdam: Rodopi.

Sauer, Hans – Ursula Lenker
2005　　"Das englische Mittelalter im Film – Perspektiven und Probleme: ein Bericht" [The English Middle Ages on film – perspectives and problems: a report], in: Gabriele Knappe (ed.), 95-117.

Umland, Rebecca A. – Samuel J. Umland
1996　　*The use of Arthurian legend in Hollywood films from Connecticut Yankees to Fisher Kings.* Westport, CT: Greenwood Press.

Alfred Tennyson's "Vivien" and "Guinevere": sensation stories in medieval setting[1]

Agnieszka Setecka, Poznań

In an unsigned review from *Quarterly review* of 1859, William Ewart Gladstone praised Alfred Tennyson for the choice of subject for his *Idylls of the King* (1859), saying that "[t]he Arthurian Romance has every recommendation that should win its way to the homage of a great poet" (1859 [1967]: 250), and for his ability to reconstruct the world of the Middle Ages: "[a] poet of the nineteenth century, the Laureate has adopted characters, incidents, and even language in the main, instead of attempting to project them on a basis of his own in the region of illimitable fancy" (1859 [1967]: 250-251). Still, Gladstone points to a number of alterations introduced to the medieval legend: "[Tennyson] has claimed and used the right to sever and recombine, to enlarge, retrench and modify, for the purposes of at once more powerful and elaborate art than his original presents, and of yet more elevated, or at least of a far more sustained, ethical and Christian strain" (1859 [1967]: 251). Whether the art of Tennyson is more elaborate and powerful than the original remains arguable,[2] but one thing is certain: the severing and recombining, retrenching and modifying[3] that Gladstone refers to result in a poem that is unquestionably Victorian in spite of its medieval setting, legendary characters, and events based on Malory's *Morte*

---

1   This article was first presented at the 2006 MESS conference in Poznań. I am particularly grateful to Professor Andrzej Wicher, Professor Barbara Kowalik and Mr Piotr Spyra for their helpful comments.

2   Another Victorian reviewer claims that "when we come to examine the chivalric romance, we shall find that, though dull and tedious in its actual form, it contains many elements of great artistic value; that, though it can never again be popular itself, something more than accident has attracted our poets to it" (Bagehot 1859 [1967]: 221). Thus, he seems to believe that Arthurian romances can only be popular in a new form, adapted to the tastes of a new reading public.

3   One of Tennyson's contemporaries insisted on poets' right to select and to exaggerate when they speak of the past. His argument is that the past of the kind found in romances is better suited for poetry than the present, which is overloaded with unnecessary mundane details that only blur the picture that a poet wants to present. He does not, then, expect Tennyson to be particularly "realistic" about the Middle Ages: "We rise from the romance with the idea that some centuries ago there were black horses, and large lances, knights in armour, and beautiful ladies: and that there was little else. ... If King Arthur existed, there were peasants in his time, and these peasants had wives, and these wives had children, and these children had measles; but no one wishes to hear of the peasants, the wives, or the babies, but of Queen Guinevere and Lancelot, of the king himself, and all the 'Table Round'" (Bagehot 1859 [1967]: 222).

d'Arthur and other medieval sources. An analysis of the points where Tennyson interfered with the original story and of the kind of alterations that he made offers significant information as to which elements of the medieval romance were still attractive to a nineteenth-century reader, and which needed to be modified in order to appeal to the Victorian imagination and moral sense. The *Idylls*, therefore, show how Tennyson's reading of a literary text from the past was influenced by his own cultural and ideological position.

This article will analyse two of the *Idylls* from the 1859 edition, "Vivien" and "Guinevere", with the objective of showing them to be, in spite of their remote setting and apparently equally remote preoccupations, a part of the Victorian discourse concerning the position of women in society, their relations with men, and morality. Comparing the medieval romance and its nineteenth-century version only throws into full relief aspects of Victorian morality which seemed incompatible with medieval views, and a nostalgic desire for the return of chivalric ideals. Much like Malory's *Morte d'Arthur*, which bemoaned the deterioration of chivalric ideals, the *Idylls* might be seen both as an apology for typically Victorian (and chivalric) values and as an expression of anxiety about their decline. As such they seem to oppose sensation fiction, those "feverish productions" (Bernstein 1994) rendering the bodies of their readers "theatres of neurasthenia" (Miller 1986: 95), which were seen as epitomising both aesthetic and moral decay. The sensation novel scandalised Victorian reviewers not only by its relatively explicit references to female sexuality, desires and passions, but also by its rather lenient approach to moral standards and indulgence toward transgressive characters. Yet despite obvious differences, Tennyson's poems resort to topics and construct characters that in fact are similar to those found in sensation fiction. Placing the *Idylls* in the legendary past undoubtedly diminishes their "sensational" appeal, but they nevertheless do feature secrets and betrayal, passionate and voluptuous women and a broken marriage, sensuality and crime, subjects which made Victorian critics so indignant about the sensation novel. Moreover, although they might be read just as an expression of the Victorian ideology, the *Idylls*, much in the manner of sensation fiction, expose its frailty.

In fact, the weakness of Victorian ideology became more and more evident in the 50s and 60s of the nineteenth century, with a growing number of divorce cases (following the 1857 Matrimonial Causes Act) and headline-making scandals. Tennyson's rendering of the story of the fall of the Round Table might be seen as an allegorical representation of the decline of moral standards in his age. Much like Malory, Tennyson might be seen as a eulogist of days gone by. Malory wrote

> for an age whose feudal polity, based on the ownership of land, was being rapidly transformed by the mercantile economy on which it now rested and whose idealisation of the personal virtues of the mounted knight was contradicted by the increasingly tactical and mechanized nature of war, a display of chivalry so comprehensive as to contain its own critique of the code. Chivalry fascinated the fifteenth century as a historical ideal ...

> Whatever its continuing value as a personal code its limitations as a political model
> were as apparent to Malory in the failure of the dynastic dream of Arthurian Britain as
> in the chaotic nightmare of contemporary England.
>
> (Barron 1987: 148)

However, although both Malory and Tennyson use Arthurian legends to present the decline of values, the alterations that the Poet Laureate introduced to the medieval version of the legend point to his different understanding of the reasons for the fall of the ideals represented by the Round Table and to his stress on values closely related to Victorian domestic ideology.

Tennyson's "Guinevere" tells a story of the Queen entering a convent and her subsequent meeting with King Arthur, who comes to see her before his "last tournament", an episode which corresponds to Book XXI, chapter 7, of Malory's narrative. J.M. Gray, in his very comprehensive study of the *Idylls*, points out a number of changes from the original source that Tennyson introduced: the order of events (in Malory's version Guinevere enters the nunnery only after the King's death), and the farewell kiss of Lancelot and Guinevere (the Queen denies Lancelot the kiss in *Le Morte d'Arthur*). Gray claims that these alterations were introduced because they "are vital for [Tennyson's] design" (1980: 19), and for the sake of artistry, which "prescribes that [Lancelot and the Queen's] relationship should close as it opened, with a kiss" (1980: 20). Gray does not provide the reason for other alterations that he mentions, like Mordred being the only knight of the Round Table to attack Lancelot when he is discovered with the Queen, rather than following Malory's version in having fourteen knights present, and Tennyson's shift of scene from the Queen's chamber to a tower (1980: 19-20). In all probability these alterations could also be attributed to Tennyson's artistry.

Like "Guinevere", "Vivien" is based on *Le Morte d'Arthur*, and it retells the story from Book IV, chapter 1, of Malory's narrative, of "[h]ow Merlin was assotted and doted on one of the Ladies of the Lake, and how he was shut in a rock under a stone and there died". The alterations that Gray points out in this case refer mainly to the origins of the Vivien figure. Gray indicates that in Malory the damsel who managed to seduce Merlin was called Nimue, "one of the damosels of the lake" (*Le Morte d'Arthur*, I: 117);[4] that Tennyson "splits Vivien into two strongly contrasting characters. One is now called the Lady of the Lake while the other retains the name Vivien" (Gray 1980: 13); furthermore, the motif of Vivien's attempt to seduce Arthur is altered from the source episode in Malory's texts when another enchantress tries to seduce the King.

---

4   Sir Thomas Malory. 1986. *Le Morte d'Arthur*. (Edited by Janet Cowen, introduction by John Lawlor.) 2 vols. London: Penguin Books. All the quotations from the text are from this edition. References include the title followed by volume number and page number(s).

Gray does not mention other changes that Tennyson introduces to Malory's romance, which, subtle and even insignificant as they might appear, nevertheless transform the narrative into a Victorian text. The alterations do not necessarily affect the plot but simply cater to the tastes and sentiments of the Victorian reading public and conform (at least seemingly) to Victorian ideology. Thus, by retouching the original, Tennyson produces a Victorian sensation narrative in a medieval setting, a narrative which involves legendary characters expressing Victorian sentiments and which participates in nineteenth-century debates concerning moral standards and position of women in society.

One of the alterations that Tennyson introduces to Malory's text involves the construction of characters. Arthur, idealised in *Le Morte d'Arthur* after an uncouth medieval fashion, is transformed by the Laureate into a figure that is consistent with the Victorian imagination of an ideal knight. Consequently, the Arthur of the *Idylls* may remind the readers more of a Victorian gentleman than of the less refined hero of a medieval narrative. Malory's Arthur, who agrees to burn his wife for treason (*Le Morte d'Arthur*, II: 469)[5] becomes Tennyson's "blameless King and stainless man" ("Guinevere", 489)[6] who forgives his wife "as Eternal God forgives" ("Guinevere", 539) and claims that he loves her still:

> For think not, tho' thou would'st not love thy lord,
> Thy lord has wholly lost his love for thee.
> I am not made of so slight elements.
> Yet must I leave thee, woman, to thy shame.
>
> ("Guinevere", 538)

Presenting Arthur as a "great pillar of the moral order, and the resplendent top of human excellence" (Gladstone 1859 [1967]: 258) in the Victorian sense, required Mordred to be Arthur's nephew rather than his illegitimate son.[7] Thus, Tennyson's Arthur can say of himself that he was "ever a virgin save for thee [Guinevere]" ("Guinevere", 539) and of his heart that it is "[t]oo wholly true to

---

5   There is a reference to this passage in "Guinevere". However, the decision to burn his wife would be inconsistent with Arthur's saintliness, so in Tennyson he says: "The wrath which forced my thoughts on that fierce law,/ The doom of treason and the flaming death, / (When first I learned thee hidden here) is past" ("Guinevere", 538).

6   Alfred Tennyson. 1994. *The collected poems*. Ware: Wordsworth Editions, 526-542. All the quotations from "Guinevere" come from this edition. Reference include the title and page number(s).

7   Swinburne indicates that Tennyson does not mention an important fact that was, in Malory's text, the reason for the decline of the Round Table: "The hinge of the whole legend of the Round Table, from its first glory to its final fall, is the incestuous birth of Mordred from the connection of Arthur with his half-sister unknowing and unknown; ... from the sin of Arthur's youth proceeds the ruin of his reign and realm through the falsehood of his wife, a wife unloving and unloved" (Swinburne 1872 [1967]: 318).

dream untruth in thee [Guinevere]" ("Guinevere", 539). He acquires features of a saint when he claims that he loves Guinevere in spite of her sins, but spiritually rather than physically ("Guinevere", 539).[8]

Arthur's saintliness, his "blamelessness", shifts the responsibility for the fall of the Round Table on his wife, repeatedly referred to as "the sinful Queen" (in contrast to Arthur, "the blameless King"). Arthur claims that "all this [the Round Table and its ideals] throve until I wedded thee [Guinevere]" ("Guinevere", 537) and that

> Well it is that no child is born of thee.
> The children born of thee are sword and fire,
> Red ruin and the breaking up of laws,
> The craft of kindred and the Godless hosts
> Of heathens swarming over the Northern Sea.
>
> ("Guinevere", 536)

He lays the blame at Guinevere's door both for the decline of morals and the resulting wars. Similarly, the maid who is Guinevere's companion at the convent claims that the Queen is

> woman, whose disloyal life
> Hath wrought confusion in the Table Round
> Which good King Arthur founded, years ago,
> With signs and miracles and wonders, there
> At Camelot, ere the coming of the Queen.
>
> ("Guinevere", 531)

Victorian critics share the idea of the Queen's guilt, one of them declaring that in Tennyson's rendering of the story she has "a rooted ethical defect in her nature" (Gladstone 1859 [1967]: 259). Guinevere herself internalised the conviction of her responsibility, and calls herself "one pollution" ("Guinevere", 540). She is presented as more to blame than Lancelot. By her own admission, "[hers] is the shame, for [she] was wife, and [he] / Unwedded" ("Guinevere", 529). Interestingly enough, the negative presentation of Guinevere in Malory's *Morte d'Arthur* (when she is not absent) is not, according to Fisher, motivated so much by the need to attribute the responsibility for the fall of the Round Table on the Queen as by the desire on the part of the narrator to vindicate Lancelot: "Malory can make political and ideological capital out of Guinevere's personal weakness because they go a distance toward constructing and reinforcing Lancelot's heroism, loy-

---

8   The transformation of Malory's Arthur to a higher level of perfection was noted by a few Victorian critics: Knowles (1970 [1967]: 313), Gladstone (1859 [1967]: 257-258).

alty, and unswerving fidelity to his queen, who also happens to be his lover" (2000: 160). Lancelot's virtues, then, stand out against her imperfections.

And yet, in Malory Guinevere is presented only as an indirect cause of the downfall of the Round Table and Arthur's death, a passive object of the quarrel between Arthur and Lancelot rather than an agent. Guinevere's marginality shows her to be just "an object of men's desire", and points to "a world of loyal friendship and masculine self-restraint, the shared values of noble companionship between men and prowess dedicated to virtue", taken as the ultimate ideal (Belsey 1994: 115). Malory's Arthur is not so much affected by Guinevere's sin as by the loss of his knight: "much more I am sorrier for my good knight's loss than for the loss of my fair queen; for queens I might have enow, but such a fellowship of good knights shall never be together in no company" (*Le Morte d'Arthur*, I: 473),[9] which attests to "the exchangeability and the interchangeability of women (even, perhaps especially, the highest)" (Fisher 2000: 159). It is Sir Mordred that bears the greatest responsibility for the catastrophe in the medieval text. He is the one who conspires against King Arthur, whose forces are weakened by Lancelot's departure. Moreover, Sir Mordred is Arthur's illegitimate son, and thus the destruction of the Round Table brotherhood might be interpreted as the effect of Arthur's sin (Swinburne 1872 [1967]: 318). In the *Idylls*, however, Mordred merely reveals the Queen's shameful secret. Interestingly, his role can be actually reduced to embodying Guinevere's guilt, she is "guilt-ridden in the face of Mordred (as in a mirror) and haunted – night and day, waking and sleeping – by images of guilt" (Buckler 1984: 127).

A similar shift of responsibilities is seen in "Vivien". Tennyson presents Merlin as a man taken off his guard by his attraction to "lissome Vivien", in contrast to Malory's Merlin who "would let have [Nimue] no rest, but always he would be with her," and who "was assotted upon her, that he might not be from her" and who pursues Nimue, and "always ... lay about the lady to have her maidenhood" (*Le Morte d'Arthur*, I: 117-118). Tennyson's Merlin seems older, so that he appears more vulnerable, and, although he is flattered by Vivien's attentions, his relation towards her is fatherly rather than sexual. Whereas in the *Idylls* Vivien seeks Merlin's company and he merely "grew / Tolerant of what he half disdain'd" ("Vivien", 476)[10], in *Le Morte d'Arthur* it was Nimue who "was ever passing weary of [Merlin], and fain would have been delivered of him" (*Le Morte d'Arthur*, I: 117). Moreover, Tennyson makes Vivien betray Merlin's trust, as he "half believed her true" ("Vivien", 476), while in the medieval narrative the wizard knows his future beforehand and thus Nimue is merely a means of fulfilling the prophecy.

---

9   In his review Gladstone points to the medieval Arthur as sorrier for the loss of Lancelot (1859 [1967]: 259).

10   Alfred Tennyson. 1994. *The collected poems*. Ware: Wordsworth Editions, 475-494. All the quotations from "Vivien" come from this edition.

Tennyson makes Vivien into an evil character, poisoning the atmosphere of Camelot with slander and malice. She is the devil's accomplice and she is therefore compared more or less explicitly to a serpent: not only does she tempt Merlin, like the serpent in Paradise tempted Eve, but is "lissome" and "wily", as she is described, and her movements are those of a snake:

> And lissome Vivien, holding by his [Merlin's] heel,
> Writhed towards him, slided up his knee and sat,
> Behind his ankle twined her hollow feet
> Together, curved an arm about his neck
> Hung like a snake.
>
> ("Vivien", 477)

In *Le Morte d'Arthur*, however, the associations with the devil rest solely on Merlin's side: Nimue "was afeared of him because he was the devil's son" (*Le Morte d'Arthur*, I: 118).

The Arthurian legend, as Tennyson presents it, is far from being merely escapist. The modifications that the poet introduced result in a work that is of great significance to his reading public as it provides a comment on the world they live in. Shifting the responsibility for the decline of the Round Table on the female characters is not merely Tennyson's whim, but it coincides with Victorian ideology. Not only does the prominence of the female characters in Tennyson's *Idylls* reflect transferring of interest from the homosocial relations in the medieval text to the relations between female and male characters but it also shows that the two texts concentrate on two different kinds of conflict: in Malory it is the conflict between love and loyalty (chivalry) and in Tennyson it is the conflict between pure love, "legitimized by the state and sanctified by the Church" (Belsey 1994: 118) and adulterous love. Belsey indicates how the conceptions of love and marriage, which in the Middle Ages "are not yet indissolubly linked" (1994: 107) are transformed in the Victorian period into "the central myth of bourgeois society: passion and property harmoniously aligned; love, loyalty and the reproduction of the next generation all in one place" (1994: 118). Moreover, the Victorian marriage required a new kind of feminine ideal, a woman who is unpolluted by the worldliness and desires of the flesh, a figure closer to angels than humans. An angelic woman was supposed to be pure herself and a guardian of purity in others; she should protect her home from evil influences from the outside. Consequently, for Victorian readers, decline in moral standards is always blamed on women (which becomes evident in the discourse concerning divorce and illegitimacy), and "improper" female characters are objects of censure and scandal.

Scandal (especially sexual scandal), in turn, is the subject of the Victorian sensation novel, attacked, for that very reason, by critics who deemed it trash. As Susan David Bernstain indicates, Victorian critics saw the appearance of sensation fiction as "a social catastrophe that threatened to erode literary standards and to undermine domestic tranquility, the guiding fiction of middle-class life" (1994).[11] Critics objected to its subject matter, to the poor aesthetic quality of this kind of fiction,[12] and to its power to excite the nerves of readers. The heroines of sensation fiction in particular met with disapproval as they are

> Women driven wild with love for the man who leads them on to desperation.... Women who marry their grooms in fits of sensual passion; ... who pray their lovers to carry them off from husbands and homes they hate; ... who give and receive burning kisses and frantic embraces, and live in a voluptuous dream ... the dreaming maiden waits. She waits now for flesh and muscles, for strong arms that seize her, and warm breath that thrills her through, and a host of other physical attractions.
>
> (Oliphant quoted in: Pykett 1994: 7)

The figure of a sensation heroine as drawn by Oliphant opposes the feminine ideal as it presents women who go against all that is held most sacred in Victorian society: family and home.

Tennyson's *Idylls*, praised for the "sustained, ethical and Christian strain" (Gladstone 1859 [1967]: 251), "[t]he chastity and moral elevation" (Gladstone 1859 [1967]: 263) and for "[t]he fine and wholesome moral breeze which always seems to blow about the higher realms of Art" (Knowles 1870 [1967]: 312) can hardly be said to share the notoriety of sensation fiction. In spite of the fact that the poet places his story in the past, he nevertheless dwells on topics and events that are sensational and he constructs his two heroines much after the fashion of sensation novels. Interestingly enough, although Victorian critics tended to praise the *Idylls*, many complained about "Vivien" much in the same manner as they might have complained about a sensation novel. Bagehot describes Vivien as "more fitted for the court of Louis Quinze than for that of the saintly king of chivalry" (1859 [1967]: 228). He adds that "[i]t rather mars our enjoyment of the new book of chivalry, to have a character so discordant with its ideal placed in such prominence, and drawn in such development" (Bagehot (1859 [1967]: 228). Another critic writes, in a similar vain, that "[n]o pleasure, we grant, can be felt from the character either of the wily woman, between elf and fiend, or the aged magician, whose love is allowed to travel whither none of his esteem or regard can follow it; and in reading this poem we miss the pleasure of those profound moral harmonies with which the rest are charged" (Gladstone 1859 [1967]: 252). Indeed, the wily Vivien, the "harlot" ("Vivien", 490, 494) ready to barter her love to gain power, appears to be taken straight from sensation fiction, which so often features women who sell themselves into marriage.

---

11   http://www.questia.com/PM.qst?a=o&d=5000210746 (date of access: 20th October 2006).
12   Ann Cvetkovich points out that there existed "mechanisms by which aesthetic distinctions mask moral and political ones" (1992: 15).

Fewer reviewers bring themselves to criticise "Guinevere" on similar grounds. Gladstone indicates that although the subject is difficult, Tennyson manages to handle it with propriety: "[Tennyson] has had to tread upon ground which must have been slippery for any foot but his. We are far from knowing that either Lancelot or Guinevere would have been safe even for mature readers, were it not for the instinctive purity of his mind and the high skill of his management" (Gladstone 1859 [1967]: 264). However, Algernon Charles Swinburne claims that in Tennyson's version of the story the Queen is just an adulteress: "[r]emove ... the plea which leaves the heroine less sinned against than sinning, but yet not too base for tragic compassion and interest, and there remains merely the presentation of a vulgar adulteress" (Swinburne 1872 [1967]: 318-319). In fact, Swinburne believes that "Mr. Tennyson has lowered the note and deformed the outline of the Arthurian story, by reducing Arthur to the level of a wittol, Guenevere to the level of a woman of intrigue, and Launcelot to the level of 'co-respondent'. Treated as he treated it, the story is rather a case for the divorce-court than for poetry" (Swinburne1872 [1967]: 319), or for sensation fiction.

Indeed, Tennyson shapes the Queen into a morally ambiguous character. Although, like Vivien, she disgraces herself, her suffering and her repentance extenuate her sin.[13] At court she is presented as sitting "betwixt her best / Enid, and lissome Vivien, of her court / The wilest and the worst" ("Guinevere", 527) and this is the place that she occupies in moral hierarchy. Guinevere belies the ideal represented by Enid, the embodiment of wifely obedience, but she cannot be so unequivocally denounced as Vivien. Paradoxically, her ambiguous moral position makes the Queen even more suited for a sensation heroine. As a number of contemporary critics indicate, the downright disapproval of sensation fiction might have resulted from the fact that it shows a rather equivocal attitude towards disreputable women. Not only is the reader often wheedled into taking sides with an "improper" heroine, but also the categories of "proper" and "improper" behaviour are redefined.[14]

---

13   Professor Andrzej Wicher suggested that Vivien and Guinevere might be analysed as two female archetypes, one fallen and beyond redemption, like Lilith, and the other fallen but redeemed, like Eve.

14   Margaret Oliphant, when commenting on *East Lynne*, indicates that the figure of Isabel is constructed in such a way that she earns the sympathy of the reader: "The Magdalen herself, who is only moderately interesting while she is good, becomes, as soon as she is a Magdalen, doubly a heroine. It is evident that nohow, except by her wickedness and sufferings, could she have gained so strong a hold upon our sympathies. This is dangerous and foolish work, as well as false, both to Art and Nature. Nothing can be more wrong and fatal than to represent the flames of vice as a purifying fiery ordeal, through which the penitent is to come elevated and sublimed" (Oliphant 1862 [1995]: 114).

> The sensation heroine ... cannot easily be accommodated either to the category of normal, proper femininity, nor to that of deviant, improper femininity. Sometimes ... she might appear to be a combination of both versions of femininity, which are put into play by the complex machinery of the sensation plot. On other occasions an apparently, or actually, 'improper' heroine may be juxtaposed with the epitome of proper femininity in such a way as to redefine both categories. ... In each of these cases, as the plot unfolds, the reader is continually required to rethink her conceptions of femininity and proper feminine behaviour.
>
> (Pykett 1992: 19)

Thus, sensation novels render the very category of respectability and propriety problematic; they are attacked because they blur the boundaries between respectable and disrespectable, moral and immoral.

The ambiguity of Guinevere's position is reflected in the equivocal critical response to her and her sin. Bagehot, for example, after criticising "Vivien" on moral grounds, indicates that "[a] similar charge cannot ... be justly brought against the main story of the poem" (Bagehot 1859 [1967]: 229). He observes that Guinevere's choice of Lancelot is simply a choice between two kinds of goodness represented by Arthur and Lancelot respectively. He mentions Tennyson's "moral tact of making the Queen see Lancelot first" which "was necessary as an artistic palliation for her" (Bagehot 1859 [1967]: 229). Another Victorian critic, similarly, cannot bring himself to condemn her wholly when he writes that Tennyson "means Guinevere for the impersonation of that highest form of woman's beauty, which is the noblest embodiment of purity and therefore shows more sadly the flaw of passionate sin" (Hutton 1888 [1967]: 386). And yet, Tennyson's Guinevere commits adultery, a sin to be decried in the Victorian world.

As an adulteress who managed to keep appearances of innocence, Guinevere is like a sensation heroine, who is "on the surface, the quintessential Victorian angel-in-the-house, but underneath an appealing demon of domestic crimes for which she is never convincingly punished" (Bernstein 1994). Consequently, she is even more dangerous than Vivien; her immoral behaviour becomes an inimical example to follow:

> Then came thy [Guinevere's] shameful sin with Lancelot;
> Then came the sin of Tristram and Isolt;
> Then others, following these my mightiest knights,
> And drawing foul ensample from fair names
> Sinn'd also, till the loathsome opposite
> Of all my heart had destined did obtain,
> And all thro' thee!
>
> ("Guinevere", 537)

In fact, Arthur's speech reflects nineteenth-century fears of immorality that threatens from the quarter where it is least expected, home. Sensation fiction thrived on such fears, presenting vile women who insidiously manage to become members of respectable households only to destroy them from within. Arthur's speech echoes Victorian discourse, which often presents immorality in terms of infectious disease that attacks stealthily:[15]

> I hold that man the worst of public foes
> Who either for his own or children's sake
> To save his blood from scandal, lets the wife
> Whom he knows false, abide and rule the house:
> For being thro' his cowardice allow'd
> Her station, taken everywhere for pure,
> She like a new disease, unknown to men,
> Creeps, no precaution used, among the crowd,
> Makes wicked lightenings of her eyes, and saps
> The fealty of our friends, and stirs the pulse
> With devil's leaps, and poisons half the young.
>
>   ("Guinevere", 538)

Moral integrity, then, is threatened by any contact with a sinful woman like Guinevere, much in the manner that physical integrity is threatened by contact with the diseased.

Yet, neither is the Queen "convincingly punished" for her sin nor is she deprived of the reader's sympathy. Though the perfect Arthur was interpreted as an idea, who "stands obviously for no mere individual prince or hero, but for the "King within us" – our highest nature, by whatsoever name it may be called – conscience; spirit; the moral soul; the religious sense; the noble resolve" (Knowles 1870 [1967]: 313), Guinevere in her passionate love for Lancelot, however sinful, marks her as fallible, and therefore human. Arthur's perfection, paradoxically, might estrange him from the readers and earn him the epithet of "an impeccable prig" (Knowles 1870 [1967]: 386). By contrast, Guinevere, through her sorrow and pain, seems to atone for the wrong she did. Like the heroines of Wilkie Collins' *No Name* and Ellen Wood's *East Lynne*, the Queen cannot be condemned downright.[16] Moreover, Guinevere regains a respectable place in society:

---

15 In her article on *Bleak House* and *Dombey and Son*, Deborah Epstein Nord argues that in these two novels "various threats of moral and physical contamination are clustered around fallen female sexuality, that the danger to the middle-class survival and renewal is posed in the form of debased womanhood, and that each novel prescribes the redemption of chaste, reproductive female sexuality as the antidote to middle-class barrenness and moral bankruptcy" (Nord 1995: 40). In a similar fashion, sensation novels couple moral and physical pollution.

16 As Mr Piotr Spyra suggested, the stories of Guinevere and sensation heroines might have appealed to the readers' emotions and sympathy in a similar way. Miller states that while reading sensation novels "we are perturbed by what we are watching. We remain of course unseen, but not untouched: our bodies are rocked by the same 'positive personal shocks' as

> Then she [Guinevere], for her good deeds and her pure life,
> And the power of ministration in her,
> And likewise for the high rank she had borne,
> Was chosen Abbess.
>
> ("Guinevere", 542)

Thus, Guinevere's past trespasses seem to be wiped out and forgotten, her life again becomes pure as if she had never been stained. Significantly enough, such an ending is exactly what Victorian critics saw as immoral in sensation novels.

Tennyson's two idylls are not merely escapist and their remote setting and legendary characters do not preclude them from being a commentary on Victorian morality. Far from merely transcribing the medieval story, the poet offers a comprehensive re-reading of Malory's romance through the prism of his own culture. Both idylls shift responsibility by imputing a moral decline in women, who have marginal roles in *Le Morte d'Arthur*. Tennyson's Guinevere and Vivien, whose passions cannot be controlled or contained, are instigators of scandal rather than angelic models to follow and as such they are not unlike sensation heroines so harshly judged by Victorian critics. Paradoxically, Vivien, who is so unquestionably wicked, proves less dangerous than Guinevere, who incorporates qualities both of a saint and sinner. Thus, while seemingly just an expression of Victorian ideology, Guinevere's story, like sensation novels, serves to subvert its tenets as the poem blurs the boundaries between the proper and improper femininity, between moral and immoral behaviour.

References

Bagehot, Walter
 1859 [1967] "On the *Idylls of the King* [1859]", in: John D. Jump (ed.), 215-240.
Barron, W. R. J.
 1987 *English medieval romance*. London – New York: Longman.
Belsey, Catherine
 1994 *Desire. Love stories in Western culture*. Oxford – Cambridge, Mass.: Blackwell.
Bernstein, Susan David
 1994 "Dirty reading: Sensation fiction, women, and primitivism", *Criticism* 36: 2. http://www.questia.com/PM.qst?a=o&d=5000210746 (date of access: 20th October 2006).

---

the characters are said to be" (Miller 1986: 106). Similar emotions might have been experienced by Tennyson's readers.

Buckler, William E.
    1984   *Man and his myths. Tennyson's* Idylls of the King *in critical context.* New York – London: New York University Press.

Cvetkovich, Ann
    1992   *Mixed feelings: Feminism, mass culture, and Victorian sensationalism.* New Brunswick, NJ: Rutgers University Press. http://www.questia.com/PM.qst?a=o&d=15245312 (date of access 24th October 2006).

Gladstone, William, Ewart
  1859 [1967] "On the *Idylls of the King* [1859] and earlier works", in: John D. Jump (ed.), 241-266.

Fisher, Sheila
    2000   "Women and men in late medieval English romance", in: Roberte L. Krueger (ed.), 150-164.

Gray, J.M.
    1980   *Thro' the vision of the night. A study of source, evolution and structure in Ttennyson's* Idylls of the King. Edinburgh: Edinburgh University Press.

Hawthorn, Jeremy
    1986   *The nineteenth-century British novel.* London: Edward Arnold.

Hutton, Richard Holt
  1888 [1967] "Tennyson", in: John D. Jump (ed.), 352-394.

Jump, John D.
    1967   *Tennyson. The critical heritage.* London – New York: Routledge – Kegan Paul – Barnes & Noble.

Knowles, James Thomas
  1870 [1967] "On the *Idylls*", in: John D. Jump (ed.), 312-317.

Krueger, Roberta L. (ed.)
    2000   *The Cambridge companion to medieval romance.* Cambridge: Cambridge University Press.

Malory, Sir Thomas
    1986   *Le Morte d'Arthur.* (Edited by Janet Cowen, introduction by John Lawlor.) 2 vols. London: Penguin Books.

Miller, Andrew H. – James Eli Adams (eds.)
    1994   *Sexualities in Victorian Britain.* Bloomington – Indianapolis: Indiana University Press.

Miller, D. A.
    1986   "*Cage aux folles*: Sensation and gender in Wilkie Collins's *The Woman in White*", in: Jeremy Hawthorn (ed.), 95-124.

Nord, Deborah Epstein
    1994   "'Vitiated Air'. The polluted city and female sexuality in *Dombey and Son* and *Bleak House*", in: Andrew H. Miller – James Eli Adams (eds.), 38-59.

Oliphant, Margaret
  1862 [1995] [from an unsigned review] "Sensation novels", in: Norman Page (ed.), 110-121.

Page, Norman (ed.)
   1995   *Wilkie Collins*: *The critical heritage*. London: Routledge.
Pykett, Lyn
   1992   *The "improper" feminine: The women's sensation novel and the New Woman writing*. New York: Routledge.
   1994   *The sensation novel. From* The Woman in White *to* The Moonstone. Plymouth: Northcote House Publishers.
Swinburne, Algernon, Charles
   1872 [1967]   "On the *Idylls*", in: John D. Jump (ed.), 318-321.
Tennyson, Alfred
   1994   *The collected poems*. Ware: Wordsworth Editions.

The alchemy of love: Representing desire in a medievalist (con)text.
Lindsay Clarke's *The Chymical Wedding*

Liliana Sikorska, Poznań

"First she loved a tree." This sentence appears several times in two texts narrating a love story between a young man, Mircea Eliade, and his host's daughter, Maitrei Devi.[1] For him, the European, soon to be one of the greatest professors of world religions, such a pronouncement sounds ridiculous. How can anyone love a tree, or be in love with a tree? For her, a poetess, a future translator of the national Bengal poet, Tagore, love is something one gives to the world, the entire world, animate and inanimate, without the expectation of reciprocation. Paradoxically, for Devi, a girl of Brahmin caste, it was possible to fall in love with a tree, but she was forbidden to love a man of a lower caste and, to make matters worse, a foreigner. Such a dissimilar understanding of love can be linked to the inherent differences between the Western and the Eastern ideas concerning love and relationships. Like many other things in our lives, love is a codified concept. Certain expectations are perpetrated by literary texts, films and various cultural artifacts. Thus, the status quo is the outcome of a long civilizing process, during which such concepts were formed and developed. The difference in reception toward love for a tree highlights yet another aspect of the Western idea of love, the disparity between love and passion, duty and pleasure, in short, the mind and the heart, so aptly presented by the courtly poets of the Middle Ages and captured in the Arthurian tradition. The present paper analyzes the notions of love and passion in the contemporary novel *The Chymical Wedding* (1989) by Lindsay Clarke. *The Chymical Wedding* tells two love stories, which happen in the twentieth and the nineteenth century. In what follows, I shall investigate medieval(ist) overtones in the nineteenth-century narrative, in certain ways related to the sculpture of Gypsy May, which bears a strong resemblance to the so-called *sheilas*, stone carvings of women in seemingly indecent postures.

The medieval sheilas found in many churches in Ireland, England, France and Spain remain one of the most elusive phenomena of the Middle Ages. As Weir and Jerman assert, "[t]o twentieth-century eyes these seem like sculptural caprices, carved by exuberant masons out of sheer fun and devilment, and we may be inclined to dismiss them as nothing more than creations of whim and whimsy" (1993: 8). The most common view is that the early church tried to "Christianize" festivals and old religious symbols, which went back to the Bronze Age, as Weir

---

1   Mircea Eliade. 1994. *Bengali Nights*. Chicago: The University of Chicago Press.
Maitreyi Devi. 1994. *It Does Not Die. A Romance*. Chicago - London: The University of Chicago Press.

and Jerman claim (1993: 10). Concurrently, such symbols "may have received fresh injections of vitality from the pagan Celtic and Scandinavian settlers (after all, our days of the week, and festivals like Easter are named after pagan gods and goddesses)" (1993: 10). Another possible explanation is that these figures were symbols of ancient powers.

> As 'fertility' symbols they have the power to turn aside the forces of evil, the malefi-cient glance of the Evil Eye. They are protective, tutelary, apotropaic. Perhaps we do not like to admit it, say the adherents of this theory, but most of us cling to superstitious practices. With a wry smile we touch wood, or throw salt over left shoulder, in order to placate the mysterious forces of darkness.
>
> (Weir – Jerman 1993: 10)

These views are shared by the twentieth century characters from Lindsay Clarke's novel. "'A Gypsy May', Bob had said. 'Now thereby hangs a tale'" [2] (*Chymical Wedding*, 23).[3] Finding himself in Munding, St. Mary's church, Alex Darken, a contemporary poet currently suffering from a writer's block, is still amazed at the sight. "It took a moment or two to distinguish the slab of stone from the surrounding flints, but there was shadow enough to define the rough contours of the figure carved there. I was uncertain whether to simply gasp or to laugh at the improbable sight of it" (*Chymical Wedding*, 25-26). The twentieth-century characters adhere to the popular view that Gypsy May was a pagan figure Christi-anized. Neville Sallis, the current rector of Munding church, claims that "[t]he best way to convert the heathen was to consecrate their holy sites" (*Chymical Wedding*, 49). He also maintains that: "I think May is a corruption of Mary, and of course there was more than one St. Mary. Do you know about Maria Aegyptica? ... The carving's clearly of the old Mother goddess. She couldn't be entirely sup-pressed so some progressive priest blessed her instead, and there she sits. Good thinking really" (*Chymical Wedding*, 50).

From the onset of Christianity in England and elsewhere the sublime spiritual culture was countered by gay, anarchic subculture.[4] In other words, the rigid offi-cial moral system of the church and religion was always defied by the carnival, which though lax and promiscuous, was approved of by the church authorities. In opposition to chivalric romance, there are fabliaux and comic tales which popular-ized the elevated subject to fit the plebeian taste. The high culture is always coun-

---

2   Clarke's novel takes place in two periods simultaneously: the nineteenth and the twentieth century. The nineteenth-century story has a lot of references to the predecessor of the main character Louisa Agnew, her great grandfather Madcap Agnew.

3   Lindsay Clarke. 1989. *Chymical Wedding*. London: Picador. All the quotations from the novel are from this edition. References include the title and page number(s).

4   See Barbara Nolan and her discussion of the promiscuous fictions: medieval bawdy tales and their textual liaisons (1999: 79-105).

terbalanced by the low culture. Thus, for medieval spectators, grotesque figures, comic and fearful at the same time, must have been a frequent sight. The question remains, if the sheilas and the like were designed to enlighten the illiterate, and what was the significance of the obscenity. Weir and Jerman argue that not all the churches accepted the figures, as is the case in the fictional Munding in Clarke's novel. They claim that the church in Ireland tried to get rid of them, efforts indicating that the figures might be relics of the fertility cults of the pre-Christian era, as origin which would date them much earlier than the twelfth century. If their source was the twelfth century, they must have been part of the iconography exposing the sins of the flesh, and as such they can be seen as part of the battle against lust, luxury and fornication. Thus, their appearance (there are various male carvings in indecent postures as well as the female ones) is necessarily linked to many other art forms representing evil (Weir - Jerman 1993: 17).[5] The female was commonly associated with the Supreme Temptress of the Garden of Eden and always defamed in sermons, and, as Weir and Jerman assume, masons might have been asked to use various images to mark the vices and "to depict human behavior at its worst, and not to be too fastidious in their efforts to vilify Women, the cause of the Fall of Men" (1993: 22). All of the presented views are hypotheses; none of the sources presume to say authoritatively what the sheilas signify. In Umberto Eco's manner, such views have to be consigned to the realm of misreadings.[6] In Clarke's novel the carving called Gypsy May is identified with the eternal Mother Goddess, both holy and profane, symbolizing the fusion of the spiritual and the bodily element in human life, the synthesis of sublime love and earthly passion.

---

5   The Irish sheilas testify to the hypothesis of their Celtic origin (Weir - Jerman 1993: 18). Many of the "obscene" figures appear in other cultures. One can find a tenuous analogy with figures in Teutonic or Celtic art which have a phallic form - pillars, face-pots and the like. Weir and Jerman claim that experts on Roman art generally agree that the Celts did not have a native cult, and that any overtly sexual imagery in their art is derivative and due to contact with the Roman world (1993: 18). Weir and Jerman assume that the spread of Greco-Roman culture from the Mediterranean contributed, in turn, to the transformation of classical motifs into Christian symbols: "an obsession with mortal sin distorted the 'micro-phallic' Classical prototypes into the all-too-glaring 'macrophallic' grotesqueness that adorns Romanesque churches" (1993: 20).

6   "And so we come full circle. The darkest mystery has always enshrouded Italian pre-Explosion culture, even though for the early centuries the cryptolibraries of other countries supply adequate documentation ... Kosamba also found the jacket of a volume, obviously a treatise on horticulture, entitled *The Name of the Rose*, by a certain Ache or Eke (the upper part of the relic is unfortunately torn, so the exact name is uncertain, as Strug indicates). And we must remember how Italian science in that period had clearly made great progress in genetics, even though this knowledge was employed in racial eugenics, as we can infer from the lid of a box that must have contained a medicine for the improvement of the race, bearing the words WHITER THAN WHITE accompanied by the letters AJAX (a reference to the first Aryan warrior)" (Eco 1993: 19-29).

She is the principal figure that dominates all the others in Lindsay Clarke's works, as he himself asserts:

> Firstly, you are correct to identify the figure of Gypsy May as the key motif of the book. And not only of this book, for in one form or another she seems to haunt all my work. She is present as the outcast witch in *Sunday Whiteman*, as the bag-lady manifestation of the Loathly Lady archetype in *Alice's Masque*, as Cundrie in *Parzival*, and as Eris (modulating into the figures of Thetis, Clytaemnestra and Circe) in the *Troy* books. (She is also the Celtic *Cailleach* figure in stories I retell in *Essential Celtic Mythology*.) So it seems that I'm a hag-ridden writer if ever there was one. What's this about then? For me, each of these figures is an attempt to retrieve from the shadows the demeaned, neglected, sometimes sternly repressed feminine principle that has been left so disastrously out of count by our patriarchal culture, and without whose honoured presence our feeling life is in deep trouble; as is our grasp of the full dimensionality of what masculinity - 'the man in man' as Nietzsche puts it - may mean. I speak personally as well as culturally of course.[7]

In *The Chymical Wedding*, which is subtitled "a romance", love and passion have special significance. In the book, love is identified with spiritual love, the love that should be present in our everyday lives, friendly "ennobling" love (to use Stephen Jaeger's expression) more akin to the Greek concept of *agape* and Christian concept of *caritas*, sanctioned by the institutions of the Church and the State. Passion always carries the flavor of desire, sometimes of forbidden love and transgression, and is linked to the concept of erotic love. To quote Lindsay Clarke again:

> Whatever the case, though the manner of its expression may have been literary, even ludic, in its conventions (how else could it have expressed itself in the world?) I'm pretty sure that the tradition of *amour courtois* began as much more than a literary conceit. The most powerful of the poems and romances it inspired were the fine flower of actual, lived experiences - experiences at once taboo within the strict controls of the feudal order and also perilously heretical in the inquisitorial eyes of Christian orthodoxy. Hot stuff indeed, and too wild for Andreas Capellanus to tame! Meanwhile, as you will know, similar seismic eruptions of transgressive, erotico-spiritual experiences were recorded in the poetry of other rigidly structured societies around that time – e.g. among the Sufis of the near East, in the heraldic courts of Japan, and in the caste-dominated culture of Bengal. Is it possible that some vital, compensatory evolution of consciousness was beginning to take place on a planetary scale in the early Middle Ages? Is it still trying to happen?[8]

---

7   The quotation comes from private correspondence, used by permission of the author (26. 03. 2007).

8   The quotation comes from private correspondence, used by permission of the author (26. 03. 2007).

The Chymical Wedding is a story, or two separate stories, about the search for harmony and happiness in life, about writing and inspiration, about the inborn human need for the spiritual element in life, about love and passion. The title itself evokes the alchemical "wedding" of the male and female elements as the nineteenth and the twentieth-century characters are involved in the Hermetic pursuit to re-establish the pre-Adamic unity of matter and spirit. The novel describes the transformations of the main characters, transformations which are made possible by various relationships or, to use alchemical terminology, "marriages" or "conjunctions". It is in the nineteenth-century story that the Gypsy May figure is crucial.

In 1848, the new priest Edwin Lucas Frere comes to Munding to take over the position of rector in a small local community. From documents read by the twentieth-century characters, the reader finds that Frere becomes rector of Munding for only two years. He leaves in 1850. The placing of the action of the novel in a period of reawakened interest in the literature and culture of the Middle Ages typifies Clarke's manner of juxtaposing of the spiritual and the material. The story of Frere, is based on the life of a troubled Anglican priest, a deceased friend of Lindsay Clarke, "who authorized me to tell his story - which I did by attributing it in disguised form to the fictional Victorian parson Edwin Frere".[9] Placing the action of the novel in the industrialized world of new technologies, manufacturing, and Darwinian theories highlights the gap between the real and the ideal. For Victorian society medieval texts expounded the values of selflessness, devotion and service vital for (ideal and idealized) chivalric society, despite the fact that both chivalry and courtly love might have been solely literary concepts. For the nineteenth-century genteel classes, the feudal hierarchy guaranteed order within the universe and society. Writers and poets such as Alfred Tennyson, Robert Browning, Charles Algernon Swinburne and others assumed the function of preachers in attempting to revive and re-inscribe medieval ideas and the seemingly ideal moral order of the feudal *body politic* onto their contemporary society. Clarke does not reproduce the religious/philosophical debates of the nineteenth century but draws attention to moral issues ever present in the Victorian mentality. He does this, for example, by presenting an argument over Ann Brontë's book *The Tenant of Wildfell Hall* (1848), whose heroine leaves her drunkard adulterous husband and so contravenes the Victorian principle of the silent suffering of women.[10] Frere's wife, Emilia, is appalled by the book, yet as it turns out she leaves her husband for

---

9   The quotation comes from private correspondence, used by permission of the author (26. 03. 2007).

10   During their first conversation Louisa Agnew disagrees with the Reverend's wife, Emilia Frere, on the subject of *The Tenant of Wildfell Hall* by Ann Brontë. Truly appalled to find that Emilia Frere looked with righteous indignation at the unfortunate heroine, Helen Huntingdon, Louisa is much more understanding towards the situation presented in Brontë's novel (*Chymical Wedding*, 267).

much more selfish reasons. All of the nineteenth-century characters, however, unanimously conform to the notion that both past as well as present society requires values such as honor, loyalty and honesty and balance between the spiritual and material worlds.

At the onset of his career in Munding, Frere is frightened by Gypsy May. For him she represents all that is pagan and alien in Christian culture. "… Only Edwin Frere knew how violent had been the shock when he gazed up at the crude down-lit figure of Gypsy May" (*Chymical Wedding*, 67). Louisa asks him not to let Gypsy May mortify him (*Chymical Wedding*, 45). "He stood, dumbfounded by her frank smile – utterly other than the grotesque staring head of Gypsy May where the image squatted, high on the church wall, naked with drooping dugs and both hands holding open the organ of her sex, as though she were about to drop a child in labour, or as though she might engorge a man" (*Chymical Wedding*, 46). Edwin Frere, for reasons implied but never fully explicated in the book, feels that Munding is his second chance after his apparent "failure" in India. "Frere was resolved: here, in Munding, his ghosts would be laid. Alone, by dusk, he would stand beneath Gypsy May and christen her, as once, centuries before, the first founder of the little parish had elected to do. He would make a reconciliation there" (*Chymical Wedding*, 87). The remoteness of the place together with its beauty gave him hope for peace and happiness in the family. His needs, however, are not compatible with those of his wife, Emilia. Edwin seeks the simple pleasures of life: the quiet ordinariness of the family life of a village priest. Emilia dreams of the city. She feels she is locked in and forlorn in the little rectory and wants to be part of fashionable Cambridge society. For her, the child is yet another limitation, hence the loss of it is not a tragedy of the mother losing a child but of a woman who has failed again. She mourns her vanished opportunities, her failed life and not the loss of their child.

Feeling the overbearing power of Gypsy May, whose very presence is for Edwin the sign of the bodily, uncontrollable element in his life, Edwin turns to Emilia for love and understanding. In his approach to Gypsy May he seems to be recasting the medieval ideas of the corrupted and corruptible body and divine soul. "Not only did theology, natural philosophy and folk tradition mingle male and female in their understanding of human character and human physiology, theological and psychological discussion also sometimes mingled body and soul. The spirituality of medieval women owed its intense bodily quality in part to the association of the female with the fleshly made by philosophers and theologians alike" (Bynum 1992: 183). The genre of the debate between body and soul, popular both in Latin and in vernacular languages in the Middle Ages, reappears in the Victorian period with religious debates surrounding Darwin and Evangelicalism. Frere is not particularly concerned about theological debates, but he does enter a number of discussions on Hermetic philosophy. The figure of Gypsy May in "his" church seems to remind him constantly of the ongoing struggle between the Christian idea of the divine spirit in man and of what he perceives to be the pagan element of extreme corporeality. As he apparently sees his past "failures" in bodily terms, in Munding he aspires to transform his sexual instincts into the chaste love for his wife. Emilia, however, feels trapped in a loveless marriage in which Edwin does not understand her needs, while Edwin (who sees himself as weak and fallible) feels he is failing again, failing to understand and be understood. Emilia, an Emma Bovary-like figure, disenchanted with life and bored by Munding society, feels buried alive in this dismal place. She wants excitement in her life and undoubtedly visualizes marriage as a kind of romance, an inextinguishable flame, whereas Edwin seeks peace and temperance. In short, Edwin wants love and Emilia wants passion.

As a priest, Edwin Frere tries to adhere to the ideals of temperance and propriety as the chief features of a noble union of male and female, features which are surprisingly akin to the medieval ennobling love. Payer (1993: 133) claims that the idea of temperance was formed on the basis of the Roman ideals of moral uprightness (*honestas*) as well as decorum and propriety (*décor*). In medieval society temperance conveyed a number of ideas, measure and moderation in particular, and covered a considerable area of human affairs, including sex, but also referred to such areas as eating, dress, language and human interrelations. New Testament Christianity offered the model of the spiritual life in which, unlike in the Old Testament, family relations, and consequently matters of sexual contact become of secondary importance.[11] What is more, for the New Testament virginity and not marriage won the highest approval. In the writings of the church fathers, sexual drives and bodily needs demand constant controlling.[12] There is a popular definition of temperance in the *Ordinary Gloss* on Matthew 15:38: "Temperance is the restraining of desire from things that give pleasure in a temporal manner" (Payer 1993: 135-136). According to Thomas Aquinas, through virtues "the passions are moderated lest they lead man away from the good of reason" and moreover "temperance is a disposition of the spirit that imposes measure on certain

---

11   In the Middle Ages, theologians talk about three states of chastity: "1) those who never have sex and who propose never to experience sex willingly (virgins), 2) those presently unmarried who have experienced sex willingly and who propose never more to experience it (widows) 3) those who are married and who legitimately exercise their rights to sex" (Payer 1993: 160-161).

12   For example, there is St. Augustine's analysis of the term "temperance" in *The City of God* (Payer 1993: 135). Yet another medieval authority, Macrobius, divides temperance into nine parts: modesty, sense of shame (*verecundia*), abstinence, chastity, uprightness (*honestas*), moderation, frugality (*parcitas*), sobriety, purity (*pudicitia*) (Payer 1993:136). "Latin word for 'temperance' is *temperantia*, a term used by both Stoic and Christian authors. The Greek used by Aristotle for what I have called temperance is *sophrosune*, the voice of excess is *akolasia*. Robert Grosseteste translates these terms by *temperantia* and *intemperantia*; in earlier *Ethica vetus* they are translated as *castitas* and *incontinentia*, respectively" (Payer 1993: 142-143).

passions or operations lest they be borne beyond what is due" (quoted in: Payer 1993: 151). The virtue of temperance as self-imposed underlines the Christian ideal of integrity and moderation in almost every area of life which refers to bodily needs.[13] In the course of the thirteenth century a lot of treatises on vices and virtues were written, which are then emulated by other religious and secular texts (drama included). The initial sophistication of theological and ethical discussions becomes lost, but the virtues are well forged along with other ideas of medieval society, such as love's partnership with decorum.[14]

> Sublime love allows the staging of relationships in what appears a prelapsarian world of passion unencumbered by sexuality, or rather, including a sexuality 'purified' of the physical by some act of moral conquest that creates complete freedom, openness and frankness in the realm of desire—as conquest in battle creates peace – eliminates guilt, humiliation, degradation, all dangers of earthly passion.
>
> (Jaeger 1999: 118)

Hailed as the highest ideals of behavior, temperance and continence are both concerned with bodily pleasures, but continence, is always related to self-restraint in sexual matters in thirteenth-century usage.[15]

Edwin Frere, who comes to Munding with new energy and a hopeful heart, is, indeed, a great exponent of Christian ideals. Paradoxically, it is the lack of love that makes his resolutions invalid. When Emilia loses her child, the last bastion collapses, and there is nothing left to keep their union together. During the period of her convalescence, Edwin is grieving for his lost child; Emilia only mourns her fleeting youth and lost opportunities for a more interesting life. She then makes use of the first opportunity to leave Munding and her husband. This leaves him feeling betrayed by his God and his wife, he is left at the mercy of overpowering Gypsy May.

According to Jaeger, ennobling love filters the "savage" elements of passion (1999: 119). Chaste love, the performance of which was common among medie-

---

13 "Strangely though" as Payer claims: "[t]his model does not apply to sex, which is the exclusive preserve of married people. Within marriage it is a matter of correctly moderating sexual behavior; outside marriage it is a matter of total restraint and repression" (Payer 1993: 153). And further: "Bonaventure notes that the definition of temperance used by Peter Lombard is given from the point of view of the state of fallen nature in which depraved pleasures arise and are bridled by the virtue of temperance" (Payer 1993: 158).

14 "Ennobling love had always been primarily a way of acting and behaving, and only secondarily a way of feeling. It was a mode into which the courtier or knight or lady entered as the dancer enters the dance. The gestures, scripts, and stage settings of the amatory mode relate to the private experience and the individual feelings of love as singing liturgy relates to religious devotion" (Jaeger 1999: 200).

15 For scholastic ideas on marriage, see Bumke (2000: 384-389); for more on marriage and love in courtly literature, see Bumke (2000: 413).

val nobles, exults in purity and offers modes of behavior accepted and acceptable in various contexts. Jaeger argues that "[t]he public performance of the rituals of courtly love, including love poetry, imply that the illicit is near at hand, but either shunned or ignored. It is managed, controlled, held in its place" (1999: 139). Passionate expressions of love are tempered by courtly etiquette as they are moderated by Victorian norms of behavior. In medieval culture as in Victorian, love becomes a social value idealized in the fusion of Eros and agape. For both Frere and Louisa love is a gift that one receives and gives to others. Love itself is not forbidden, neither is passion, yet, the fulfillment of desire and thus, the annihilating of the virtues of temperance and continence is taboo. Sexual transgression is the fundamental element of passionate immortal love stories.

All the metaphors connected with "pure love" conceptualize the values of friendship for both sexes. Hugh de St. Victor writes that "[l]ove is a fire. There is good love, a good fire, this is the fire of caritas, and there is bad love, a bad fire, this is the fire of cupiditas" (Bumke 2000: 369). Courtly love, however, was a social utopia (Bumke 2000: 376). The *locus classicus* of courtly love, Capellanus's *De Arte Honeste Amanti*, shows the subversive nature of and impossibility to control desire. One is struck by the arrow of Amor, who is a capricious god, one is hooked (amus = hook) to one's love object. Passion and desire are not the emotions one finds; Eros finds us and in a way controls our actions and, to an extent, our lives. Passionate medieval love stories are all seditious.[16] Tristan and Iseut succumb to passion because of a love potion, Lancelot and Guenever yield to desire.[17] Both pairs commit political as well as personal offenses. Neither Iseut nor Guenever betray King Mark and King Arthur respectively, they betray not only their kings but also implicitly the State.[18] None of the lovers can be justified

---

16   "The age needed the image of the two Venuses; it required distinctions between a "pure love" aimed only at perfecting the lover and "mixed love" that permits sexual union (Andreas); between "fin'amors"; between "mine" and "liebe" (Wolfram); between "high love" that raises a man to esteem and worthiness, and "low love" that reduces him to bestiality (Walther) ... The tortured disquisitions of Andreas Capellanus show us the problems of integrating the love of women into the discourse of ennobling love. They become so painful for this fainthearted voyager in new land that after two books he turned tail and headed for the safety of the unequivocal, hissing defiance and showing the flip side of exalted love for women, an ugly antifeminism" (Jaeger 1999: 158). In the chief source on love, Andreas Capellanus stressed that love should be based on renunciation of the flesh but his speakers also approve of physical love (Jaeger 1999: 115).

17   The contemplation of the story of Lancelot and Guenever ignites such passion in Paolo and Francesca that they have to pay for it in Dante's Hell.

18   The bodies of medieval queens were written into the feudal system of relations. Their bodies were to produce legitimate heirs, such was their political role. Both Isolde and Guenever deny motherhood; they are not capable of giving birth to heirs as they are entangled in illicit relationships. Tristan and Isolde's love story is touched by magic, Lancelot and Guenever commit adultery out of their own free will. Both queens transgress moral and social law, re-

in their lack of continence. It is only in Marie de France (and, to an extent, in Malory's version of Tristan's story) that love would justify such disobedience.[19]

Edwin Frere finds love outside the bounds of the church and outside the confines of his loveless marriage. His story begins with *com-passion*. A lonely and miserable Anglican pastor and an educated young woman, the daughter of the local squire in need of understanding and love, represent a clash of two worlds, two very different worlds. Louisa Agnew and Emilia Frere, could not be more different. Emilia wants to live in the big world and is stuck in provincial Munding, while Louisa wants love and a quiet family life. Neither of the women get from life what they want and deserve. Frere sees his meetings and discussions with Louisa as "ennobling" love, as *caritas* and not *cupiditas*. As Lindsay Clarke observes:

> In writing about Louisa and Frere, I had Eloise and Abelard in mind, of course, but also St Francis' struggle with his love/desire for Chiara di Offreduccio, and the way in which the Brahmin poet Chandidas was able to affirm his profound love for the low-caste washer-woman Rami only after withstanding immense, almost overwhelming pressure from his orthodox peers.[20]

Love that transcends the body defines the highest Christian ideal of purity of love and desire[21] and reverberated in the Victorian ideals of morality. Such an idea of friendship draws on the Ciceronian concept outlined in *De amiticia*, and was further delineated by various Christian and secular authors. Courtly love was, after all, also a public display of friendship (and sometimes fascination) as it renounced the physicality of desire as vulgar and affirmed "platonic" love. Frere, in order to make peace with his past and accept the present, tries to understand Gypsy May, whose figure resonates very deeply with his feeling of unspecified past transgressions.

---

maining forever torn between the state law and the laws of love. The break up between Arthur and Lancelot and Mark and Tristan reflects the break up within legitimate marriages, unions which guarantee the production of a legitimate heir and also defines the existence of a woman in the rhetorical structures of the Middle Ages (McCracken 1993: 38-64). The queen's body is marked by the metaphors of duties, transgression of which leads to the destabilization of the entire political system. In the most powerful love stories one always has to choose between the feudal oath of allegiance towards one's king and allegiance and service towards the woman one loves.

19   In Marie de France's version, Emilia Frere should consent to the presence of the other woman and sacrifice her happiness to the happiness of her husband ("Eliduc"), or the lover should overcome initial obstacles of one of them being married and be joined in a happy union when such obstacles are lifted.

20   The quotation comes from private correspondence, used by permission of the author (26. 03. 2007).

21   See Stephen Jaeger. 1999. *Ennobling love. In search of a lost sensibility*. Philadelphia: University of Pennsylvania Press, 117-127.

Finding himself approved of by Munding society, Frere assumes that happiness is possible as is the "marriage" of what he considers pagan: Hermeticism and Christianity.

> Around him the voices of his congregation swelled in jubilant carol. His own rich baritone rang out with joy, and at the works *Lo he abhors not the Virgin's womb*, Frere thought briefly, almost affectionately, of Gypsy May in the cold and dark outside those walls. Was she after all, but a crude precursor of the Divine Mother whose labours they celebrated here in a church consecrated to her name? At all times all wise men had revered the mysterious organ of generation through which alone might life be entered. It was no devourer but the very portal of life.
>
> (*Chymical Wedding*, 189)

Frere begins to perceive Gypsy May as Mother Goddess, sanctifying the primal myth of fertility. According to, Cybele signified Earth charged with celestial sanctity (1962: 20). Reading the poems of Catullus, Frere links the betrayed poet's invectives on his lover, Lesbia, and Catullus' fascination with the female element in the figure of the Mother Goddess Cybele, with his own growing acceptance of Gypsy May. The womb of the Earth mother also stands for the sexualization of the world with which Frere is fascinated and by which he is also repelled.[22]

Similarly, he is drawn to and curious about Hermetic philosophy, which preoccupy Louisa and her father. "The Hermitic tradition has always offered a vision whereby men and women might recover their experience in its wholeness. It offers a technique for achieving that vision" (*Chymical Wedding*, 180). Henry Agnew saw his daughter as his best acolyte, his *soror mystica*, an element necessary in the great experiment of nature. And yet, alchemy talks about the "marriage" of the female and male element not in platonic but physical terms.

> ...in the Hermetic Art –symbolic though its language was –the mating of Sol and Luna was a moment of great joy and exaltation. It was the healing of ills, the great mysterium. That humankind had been created male and female was, of itself, the promise that such mystery might be made flesh.
>
> (*Chymical Wedding*, 275)

After all, even in the courtly context, love was a bit of chemistry and a bit of magic. For the experiment of nature to be successful, the union of Louisa and Edwin must be consummated. They become a mystical couple only once. He becomes her *frater mysticus* and she his *soror mystica*. It is to him that she addresses her later notes, which her family views as only alchemical formulas: *Frater mysticus meus*. Because of the physical bond and not despite it, the mystical "marriage" of souls is possible. The "chymical wedding" of the title is the moment of desire

---

22   For more, see Eliade (1978: 34-42).

fulfilled for Edwin and Louisa and the example of the alchemical mystery, which Trismegistos describes as the sweet and vital act freeing the divinity in men.[23] In the words of the author himself:

> Sometimes I've found myself wondering whether, consciously or unconsciously, when a woman like Louisa Agnew receives her lover in deep erotic encounter, she requires him to pass beyond the limits of the divisive ego into that place where there is only body and soul in indissoluble union. But for a man who is identified with the executive ego or, like poor Frere, with a strong cultural super-ego, such an encounter will be experienced as the threat of engorgement, of the woman as devourer (see Edward's pathological description of Gypsy May on page 455). Perhaps only as he permits the centre of his consciousness to shift from ego to soul will he begin to see the ground of true being waiting for him there; for what is experienced by the ego as dissolution may be known to the soul as the indissoluble unity of being? And it may be that such a realization is not possible without some irrevocable act of transgression which propels him through from a world dominated by social conventions into that impersonal space where all boundaries are transcended. Gnostic space. That psychic, perhaps sacred space where knowledge and experience are one, and communicable only to those who have been similarly initiated? Such an inability to speak its name more widely is among the tragic consequences that seem almost inevitable when a transgressive love collides with the world whose prohibitions it violates. Perhaps, for all our yearning, the sacred marriage belongs in the archetypal realm of myth, not in the more refractory realm of fact.[24]

In the nineteenth-century story, love and its resulting physical satisfaction brings about only partial fulfillment, Louisa's life is fulfilled in the very moment of the alchemical/mystical union, the chymical wedding being realized through the bodies and the souls of the two characters. The mystery of love and the mystery of sex are combined in the alchemical conjunction, whose metaphysical force drives two opposite forces towards one another: "...her [Louisa's] concern was only with the sacred marriage of spirit and matter, the chymical wedding of the androgynous human soul" (*Chymical Wedding*, 380). The metaphors of marriage permeate alchemical writings. The late fifteenth-century *The Ordinal of Alchemy* by Thomas Norton talks about the mixture of different elements in sexual terms: "Another diuersite bi-twex þem finde ye shal / such as is fownde bitwen male & femal" (ll.1125-1126).[25]

---

23   "Therefore, the act of this mystery, so sweet and vital, is done in secret so that the divinity that arises in both nature from the sexual coupling should not be forced to feel the same that would come from the laughter of the ignorant if it happened in public or, much worse, if it were open to the sight of irreverent people". Brian P. Copenhaver, (ed.) 2000 *Hermetica. The Greek* Corpus Hermeticum *and the Latin* Asclepius *in a new English translation with notes and introduction.* Cambridge: Cambridge University Press.

24   The quotation comes from private correspondence, used by permission of the author (26. 03. 2007).

25   Thomas Norton's *Ordinal of alchemy.* 1975. (Edited by John Reidy.) (Early English Text Society 272.) Oxford: Oxford University Press.

For the transformation ("white work", as Norton calls it), one needs to unite the male and female elements. Louisa, therefore, does not suffer remorse, although it is she who comes to him, and undresses for him, in a physically literal as well as symbolic act of taking off layers of cultural taboos and prohibitions, the veils that cover one's true humanity. She gives herself to him in an act of love and liberation. It is also then that she becomes the Goddess, fusing the image of Gypsy May and Mother Goddess, Cybele. She tries to convince Edwin to accept Gypsy May fully and wholeheartedly as "[s]he is our Mother. The Mother of All. We are part of her, and she is of us'" (*Chymical Wedding*, 388). It is through Gypsy May that Louisa feels justified in the consummation of their union, as in Victorian reality there was no possibility for them to create something beyond the physical satisfaction of their passion. Louisa argues that "'[i]t is a great sin to deny her. She belongs on your church. A church consecrated solely to the Father is but half a church.' And having dared so much, her sadness could not restrain a further thought: 'As a life devoted to the father is but half a life'" (*Chymical Wedding*, 388), and then adds:

> She is our Mother. She is our Mother and her other face is love. And she will not be denied because she too is truth. I promise that there is great peace to be found in her. Hers is the promise that there is great peace to be found in her. Hers is the peace which passeth understanding. It was hers long before the Christian church claimed it for its own. It is her service that is perfect freedom.
>
> (*Chymical Wedding*, 392)

As they perform the act of marriage, the alchemical wedding, Louisa transforms herself into a priestess (*Chymical Wedding*, 393) and Edwin, for the first and last time, sees the figures of goddesses of love, Aphrodite, Cybele, Isis and Gypsy May, in contrast to his jealous, isolated God (*Chymical Wedding*, 393). In that moment of revelation, he discerns the validity and purity of their union, but at the same time, he is frightened by the feelings he has for Louisa, by the passion she evokes. As an Anglican pastor, Frere has failed, unable to cultivate the virtue of continence and feels himself failing again. He is scared because he can neither understand nor control his feelings. Unconsciously and unwillingly, Frere redefines the experience with Louisa; for him she turns the figure of Gypsy May into the symbol of illicit passion.[26]

---

26   Searching for the answers in the lost book of Louisa Agnew, the twentieth-century characters feel themselves lost. Just when the romance between Louisa and Frere becomes apparent, she herself and the content of the burned book become apparent. "... Louisa Agnew was long dead and gone. Back in the womb of time of the Great Mother. Silent and cold as Gypsy May, that other ever open door among the flints of Munding church" (*Chymical Wedding*, 356). Their quest resulted in the apparent failure.

Weir and Jerman, in their cataloguing and analyzing of the sheilas, put forth a hypothesis that such figures were "to give visual support to the Church's moral teaching ... That they kept their strange fascination is evinced by a few post-Romanseque examples, but to what extent this is due to folk attachment, belief in magic, or identification with primeval deities it is not for us to say, for this leads to the sort of speculation we are anxious to avoid" (1993: 10). They do not want to see the carvings as "sexual exhibitionist" but rather "as an expression of the medieval Church's campaign against immorality, and that they were not intended to inflame the passions but rather to allay them" (1993: 11). Still, for Edwin Frere, Gypsy May represents all that is repressed and should remain hidden, the emotions that lead to the release of desire and the consummation of mutual fascination.

Alchemy and Hermeticism are the grounding reasons for Louisa and Edwin's friendship, but what happens between them is the chemistry of fascination, the chemistry of infatuation, the extent of which is hard to understand for a contemporary reader. A nineteenth-century woman coming to a man and giving herself to him freely and unconditionally without any inhibitions is almost inconceivable. It represents a moral failure. They fall both literally and symbolically and such a fall must end tragically. The dire consequences of the act are similar to those who first succumbed, Adam and Eve. They lose paradise. Both of them feel that their short moment of happiness was a moment of transgression against Victorian moral norms. Although the semantic opposite of love is hate, in reality it is the lack of love. What is more, shame and guilt are two emotions which accompany the transgressions of moral norms. Edwin Frere, once again, is apprehensive of his failure, whereas Louisa Agnew believes in the power of giving and this conviction helps her overcome remorse.

Louisa Agnew and her father as well as Edwin Frere, seek spiritual renewal. Alchemy, functioning in the book not as the element of sensational or forbidden knowledge but rather a *sensu stricto* philosophical trend, is evoked by Clarke by means of various Hermetic texts, such as Hermes Trismegistos, Zosimus, Paracelsus and others, as well as through the relation with Gypsy May which reveals elements of primal magic and a pagan vision of the Mother Goddess. Writing her book, Louisa locked herself away from the world in a lodge by the lake, requiring seclusion to complete her task. If love is symbolized by the figure of a woman waiting passively and patiently for it to materialize, then indeed Louisa provides a great paradigm. Her Hermetic quest, although successful in the completion of the book, resulted in a disappointment. The book was declared to reveal secret matters and was burned by her father in front of their house (as was the original of Mary Ann Atwood's work). Edwin's quest for understanding and happiness also resulted in a catastrophe, as apparently, once more, he gave in to temptation. In a literal and symbolic act of self-castration, Edwin renounced not only manhood but also humanity. His is the greatest of failures encapsulated in the inability to accept weakness and the gift of love. Using medieval motifs in the context of the nineteenth-century love story, Clarke revives the nineteenth-century medievalism and transforms the cliché representations of a romance into a powerful and original love story. Edwin Frere fails not because he is guilty of the moral and sexual transgressions, but because he is unable to see that, in the words of Jeanette Winterson, "only the impossible is worth the effort" (2000: 54) and the impossible is the fusion of love and passion. Out of the two, it is Louisa Agnew who emerges victorious, though she feels herself guilty of the same offense; unlike Frere, she is able to accept Gypsy May's power, the synthesis of love and passion.

References

Atwood, Mary Ann
    1918   *Suggestive inquiry into the Hermetic Mystery with a dissertation on the more celebrated of the alchemical philosophers being and attempt towards the recovery of the ancient experiment of nature.* Montana, USA: Kessinger Publishing's.

Boitani, Piero – Anna Torti (eds.)
    1999   *The body and the soul in medieval literature.* Woodbridge, Suffolk: D.S. Brewer.

Bynum, Caroline Walker
    1992   *Fragmentation and redemption. Essays on gender and the human body in medieval religion.* New York: Zone Books.

Clarke, Lindsay
    1989   *The Chymical Wedding.* London: Picador.

Copenhaver, Brian P. (ed.)
    2000   *Hermetica. The Greek* Corpus Hermeticum *and the Latin* Asclepius *in a new English translation with notes and introduction.* Cambridge: Cambridge University Press.

Devi, Maitreyi
    1994   *It Does Not Die. A Romance.* Chicago – London: The University of Chicago Press.

Eco, Umberto.
    1993   *Misreadings.* (Translated from the Italian by William Weaver.) London: Picador.

Eliade, Mircea
    1978   *The forge and the crucible. The origins and structure of alchemy.* Chicago – London: The University of Chicago Press.
    1994   *Bengali Nights.* Chicago: University of Chicago Press.

Jaeger, Stephen C.
    1999   *Ennobling love. In search of a lost sensibility.* Philadelphia: University of Pennsylvania Press.

Lomperis, Linda – Sarah Stanbury (eds.)
1994　　　*Feminist approaches to the body in medieval literature*. Philadelphia: University of Pennsylvania Press.

McCracken, Peggy
1994　　　"The body politic and the queen's adulterous body in French romance", in: Linda Lomperis – Sarah Stanbury (eds.), 38-64.

Nolan, Barbara
1999　　　"Promiscuous fictions: Medieval bawdy tales and their textual liaisons", in: Piero Boitani – Anna Torti (eds.), 79-105.

Norton, Thomas
1975　　　Thomas Norton's *Ordinal of alchemy*. (Edited by John Reidy.) (Early English Text Society 272.) Oxford: Oxford University Press.

Payer, Pierre
1993　　　*The bridling of desire. Views on sex in the later Middle Ages*. Toronto: University of Toronto Press.

Weir, Anthony – James Jerman
1995　　　*Images of lust. Sexual carvings on medieval churches*. London: Routledge.

Winterson, Jeanette.
2000　　　*The Powerbook*. London: Vintage.

Medieval bestiaries and modern beasts – the making of beast fables in contemporary literature

Anna Warmuz, Poznań

> *How mony men in operatioun, Ar like to*
> *beistis in conditioun.*
> *Na meruell is, ane man be lyke ane beist*[1]
> Robert Henryson

Leslie J. Workman, the chief editor and founder of *Studies in medievalism,*[2] who initiated the academic study of medievalism as a separate scholarly discipline, in an editorial to one of the first issues defined it as "the study of the Middle Ages, the application of medieval models to contemporary needs, and the inspiration of the Middle Ages in all forms of art and thought" (Workman 1987: 1). Indeed, contemporary literature in its restless search for inspiration and universal models relies heavily on the past and specifically, consciously or not, on the medieval literary tradition. Thus, although structurally different, the contemporary novel and the medieval beast fable exhibit certain similarities, especially in the character of moral questions that they frequently pose but not always answer, as well as in the insight into the contemporary imagination and the general attitude to nature that they provide. This paper argues that two contemporary novels,[3] Anne Haverty's *One day as a tiger* (1998), and Yann Martel's *Life of Pi* (2002), retain some vestigial traces of medieval beast fables. In addition, they both make use of detailed zoological descriptions of animals typically associated with the medieval genre of bestiary. Haverty explores the very modern and controversial issue of genetic experimentation, which makes it possible to revive the typically medieval combination of the human and animal world. Martel, in turn, weaves a religious theme into his survival story promising the reader to "have a story that will make you believe

---

1   The quotation comes from the Prologue (ll.48- 50) to *The poems of Robert Henryson.* 1906. (Edited by G. Gregory Smith.) Edinburgh – London: Scottish Text Society.

2   Studies in medievalism is a series of scholarly volumes devoted to the study of the idea of the Middle Ages from about 1500 to the present.

3   According to Davenport Conrad of Hirsau distinguishes between animal fables and fables in which human beings interact with animals (2004: 68). The three contemporary novels in question exemplify the latter type of fable and it is the interpenetration or the merging of the two worlds that constitutes the background for conveying a more universal truth about human nature.

in God" (*Life of Pi*, x)[4] in the manner of a medieval extended exemplum. One unifying feature of those novels is the juxtaposition of the human and animal world for didactic purposes which gives these stories some of the generic attributes of beast fables.

Medievalism as the process of adopting and rewriting of certain medieval motifs by contemporary writers not only seems justified but also inevitable. Daniel Donoghue points out yet another quality of this scholarly discipline:

> Those of us who work in this period like to draw a distinction between medievalism on the one hand and the more serious business of medieval studies, which is what we practice. According to this distinction (and with some ironic exaggeration) medieval studies is pursued through the interpretation of empirical evidence guided by established methodologies. It has access to the real Middle Ages through old texts and other artefacts. By contrast, medievalism picks and chooses from the hard-won conclusions of medieval studies, using their gleanings as a means to a more frivolous end.
>
> (Donoghue 2002: 128)

Thus, there is a clear-cut distinction between the serious and the frivolous. On the one hand, scholars have at their disposal the "established methodologies" which are conventional, arbitrary ways of interpreting the remains of Middle Ages. Yet, there are also the things that escape scholarly research, things that can only be captured by these "frivolous" methods which can be easily applied to contemporary popular culture. Therefore, through the seemingly tenuous investigation of medieval tropes within the literary works of Martel and Haverty, their moral indebtedness to medieval fables can be discovered. The medieval matrix of the beast fable applied to current highly debatable issues reveals that the contemporary literature still poses the same moral questions but contrary to medieval beast fables it frequently leaves them unanswered. Moreover, by means of frequent references to animal behaviour the writers, just like medieval authors, attempt at social commentary and criticism making their works didactic. The main difference, however, lies in the structure of the medieval and contemporary works since medieval beast fables make no claims to authenticity in contrast to the genre of the novel which tries to be more realistic. Thus, animals in novels are anthropomorphized only to a certain degree as they do not customarily speak nor perform typically human activities. On the whole, the purpose of the application of medieval models is to rediscover the Middle Ages and at the same time to comment on the contemporary world.

In medieval culture and imagination, the relationship between the world of humans and the animal world excited intense interest which seems to be confirmed by the tremendous popularity of bestiaries, books of beasts. Contemporary

---

4   Martel, Yann. 2002. *Life of Pi*. Edinburgh: Canongate. All the quotations from the novel are from this edition. References include the title and page numer(s).

novelists explore the same interdependencies proving that literary treatment of the human and the animal has not changed much since medieval times and that literary animals still provide an opportunity for explicit moral instruction. Yet, present-day authors seem to be primarily interested in the general idea of allegorical representation of animals as a most suitable medium for conveying controversial issues and they do not attempt at retaining the structural properties of beast fables which typically had a more systematic form than the novel. In the medieval literary tradition animals were primarily perceived and treated as symbols, ideas, or images. Flores argues that the immediate association of animals with particular symbolism during this period was largely due to the significant influence of the *Physiologus* and its later development, the bestiary (1996: ix). The *Physiologus,* or *The Naturalist*, was an anonymous Greek text originating in Alexandria, possibly as early as the second century AD. It is a compilation of the supposed or imagined natural characteristics of about forty different animals, birds, reptiles, fish, and mystic stones, which are then allegorized and presented in terms of Christian dogma. The *Physiologus* is thus the ultimate source of many familiar symbols of Christianity, including the pelican, the phoenix, the unicorn, the lion, and the whale (Flores 1996: x). In the "Introduction" to his edition of *The Book of Beasts*, Frazier observes that in medieval times

> bestiaries were second only to the Bible in their popularity and wide distribution during the Middle Ages. They were catalogues of animal stories, combining zoological information, myths, and legends. Great attention was given to bizarre, exotic, and monstrous creatures.
>
> (Frazier 2002: 4)

He continues stating that "bestiary was taken seriously in its time, both as factual scholarship and as moral instruction" (Frazier 2002: 4). Bestiaries were thus the commonest of all illustrated manuscripts of the Middle Ages apart from the Bible or church service books. The sheer number of versions corroborates the great popularity of this type of texts as there exist over forty copies in Latin from the twelfth, thirteenth and fourteenth centuries (George – Yapp 1991: 5). The genre of bestiary was predominantly a compilation of a variety of accumulated folklore, legend, pseudoscience, as well as rudimentary scientific observation of an assortment of real and imaginary animals (Flores 1996: x). There was less emphasis on allegorical reading, and many animals that had not previously appeared in the *Physiologus* were given no moral interpretation at all. Having those popular, profusely illustrated books of beasts at their disposal, medieval writers made use of the animal motif mainly for didactic purposes, especially in the fables.

Throughout the Middle Ages particular animals were associated with specific human features of character and medieval authors tended to look for revelations, reading birds and beasts as signs from God. Michael Camille, who argues that the true meaning of animal motifs in medieval art should not be sought within its centre but rather on its margins as the centre is "dependent upon the margins for its continued existence" (2001: 47), observes that in the bestiaries "each beast is framed in a visual stereotype that is as strict as the theological interpretation presented in the text" and, as he further explains, "there are political and social reasons for the choice of particular beasts, especially for the landowning and hunting aristocracy" (Camille 2001: 48). Thus, the elements of nature were given great social significance and what is more, different animals had different class associations for medieval audiences; they could refer to all groups up and down the social scale as well as to the clergy (Camille 2001: 70). Moreover, many figures of saints were easily recognized by their associated beasts.[5] Interestingly, in the medieval allegorical or moral interpretation of beasts, the reduction of the formerly multiple nature of an animal to one typical trait is visible, for example, in the *The history of Reynard the Fox*[6] whose function was to trace social and political trespasses and to chastise the culprits often through biting satire, the fox's main attribute is cunning.[7] Thus, *The History of Reynard the Fox* is one of the examples of medieval pseudo-biological observations of nature on the basis of which a simple picture of the world originated which was then transferred to literature and served as a model. Medieval people must have felt themselves close to the beasts since they so often assigned them human traits and behaviour.

Since the Middle Ages,[8] the fable as a literary form has especially explored those regions of medieval culture where human and animal overlap. Beast literature at the end of the twelfth century includes three prominent genres: bestiary, beast epic, and fable.[9] In England, two basic types were present: the Anglo-French "courtly" beast fables by Marie de France and the "exempla" or beast fables found in sermons and handbooks for preachers (Honegger 1996: 175). As Henderson observes, "fable lies half-way between the poles of moralized, supposedly factual

---

5   For example, St. Mark the Evangelist by the winged lion, St. Luke the Evangelist by the winged ox, St. John the Evangelist by the eagle, St. Agnes by the lamb, St. Giles by the doe, or St. Hugh of Lincoln by the swan (Ziółkowski 1993: 34).

6   *The history of Reynard the fox* is a collection of medieval French stories which originated in the twelfth century and later permeated Western European literatures.

7   Moreover, fox as a wily animal which frequently feigns death in order to lure scavenger birds is usually allegorically interpreted as the devil's attempt to ensnare the unwary souls of those who believe him to be dead (Honegger 1996: 172).

8   Ancient roots of fable are not the concern of this paper although the didactic functions of Aesopian fable are indisputable. Holzberg explains that "the fable was not regarded in antiquity as a literary genre *per se*, but was primarily used in poetry and prose as exemplum with which to illustrate all manner of observations" (2002: 1). For more on ancient fable, see: Lewis (1996), Holzberg (2002).

9   Ziółkowski gives yet another categorization: "animals and birds are especially salient in three types of medieval literature: one is beast fable, often called Aesopic fable; another is the *Physiologus* and its close relative, the bestiary; and the third is the cycle of stories that runs around Renard the Fox" (1993: 2).

bestiary and fictionalized epic" (1981: 162). The precise generic classification of beast literature is problematic but Ziółkowski concludes that "beasts override genre" (1993: 1). In the Middle Ages a variety of longer didactic texts, such as sermons, were scattered with fables and exempla in which animals were primarily used to convey a particular meaning. Flores emphasizes (1996: x) that it is the *sensus moralis*, that is, the interpretation of animals as important symbols of moral and metaphysical truths, that lies at the very heart of the *Physiologus* and bestiary tradition. Loveridge defines fable by means of animal imagery. Fable, in his view, is a "distressingly vague, notoriously hydra-headed technical term" (1997: 2). Despite the great difficulty in delineating the precise scope and definition of a beast fable the application of certain generic properties of medieval beast fable to even recent writings seems promising in terms of establishing certain common ground for comparison between medieval and modern imagination and treatment of nature for didactic purposes.

Although it seems that our modern culture does not make use of the sophisticated allegorical and moral interpretations of literary beasts and animals which-have lost their symbolic meaning, contemporary novelists still use animal motifs for didactic purposes. *One Day as a Tiger* (1998), Anne Haverty's first novel set in rural Ireland, is a story of a clever young historian Marty Hawkins, "younger brother in the groves of academe" (*One Day as a Tiger*, 3)[10] with a bright future ahead who gives up his promising academic career at Trinity College and returns to the family sheep-farm in the heart of Tipperary where he experiences unexplained longing and meditates upon the past while being unable to cope with the present. Marty turns out to be a destructive character who being secretly in love with his brother's wife, Etti, brings about tragic events in the family. At the same time, he indulges in a strange relationship with Missy, a genetically modified sheep, whom he initially treats as a pet only to cruelly abandon her when his interest wanes. Haverty assumes the role of moral fabulist and shows the carnivalesque reversal of roles, in which Marty becomes an animal predator and Missy the sheep acquires human attributes. Their relationship resembles the one between the tiger and the sheep, at the same time referring to the Aesopian mode of moral teaching. On the one hand, the sheep's function in the novel is to teach Marty and force him to ponder the idea of human nature. On the other, the typical combination of meek animal and tigerish human being presupposes tragedy. The didacticism of the fable primarily consists of the example that it sets. When he realizes Missy's absolute dependence on him, he instantly loses his interest in grooming her concluding coldly: "she had little choice, I admit, but to love me. Who has the prisoner to turn to in the end, only his keeper, or the prey to its hunter?" (*OneDay as a Tiger*, 99).

10　Anne Haverty. 1998. *One day as a tiger*. London: Vintage. All the quotations from the novel are from this edition. References include the title followed by page number(s).

Haverty in her questioning of the idea of genetic engineering on moral grounds points to the possible interpretation of sheep as a religious symbol making her story similar to medieval beast fable. The author hints at the similarity between Missy and the sacrificial lamb, "the lamb of God" which symbolizes Christ: "She exuded a sweetish scent, bearing no relation to the oily brackish ovine smell, and quite different to the light flowery scent of the shampoo" (*One Day as a Tiger*, 101). Later, Etti observes that the sheep smells like incense: "'She smells like...' she hesitated. 'Like a saint'" (*One Day as a Tiger*, 109). Thus, since the genetically enhanced animal has great symbolic potential, outfitting the story with a universal moral seems natural. Haverty also shows the controversy surrounding the field of genetic engineering not as a remote scientific experimentation but as an inevitable part of contemporary life with which each individual has to come to terms. Henderson observes that "fables were thought of as satiric and as potential vehicles for more specific criticisms if only an author were willing to break the decorum of generality" (1981: 161). The decorum here is broken as the world presented is the world of an individual human being and a member of a small community whose case is unique and uncommon. From the beginning Marty takes the position of the animal in the fable, an animal whose function it is to reveal the truth about the elements of the beast in human nature.

In her observations, physical and psychological, concerning people Haverty uses numerous animal references. When Marty thinks about Young Delaney, his boyhood friend, he remarks in his mind "his ears were pricked, you could nearly say, like a gun-dog scenting a prey" (*One Day as a Tiger*, 11) pointing to the man's brutish qualities. And about his wish to see his ex-girlfriend Caroline he thinks, "his wish to see her was a residue of my old self, nothing more. Like an old dog leaping a wall out of habit, without enthusiasm" (*One Day as a Tiger*, 16). The image of an old dog which he applies to himself serves to underscore his lack of emotionality and lacklustre attitude towards his ex-girlfriend. Additionally, it also encourages the projection of other animal features on to Marty. Thus, the animal features of people permeate the novel and function as a reminder of the animal nature in men and as a counterbalance to Missy's human features.

> During his first encounter with the sheep he learns from the man in the Institute: They're very troublesome to manage, sheep are, Mr Hawkins, as you know yourself. But these human genes make them resistant to a lot of the usual ovine infections. Make them a bit less sheeplike, if you follow me. These little fellas here now are a fantastic improvement. They're close enough to what you could nearly call a trouble-free sheep, Mr Hawkins.
>
> (*One Day as a Tiger*, 23)

Further account of the visit to the Institute abounds in descriptive illustrative passages on typical animal behaviour which resemble bestiary passages. In the Middle Ages, the function of those lengthy explanatory sections which combined zoological observations and imagination was primarily educational. The twelfth century bestiary depicts the sheep in the following way:

> the gentle flock of OVIS the sheep, woolly, defenceless in body and placid in mind, gets its name '*ab oblatione*' –from the burnt sacrifice – because in the old days, among the ancients it was not bulls but sheep which were offered up. They call some of them 'bidents', and these are the ones which have two longer teeth among the eight. It was these which the Gentiles used principally to offer in sacrifice.
>
> (White – Frazier 2002: 72-73)

In the medieval bestiary, the author typically uses the details of the physical features of the animal projecting them on its emotional sphere or speculating about its habits and instincts. Haverty to a certain degree follows this type of presentation and also points to the fact that the passivity and silent suffering of Missy makes Marty easily offer her as a kind of sacrifice for Etti without any pangs of conscience.

From the first moment Marty sees Missy, he feels he wants her as his possession and maybe at this very moment he also invents his plan to use the animal for his own purposes to satisfy his need of understanding himself. Moreover, he focuses his entire attention on the sheep as having abandoned university career he seems to have no other goals. Marty continues:

> Her eyes were fixed on me, glittering and unfathomable, but with a look full of hope and pathos. It was a look I had seen in no lamb's eyes before. Certainly, she was as mean a specimen of a lamb as you could find. Scrawny, as if her mother had been dry as a bone, one ear floppy, and a freakish bluish tinge in those eyes of her. But almost at once, I knew I had to have her. Not for any farmer's purpose, not for meat or to breed from, but to watch and understand.
>
> (*One Day as a Tiger*, 24-25)

The detailed physical description of the animal diminishes the distance between people and genetically modified animals through the gradual process of familiarization with the strange new breed of sheep.

Apart from obvious animal associations that reappear throughout the novel, Haverty also uses another motif typical of a fable, that is the discernible nostalgia for the past which typically underlies the presentation of irretrievably lost spheres of life. As Davenport observes contemporary "[writers] have expressed a mythical or mystical interest in the past through recreations of lost realms or the pursuit of Grail quests..." (2004: 1). The fact of Marty's return to his home country in search of the "lost realm" of his childhood gives the novel yet another attribute of a fable. According to Marty's view: "Pierce was patient because my obsession with Missy he regarded as a nostalgic attempt to recreate the past" (*One Day as a Tiger*, 45). For Marty, the sheep is also an exceptional mythical animal, as he observes one evening while looking at Missy:

> I went out to the yard and saw Missy huddled on the last patch by the wall to lose the
> glow of the day, her head raised to the embers of the sun in a posture of rapt and medi-
> tative solitude. She appeared to me as a mythic creature, wild, biblical, travelling in the
> desert under a white moon, into the cold black stretches of outer space, into seasons to
> come, following each other with inexorable bleakness.
>
> (One Day as a Tiger, 78)

Marty talks to Missy like to a child, tells her fairy tales "about a goblin and a fair princess and a magic horse and a girl-sheep who saved them from the wicked wizard" (*One Day as a Tiger*, 81). He realizes that the world of fable is engrossing and believable: "I almost believed in it myself, the way the words came out soft and expressive and endlessly inventive, arriving inevitably at a happy ending for one and all" (*One Day as a Tiger*, 81). Marty is not only caught in a fable, he also consciously uses the motifs of fairy tales as when he invents a tale about her "mythic father" whom he calls Harold and makes up a body of fantastic adventures with Harold as their hero (*One Day as a Tiger*, 125).

The power relation has already started during his first meeting with the sheep, the moment he names her:

> It was then, waiting for Pierce to make his selection, staring about me with a new alert-
> ness, that my eye caught Missy's. She was not yet Missy to me but it was soon after that
> I gave her that name, inspired by some absurd but touching quality of pride and hauteur
> in her bearing.
>
> (One Day as a Tiger, 24)

In the course of the novel Marty teaches the animal how to be a sheep and by exerting more and more power on her he learns at the same time how to be a human. He wonders: "When I think of those efforts I made in my persistent attempts to induce in Missy a credible sheepiness. The misery I put her through. To prove to myself something I knew very well to be false (*One day as a tiger*, 47). The task that he undertakes of teaching Missy how to be a sheep is bound to fail as Missy is hardly a typical animal, she enjoys eating porridge, and seems to be fond of the smell of shampoo. Finally, when he feels he is losing control over the animal, he starts using force against her while giving her medicine since he realizes that she is week and helpless. He is aware of all his vices and does not refrain from openly admitting to be malicious and bestial and from chastising himself:

> What was the good of dosing Missy? She was hardly a lamb at all. I was treacherous
> and cruel and weak in attempting to force compliance on her, to impose meek ovineness
> on a creature bent on rejecting her sheep's costume, steadfast as a dissident bent on
> martyrdom.
>
> (One day as a tiger, 68)

Continuously he discovers his own capability to act in a cruel and ruthless way towards a creature which has already been ill-treated. All this time he is aware of her helplessness and transgresses the limits of nature trying to manipulate the sheep's human-animal identity. As he continues: "However, I knew she would forgive me. I felt quite confident about that. After all, she had no one else, good or bad, to depend on, or to forgive" (*One Day as a Tiger*, 71). Towards the end of the novel when Marty's friend Fintan asks what Missy actually is, Marty replies: "A monster. I suppose that's what she is. Small-sized certainly as monsters go. But a monster all the same" (*One Day as a Tiger*, 214). This scene demonstrates the man's own monstrosity which he cannot come to terms with and which he subsequently projects onto the animal. The idea of giving a sheep human attributes and thus creating a hybridized living being resembles shaping of the Frankenstein's monster and what follows, it foretells a catastrophe.

As an echo of a beast fable, Haverty's novel undoubtedly conveys a didactic message as it shows the dangers of man's violating the laws of nature and uncovers the truth about the nature of human failings and imperfections. Traditionally fables are "associated with traditional wisdom, inherited maxims, and proverbs, and often using animals to make observations on human behaviour, fables present pictures of common experience" (Davenport 2004: 67). Also, Haverty adopts a Tibetan proverb as the motto for her novel: "It is better to have lived one day as a tiger than a thousand years as a sheep". The proverb can be applied to the central character of Marty who can be compared to the tiger figure when he decides to break with his dull everyday reality, take a risk and bravely escape with his beloved. The motto of the novel, however, turns out to be an ironic remark about Marty as instead of acting in a courageous way he chooses to escape. Haverty does not judge her characters directly but rather she leaves it all to her readers, similarly to Chaucer's approach to the moralizing by means of fable. In the ending to "Nun's Priest Tale", which is a beast fable, he explains role of fabulist and instructs the audience in the reception of the genre of fable:

> But ye that holden this tale a folye,
> As of a fox, or of a cok and hen,
> Taketh the moralite, goode men.
> For Saint Paul seith that al that writen is,
> To oure doctrine it is ywrite, ywis;
> Taketh the frays, and let the chef be stifle.
>
> (ll.3438-3443)[11]

It is thus essential to take the wheat and leave out the chaff, that is to be able to distinguish the moral from the story.

---

11   "Nun's Priest Tale" from Geoffrey Chaucer's *The Canterbury Tales*, in: Larry D. Benson (ed.). 1988. *The Riverside Chaucer.*(Third edition.) Oxford: Oxford University Press.

A slightly different set of moral questions and instruction can be found in Yann Martel's story *Life of Pi*.[12] In his discussion of medieval narrative Tony Davenport points out that "a fable contains events that are untrue, and do not pretend to be true: it follows that avoiding vice in fabulous narratives means lying with probability" (2004: 11). The Canadian author in his story *Life of Pi*, gives two alternative endings to his novel and leaves it up to the reader to choose the better one. At the end of the novel, two Japanese officials interrogate the protagonist after he had spent 227 days at sea and they are rather sceptical about the truthfulness of the story. When he gives them two equally plausible accounts of what happened to him, they finally conclude that "the story of animals is the better story" (*Life of Pi*, 317). The novel, which to a large extent is designed as a survival memoir, serves as a powerful allegory in which animal imagery is skilfully employed to produce the effect of the beast fable. Martel, however, unlike typical medieval moralists, does not provide the reader with certain universal guidelines on ethical conduct and the story lacks an easily understood moral. One of the major concerns of the writer, apart from religious controversies, is the practical application of the entire science of zoology whose elements are interwoven in the narrative. Moreover, as Lewis emphasizes, "prefaces to fable collections major and minor often stressed the physical features of the texts at hand" (1996: 4). Thus, Martel, drawing on the vast fable tradition, does the same providing the reader with a fictitious framework for his exemplum.

In Martel's story the main character Piscine ("Pi") is Molitor Patel, an Indian boy from Pondicherry, who survives the sinking of the cargo ship and finds himself aboard a lifeboat together with an orangutan named Orange Juice, a wounded zebra, a hyena, and a Royal Bengal Tiger by the name of Richard Parker. The main interest of the author is the study of the unique relationship between the boy and the tiger in extreme and improbable conditions. The first part of the novel, which to a large extent takes place in a zoo, equips the reader with information typical of bestiaries and it abounds with useful observations about animal behaviour. Pi mentions that "there are many examples of animals coming to surprising living arrangements. All are instances of that animal equivalent of anthropomorphism: zoomorphism, where an animal takes a human being, or another animal, to be one of its kind" (*Life of Pi*, 84).[13] The theoretical information is further verified in the second part of the novel when Pi who was almost brought up in zoo has to put his knowledge into practice while unsuccessfully trying to tame and train the tiger. Pi in his narration rejects the medieval tradition of approaching animals, and he points out "I am not one given to projecting human traits and emotions onto animals" (*Life of Pi*, 4) but at the same time he often comprehends them in reli-

---

12   Martel's *Life of Pi* is a 2002 Booker Prize Winner.
13   Yann Martel. 2002. *Life of Pi*. Edinburgh: Canongate. All the quotations from the novel come from this edition. References include the title followed by page number(s).

gious terms: "the three-toed sloth, such a beautiful example of the miracle of life, reminded me of God" (*Life of Pi*, 5). And, what is more, he involuntarily assigns the tiger with certain human features as he often talks to the animal and is convinced that it understands him:

> Hold on tight, I'll pull you in. Don't let go. Pull with your eyes while I pull with my hands. In a few seconds you'll be aboard and we'll be together. Wait a second. Together? We'll be together? Have I gone mad?
>
> (*Life of Pi*, 99)

Only later does he realize that he is talking to a wild beast. Interestingly, in Pi's view animals not only deserve equal respect as people but in many ways they are better than humans. Moreover, he frequently emphasizes the tiger's advantage in comparison to himself as commenting on the animal's sharp senses he observes: "Next to Richard Parker, I was deaf, blind and nose-dead" (*Life of Pi*, 108). He admires and respects animals: "What a stunning creature. Such a noble mien. How apt that in full it is a Royal Bengal Tiger" (*Life of Pi*, 175). Pi's admiring attitude towards animals and nature in general reveals the imperfections of human beings who do not stand comparison.

Thus, the animal world is used throughout the novel as a commentary on human life. Especially, the improbable tale of the boy and the tiger assumes the quality of a fable of general significance. The narrative abounds in statements of general wisdom which resemble folk wisdom in medieval fables. As Pi says: "We commonly say in the trade that the most dangerous animal in a zoo is Man. In a general way we mean how our species' excessive predatoriness has made the entire planet our prey" (*Life of Pi*, 29). Martel, similarly to Haverty, investigates the fascinating nature of the predator-prey relationship. Here, however, unlike in Haverty's novel, the predator is the tiger with the little boy as his prey. On his raft, which initially allegorizes Noah's ark filled with animals, Pi confronts his zoological education with reality. He observes:

> But I learned at my expense that father believed there was another animal even more dangerous than us, and one that was extremely common, too, found on every continent, in every habitat: the redoubtable species Animalus anthropomorphicus, the animal as seen through human eyes.
>
> (*Life of Pi*, 31)

Thanks to his background and the conditions on the lifeboat Pi is able to describe animals as seen at close quarters and evaluate them through the human prism: "I am not one to hold a prejudice against any animal, but it is a plain fact that the spotted hyena is not well served by its appearance. It is ugly beyond redemption" (*Life of Pi*, 115). When the hyena attacks the orangutan he makes an observation: "to the end she reminded me of us: her eyes expressed fear in such a humanlike way, as did her strained whimpers" (*Life of Pi*, 131). Further on, Pi following the bestiary tradition produces a catalogue of the sounds made by tigers and gives adequate and sufficient explanation as to their meanings. The most important motif in the process of the main character's self-discovery is his exceptional connection with the wild animal whom he calls "my fellow castaway" (*Life of Pi*, 160) and treats it as a friend:

> It was Richard Parker who calmed me down. It is the irony of this story that the one who scared me witless to start was the very same who brought me peace, purpose, I dare say even wholeness.
>
> (*Life of Pi*, 162)

And when he realizes his strange fascination and excessive dependence on the tiger, he continues:

> I will tell you a secret: a part of me was glad about Richard Parker. A part of me did not want Richard Parker to die at all, because if he died I would be left alone with despair, a foe even more formidable than a tiger.
>
> (*Life of Pi*, 164)

Although he fears the wild animal, at some point he starts appreciating the fact that he has the tiger as his company since he believes that otherwise he would be even more alone and miserable.

Interestingly, although the unique bond between the little boy and the wild animal grows stronger in the course of time, Pi never decides to change the terms of address that he uses while talking to the animal. Throughout the entire voyage he insists on calling the tiger by his official full name preserving the well established distance while ironically, all the time he tries to domesticate the wild animal. Just like a circus trainer, he starts using the whistle and also designs a special training programme which he believes to turn out successful in taming the wild beast. However, he soon bitterly realises that he should be happy that he stayed alive:

> If I survived my apprenticeship as a high seas animal trainer, it was because Richard Parker did not really want to attack me. Tigers, indeed all animals, do not favour violence as a means of settling scores.
>
> (*Life of Pi*, 206)

Once again, the tiger turns out to be more noble and generous than his trainer. All the time Pi is perfectly aware of his position in nature and especially in the food chain which he closely observes on his raft, and fears being eaten. The medieval book of beasts, however, seems to have neglected the dangerous and predatory instincts of tigers and concentrated mainly on the animals' exceptional speed and courage. Thus, the bestiary authors rather focused on the positive and admirable qualities of tigers showing them as most exquisite and respectable species:

> TIGRIS the Tiger gets his name from his speedy pace; for the Persians, Greeks, and Medes used to call an arrow "tygris". The beast can be distinguished by his manifold specklings, by his courage, and by his wonderful velocity. And from him the River Tigris is named, because it is the most rapid of all rivers.
>
> (White – Frazier 2002: 12-13)

In Martel's novel the most frequently emphasized feature of the animal is its dignity and fierceness which stands in stark contrast to the little boy's initial innocence and incapability to kill.

At the beginning of his unintended voyage, Pi is "unable to kill the fish" (*Life of Pi*, 182) on which fact he comments: "Such sentimentalism may seem ridiculous considering what I had witnessed in the last days, but those were the deeds of others, of predatory animals" (*Life of Pi*, 183). In the course of the journey his experience changes and he acquires some of the animals features: "With time and experience I became a better hunter. I grew bolder and more agile. I developed an instinct, a feel, for what to do" (*Life of Pi*, 195). When he starts drinking animal blood he concludes: "I descended to a level of savagery I never imagined possible" (*Life of Pi*, 197). This change that he undergoes might serve as a lesson about the transgressing of human limitations and about the more savage side of human nature.

> Richard Parker has stayed with me. I've never forgotten him. Dare I say I miss him? I do. I miss him. I still see him in my dreams. They are nightmares mostly, but nightmares tinged with love. Such is the strangeness of the human heart. I still cannot understand how he could abandon me so unceremoniously, without any sort of goodbye, without looking back even once. That pain is like an axe that chops at my heart.
>
> (*Life of Pi*, 6)

This unnatural symbiosis between the boy and the tiger seems fabulous and Martel shows this almost idyllic relationship by means of puns and verbal games. Pi, who undertakes the task of feeding the tiger, observes in a frivolous manner: "Of whatever food I caught, Richard Parker took the lion's share, so to speak" (*Life of Pi*, 224). And the narrator says about Pi: "Richard parker still preys on his mind" (*Life of Pi*, 42).

At the end of the novel, when the lifeboat finally reaches the shore, Pi's greatest distress is caused by the fact that the tiger did not say goodbye: "I was certain he would turn my way. He would look at me. He would flatten his ears. He would growl. In some such way, he would conclude our relationship" (*Life of Pi*, 284). He weeps not because of the catastrophe and his hardship at sea or because of the fact that he lost his entire family in a catastrophe but "was weeping because Richard Parker had left me so unceremoniously. What a terrible thing it is to botch a farewell" (*Life of Pi*, 285). He attached so many anthropomorphic qualities to Richard Parker that he consequently expected typical human behaviour from him. Through the confrontation of a tiger and a boy in the confined space of a lifeboat tossed by the sea, Martel leads the reader into the dream-like and improbable narrative which he assigns with religious meaning and further encourages the reader to slip into a pensive reflection on issues of universal significance.

Umberto Eco stated that we can only dream of the Middle Ages since we do not even know which Middle Ages we want to approach. He calls it "dreaming"[14] which suggests some subconscious longing for the past. This search for the past can be at least partially realised by the application of medieval models to contemporary needs. The medieval beast fables related to bestiaries enjoyed great popularity in the times of their production. Similarly, contemporary novels featuring animals have become popular due to their universality and variety of possibilities of interpretation. As stressed by Ziółkowski (apart from being clearly meaningful and easily approachable to all sorts of people, animals in literature permit authors to take risks that they cannot take in stories explicitly about human beings1993: 7). Through the animal characters the medieval authors frequently revealed hidden truths about an individual and society. In their search for inspiration, contemporary novelists frequently recreate medieval motifs and ideas which still prove valid today. A fable as a genre serves well as a means for conveying difficult issues or controversies. In the texts by both Haverty and Martel certain reminiscences of the past literary tradition as well as the use of animal motifs for didactic purposes are conspicuous. The reader is thus encouraged to interpret not only human actions in the narrative but also to search for animal symbolism in contemporary culture.

References

Benson, Larry D. (ed.)
    1988   *The Riverside Chaucer.* (Third edition.) Oxford: Oxford University Press.
Camille, Michael
    2001   *Image on the edge: margins of medieval art.* London: Reaktion Books.
Clark, Willene B. – Meradith T. McMunn (eds.)
    1989   *Beasts and birds of the Middle Ages. The Bestiary and its legacy.* Philadelphia: University of Pennsylvania Press.
Davenport, Tony
    2004   *Medieval narrative: an introduction.* Oxford: Oxford University Press.
Donoghue, Daniel
    2002   *Lady Godiva: a literary history of the legend.* Oxford: Blackwell Publishing.
Eco, Umberto
    1987   *Travels in Hyperreality: Essays.* London: Picador.
Fizjolog. [*Physiologus*]
    2003   (Edited by Katarzyna Jażdżewska.) Warszawa: Prószyński i S-ka.

---

14   From Umberto Eco. 1987. *Travels in Hyperreality: Essays.* London: Picador.

Flores, Nona C. (ed.)
1996   *Animals in the Middle Ages. A book of essays*. New York – London: Garland Publishing, Inc.

Frazier, Kenneth
2002   "Introduction," in: Terence Hanbury White – Kenneth Frazier (eds.), [unpaged].

George, Wilma – Brundson Yapp
1991   *The naming of the beasts. Natural history in the medieval bestiary*. London: Gerald Duckworth and Co Ltd.

Goossens, Jan – Dodmann Timothy (eds.)
1981   *Proceedings/Third international beast epic, fable and fabliau colloquium*. Köln – Wien: Böhlau.

Hassig, Debra
1995   *Medieval bestiaries. Text, image, ideology*. Cambridge: Cambridge University Press.

Haverty, Anne
1998   *One Day as a Tiger*. London: Vintage.

Henderson, Arnold Clayton
1981   "Animal fables as vehicles of social protest and satire: twelfth century to Henryson," in: Jan Gossens – Timothy Dodmann (eds.), 160-173.

Holzberg, Niklas
2002   *The ancient fable: an introduction*. Bloomington: Indiana University Press.

Honegger, Thomas
1996   *From Phoenix to Chanutecleer. Medieval English animal poetry*. Tübingen – Basel: Francke Verlag.

Lewis, Jayne Elizabeth
1996   *The English fable: Aesop and literary culture, 1651-1740*. Cambridge: Cambridge University Press.

Loveridge, Mark
1997   *A history of Augustan fable*. Cambridge: Cambridge University Press.

Martel, Yann
2002   *Life of Pi*. Edinburgh: Canongate.

Smith, Gregory, G (ed.)
1906   *The poems of Robert Henryson*. Edinburgh – London: Scottish Text Society.

White, Terence Hanbury – Kenneth Frazier (eds.)
2002   *The book of beasts: being a translation from a Latin bestiary of the twelfth century*. Madison: University of Wisconsin Madison Libraries Parallel Press.

Workman, Leslie, J.
1987   "Editorial," in: *Studies in Medievalism* 3, 1.

Ziółkowski, Jan
1993   *Talking animals. Medieval Latin beast poetry 750 – 1150*. Pennsylvania: University of Pennsylvania Press.

Some Boethian and ecclesiological themes in C.S. Lewis's *Screwtape Letters*

Andrzej Wicher, Łódź

This probably the most popular of C.S. Lewis's religious and moral treatises is based on the author's own conception of Christianity, and of good and evil, a conception that cannot be fully identified with the teachings of any particular branch of Christianity, or any particular variety of Christian philosophy. This seems to have been, in a high degree, the author's conscious decision, it is clear that he was afraid of what he called "faction", or "coterie". The following is what Screwtape, the mentor devil, has to say on the subject:

> We want the Church to be small not only that fewer men may know the Enemy but also those who do may acquire the uneasy intensity and the defensive self-righteousness of a secret society or a clique. The Church herself is, of course, heavily defended and we have never yet quite succeeded in giving her all the characteristics of a faction; but subordinate factions within her have often produced admirable results, from the parties of Paul and of Apollos at Corinth down the High and Low parties in the Church of England.
>
> (*Screwtape Letters*, 33)[1]

It is, most likely, Screwtape's, and Lewis's, deliberate strategy that he talks about small, or relatively small, groups within Christianity, but it should not escape our attention that the factions of Paul and of Apollos in Corinth, though small in themselves, are comparable to the later division into the Latin and Eastern Orthodox Church, or into Catholicism and Protestantism. This is because the Christian Church in St. Paul's times was itself still very small, and, besides, contrary to Screwtape's suggestion, there is nothing in St. Paul's *Epistles* that would exclude the possibility that those two factions were not in fact limited to the town of Corinth and could also be found in other centres of early Christianity. Thus, it would appear that Screwtape is inclined to praise, and Lewis – who is Screwtape in reverse – to condemn, all identification with any of the existing denominations into which Christianity is divided. Lewis's use of the term "the Church" is highly characteristic, it seems to refer either to the whole of Christianity, or to some kind of common denominator that captures the essence of Christianity, irrespective of any divisions in it, in other words, Lewis uses this word in a way that is rather

---

1   Lewis, C.S. 2002. *The Screwtape Letters* (with *Screwtape Proposes a Toast*). London: HarperCollins Publishers. All the quotations from the text are from this edition. References include the title followed by page number(s).

uncommon in Catholic countries, but can be found in Protestant ones.[2] Lewis's ec-
clesiology does not seem, indeed, very distant to that of Calvin, who insisted on the
Church's complete lack of any necessary connection with any priestly hierarchy, or
any institutions. For Calvin, the Church was the society of believers in which God's
word is taught and sacraments administered, but Calvin distinguished between the
invisible, ideal Church, and the Church understood as a visible congregation of real
people (Todd 1974: 301-303), while for Lewis "the Church" seems to be an entirely
abstract mental construct. It might be considered a little disturbing to think that
Lewis, while nominally a member of the Church of England, was apparently quite
prepared to think of this Church, or denomination, as a mere faction, and would
never refer to it as "the Church". On the other hand, however, Lewis does refer to
the Church of England as "my own church", with a small 'c' (*Mere Christianity*,
54),[3] which seems to imply that the difference between the Church of England and
the Christian Church in Lewis's writings can be understood as analogous to Calvin's distinction between the visible and invisible Church.

It is, of course, quite likely that what Lewis means by "the Church" in *Screwtape Letters* is simply his idea of "mere Christianity" explained in the book under
the same title. There he says the following:

> I hope no reader will suppose that 'mere' Christianity is here put forward as an alterna-
> tive to the creeds of the existing communions – as if a man could adopt it in preference
> to Congregationalism or Greek Orthodoxy or anything else. It is more like a hall out of
> which doors open into several rooms. If I can bring anyone into the hall I shall have
> done what I attempted. But it is in the rooms, not in the hall, that there are fires and
> chairs and meals. The hall is a place to wait in, a place from which to try the various
> doors, not a place to live in.
>
> (*Mere Christianity*, xv)

This would imply that "the Church" is a mere waiting room, a kind of Dantesque
limbo, and that the real Christian life begins the moment we embrace one of the
"communions" or denominations. After all, the factions Lewis condemns are
called "subordinate" which probably means that they are subdivisions in relation
to the basic and fundamental divisions within the Christian Church. Thus, not the
Church of England is pernicious but various groups within it, even though, to continue the "hall and rooms" metaphor, those groups may be thought as pleasant
corners, "nooks and crannies", within the rooms. This is, I must admit, a rather
strange theology, a theology that makes much of the idea of the one and undivided

---

2   This is apparently the way the word "Church" is used in the title of *The Oxford Dictionary of
     the Christian Church*, edited by F.L. Cross, upon which E.A. Livingstone's *Concise Diction-
     ary of the Christian Church* (1996) is based.
3   C.S. Lewis. 2002. *Mere Christianity*. London: HarperCollins Publishers. All the quotations
     from the text are from this edition.

Christian Church while according, at the same time, some supreme value to the divisions within that Church, and treating those divisions as if they were perfectly natural, and God given, as opposed to the subdivisions within them which, for some obscure reason, are qualified as diabolical.

It might appear then that the well-known prophecy from St. John's Gospel: "there shall be one fold and one shepherd" (10: 16)[4] failed to influence Lewis's style of theological thinking. But such an impression would probably be false, here is the same old devil describing his experiences of direct contact with the Church:

> One of our great allies at presents is the Church itself. Do not misunderstand me. I do not mean the Church as we see her spread out through all time and space and rooted in eternity, terrible as an army with banners.

> *(Screwtape Letters, 5)*

Thus, the Church, in Lewis's understanding of the term, seems to have much to do with the conception of "the Church militant", that is, Church on the Earth, as opposed to "the Church suffering", in Purgatory, and "Church triumphant", in Heaven. Naturally, the phrase "terrible as an army with banners" comes from *The Song of Solomon* (6: 4) and contains an allusion to the traditional Christian interpretation of this book of the Bible as an allegory in which the male lover stands for Christ and his female beloved for the Church. It also shows Screwtape as a devil who is thoroughly steeped in biblical lore, and can sometimes speak as if he were an "unfallen" angel. At any rate, it is rather hard to reconcile this vision of the "terrible" Church, and all its impressive, albeit only metaphorical, military capability, with the rather supine acceptance of the debilitating divisions in the Church, which Lewis seems to advocate in the "Introduction" to *Mere Christianity*.

We may, indeed, find, in *Screwtape Letters*, passages that seem intended to strike a balance between the traditional Catholic and Protestant sensibilities so that the author emerges as someone who can stand either halfway between them, or above them. In this way, Lewis, contrary to his assurances that he is not after giving us an alternative creed, does sometimes appear to offer the reader a position that is more mature than the traditional Catholic and Protestant positions, and from the perspective of which the traditional differences between denominations fade into insignificance. Let us consider the following passage in which Screwtape teaches Wormwood, the young devil, about the nature of prayer:

> The best thing, where it is possible, is to keep the patient from the serious intention of praying altogether. When the patient is an adult recently reconverted to the Enemy's party, like your man, this is best done by encouraging him to remember, or to think he

---

4   All quotations from the Bible follow the *Authorized King James Version*. 1997. (Edited by Robert Carrol and Stephen Prickett.) Oxford – New York: Oxford University Press.

remembers, the parrot-like nature of his prayers in childhood. In reaction against that, he may be persuaded to aim at something entirely spontaneous, inward, informal, and unregularised; and what this will actually mean to a beginner will be an effort to produce in himself a vaguely devotional mood in which real concentration of will and intelligence have no part.

(Screwtape Letters, 15-16)

Lewis establishes here two extremes, poles apart, with regard to the subject of prayer, one is represented by "parrot-like prayers", and may be called the Catholic extreme, the other by "devotional mood", and may be justly called the Protestant extreme. It is well-known that the Protestants, especially the radical ones, distrusted the idea that the believers should use established and written texts of prayers, they suspected that the "dead letter" may kill the spirit of such a prayer and so it will degenerate into some automatic, thoughtless, parrot-like repetition, the form of prayer they preferred consisted in spontaneous and extemporary invocations either using one's own words, or wordless. It is clear enough that in the first case form triumphs over content, and in the other one content is treated as far more important than form. It is certainly significant that Lewis devotes much more attention to the latter case than to the former one. The "formalistic" danger is easy to identify, while the case of privileging the content of prayers is more difficult to deal with. Certainly a prayer that is not based on a fixed text may be described as "advanced", "spiritual", or "mystical", but Lewis quickly spots its diabolic potential, the fact that it can be merely a cover up for spiritual laziness and loss of faith.

Lewis describes this watered down form of prayer pointing to S.T. Coleridge as its main advocate:

> One of their poets, Coleridge, has recorded that he did not pray 'with moving lips and bended knees' but merely 'composed his spirit to love' and indulged 'a sense of supplication'.

(Screwtape Letters, 16)

To this we may add the well-known statement from Coleridge's *The Rime of the Ancient Mariner*:

> He prayeth well, who loveth well
> Both man and bird and beast.
> He prayeth best, who loveth best
> All things both great and small...

(Coleridge 1973, 2: 254; Part 7, ll. 612-615)

In this context, Screwtape's verdict: "This is exactly the sort of prayer we want" (*Screwtape Letters*, 16) may strike us as rather rash and unfair, suggesting clearly that Coleridge was, like Milton in Blake's well-known opinion, "of the devil's party without knowing it". Thus, Lewis insists on the rather old-fashioned style of praying "with moving lips and bended knees" because human beings: "are animals and ... whatever their bodies do affects their souls" (*Screwtape Letters*, 16). This clear tendency to unite matter with spirit, gesture and word with the inner disposition, the ritual with what it is supposed to stand for, may indicate either an attitude sympathetic to the traditional Roman Catholic position, or a desire to reunite form and content, as perhaps standing for Catholicism and Protestantism respectively. Coleridge's spiritualization and moralization of prayer was then, from Lewis's point of view, an act of sabotage directed against the synthesis that allows Lewis to feel safe on the territory of "mere Christianity".

A similar synthesis concerning the matter of prayer can be found in St Augustine, later quoted by St. Thomas Aquinas, or rather in St Augustine's formula: "Whatsoever words we use in prayer, we cannot but repeat what is found in Our Lord's Prayer, if we pray suitably and worthily" (Aquinas 1988: 529). Thus, it seems possible to tolerate any amount of formal freedom in the use of words, or even complete lack of words. As long as the believer's attitude to God is correct, whatever he may say will be somehow not only perfectly orthodox, but will be, as it were, virtually present in the Lord's Prayer, that is in a traditional, written text perfectly suitable for thoughtless repetition. The philosophy behind this Augustinian formula is of course encapsulated in the famous Augustinian slogan: "Love, and do what you will", but it is clear enough that St. Augustine's way of thinking, at least on this point, is closer to S.T. Coleridge than to C.S. Lewis. St. Augustine is also a highly ambiguous saint from the point of view of the relationship between Catholicism and Protestantism, fundamentally a Catholic saint, he was also one of the chief sources of inspiration for Protestant Reformers, such as Luther or Calvin, who both quoted St. Augustine extensively.

Naturally, the whole of Lewis's theory of evil is essentially Augustinian, it is the famous negative theory of evil according to which whatever exists is intrinsically good, and that evil consists in perverting goodness, or in a lack of good. Thus, according to Augustine:

> Take away all good, and absolutely nothing will remain. All good is from God. Hence there is no natural existence which is not from God. Now that movement of "aversion," which we admit is sin, is a defective movement; and all defect comes from nothing. Observe where it belongs and you will have no doubt that it does not belong to God.
>
> (quoted from St. Augustine's *On Free Will* in Hyman – Walsh 1983: 55-56)

And, according to a critic writing about the Augustinian doctrine of good and evil:

> The world is good, manifesting measure, form, and order; and any evil appearing in it is the privation of some good, not the creation of some independent principle of evil.
>
> (Hyman – Walsh 1983: 17)

It is well known that this doctrine is, first of all, directed against the Manicheans and their tendency to treat good and evil as more or less symmetrical entities, often embodied in rivalling gods, one of whom stands for the forces of Light, and the other for those of Darkness. This structure Augustine destroys by linking morality with ontology, goodness with existence and evil with some kind of "defective" or "perverted" existence that is always on the brink of non-existence. This may be compared with the following statement concerning God and made by Screwtape, whose very name of course denotes distortion:

> He's vulgar, Wormwood. He has a bourgeois mind. He has filled His world full of pleasures. There are things for humans to do all day long without his minding in the least – sleeping, washing, eating, drinking, making love, playing, praying, working. Everything has to be twisted before its any use to us. We fight under cruel disadvantages. Nothing is naturally on our side.
>
> (*Screwtape Letters*, 118-119)

What is implied here is clearly that the so called neutral activities, which are not intrinsically either morally good or evil, are, in fact, much closer to the pole of goodness than to that of evil, their simple and unperverted existence makes them essentially good, even though they are nothing to boast of. Another problem is why this neo-Augustinian position should be called "vulgar" and "bourgeois". The answer might be that to ascribe goodness to "mere existence" is contrary to what might be called blown up "party politics", that is a partisan position which says that almost nothing is neutral because everything may be construed as serving a particular cause or being detrimental to it. Lewis often warned against approaching religion in the spirit of party politics: "Most of us are not really approaching the subject (social morality) in order to find out what Christianity says: we are approaching it in the hope of finding support from Christianity for the views of our own party" (*Mere Christianity*, 87). In another place, he says the following about a soul that did not escape damnation: "Toeing the party line, self-importance, and above all mere routine, were what really dominated his life" (*Screwtape Letters*, 189).

A Polish poet with strong Marxist leanings, Julian Tuwim, once defined a bourgeois as somebody who "sees all things as separate from one another" and of course made fun of this attitude as denoting a typical, bourgeois, narrow-mindedness.[5] It seems that, from Lewis's point of view – and Lewis was, no doubt, a bourgeois thinker – there is something to be said in favour of this "seeing things separately", its counterpart, that is "seeing all things as interconnected", and therefore plagued by dualism, makes you, at least potentially, into an abject

---

5   I allude of course to the line "A patrząc-widzą wszystko oddzielnie" [And when they look, they see everything separately] from the well known (in Poland) poem *Mieszkańcy* [Dwellers] by Julian Tuwim (Tuwim 1986: 216).

slave of some "party line", in other words, a political, or ideological, fanatic, a Manichean, in fact, who neatly divides the whole world into the zone of light, and that of darkness.

At this point, we may return to the doctrine of "mere Christianity" as it is defined both in *Mere Christianity* and in *Screwtape Letters*. In the latter book, we find the following passage:

> The real trouble about the set your patient is living in is that it is *merely* Christian. They all have individual interests, of course, but the bond remains mere Christianity. What we want, if men become Christians at all, is to them in the state of mind I call 'Christanity And'. You know – Christianity and the Crisis, Christianity and the New Psychology, Christianity and the New Order, Christianity and Faith Healing, Christianity and Psychical Research, Christianity and Vegetarianism, Christianity and Spelling Reform. If they must be Christians let them be Christians with a difference. Substitute for the faith itself some Fashion with a Christian colouring. Work on their horror of the Same Old Thing.
>
> (*Screwtape Letters*, 135; original emphasis)

Lewis's horror of "Christianity And" seems to include probing into the differences dividing particular Christian denominations, but, first of all, we have to do here with a good example of how the devil, or devils deal with the problem of "twisting" things that originally were good, or God's own. Something is added to them, which apparently enriches "the Same Old Thing" and makes it more attractive. In reality, however, this added element acts as a virus or a cancerous cell; it destroys the thing it attaches itself to. This "added element" in itself is not evil – in the Augustinian structure of good and evil, nothing can be evil in itself – but somehow when combined those two elements produce an expansion of devilish nothingness.

A whole nihilistic vision is to be found in the essay *Screwtape Proposes a Toast* where the word "democracy" is shown as a cover up for the base feeling of envy, and as legitimising a system based on the idea of nothingness, or rather on that of debilitating mediocrity that is, in this case, on a liquidation of social differences that make any real development possible:

> I am credibly informed that young humans now sometimes suppress an incipient taste for classical music or good literature because it might prevent their Being like Folks; that people who would really wish to be – and are offered the Grace which would enable them to – honest, chaste, or temperate, refuse it. To accept might make them Different, might offend against the Way of Life, take them out of Togetherness, impair their Integration with the Group. They might (horror of horrors!) become individuals.
>
> (*Screwtape Letters*, 200)

Lewis's vision of nihilism is not then founded on mere absence or void, but rather on the idea of false, inauthentic presence, which may easily be described as following the herd instinct. A member of the herd derives his values from the behaviour of the herd. In extreme cases, such an individual loses completely the power of thinking and is driven only by primitive instincts, in other words, he gives up his humanity and embraces animality, and a rather simplified animality to boot, that of ants for example, even though his behaviour may superficially resemble that of a human being.

Lewis, in *The Screwtape Letters*, provides us with another vision of human enslavement, this time concerned with the conception of time. According to Screwtape, man: "takes Time for an ultimate reality" (*Screwtape Letters*, 149), which is why he expects God to do something, in connection with his prayers, and is sorely disappointed if he does not, as if our prayers had the power to make God change His mind, while, in reality, God does not divide time into the past, present, and future, He rather sees everything as part of what Lewis calls "unbounded Now" (*Screwtape Letters*, 150).

This situation makes Lewis think of the early sixth-century Latin author, Boethius, the author of *The Consolation of Philosophy*, who apparently correctly diagnosed the Human Condition, even though, as Lewis emphasises, hardly anybody thinks of him as an author who has something valuable to say to ourselves and our generation. This devilish trick is called, in *The Screwtape Letters*, "the Historical Point of View":

> The Historical Point of View, put briefly, means that when a learned man is presented with any statement in an ancient author, the one question he never asks is whether it is true. He asks who influenced the ancient writer, and how far the statement is consistent with what he said in other books, and what phase in the writer's development, or in the general history thought, it illustrates, and how it affected later writers, and how often it has been misunderstood (specially by the learned man's own colleagues) and what the general course of criticism on it has been for the last ten years, and what is the 'present state of the question'.
>
> (*Screwtape Letters*, 150-151)

This condemnation of a certain, perhaps the most important, variety of historicism in literary studies seems to be a covert plea for a return to the way ancient authors were treated in the Middle Ages. The considerations concerning the historical context of a given literary work, no matter how ancient it was, were in those times completely disregarded, but it can hardly be said that the texts were valued for the sake of some abstract or objective truth that they might contain. They were rather used for ideological or didactic purposes, sometimes substantially changed to render them more amenable to a pragmatic use – we may mention at this point the famous *Ovid Moralisé*, – or they were rejected if it was considered too difficult to make them compatible with the dominant ideology, or the dominant mentality. Lewis, by saying that a given text should be, first of all, appreciated for the sake of the truth that it contains, if of course it contains any, also implies that it can and should be used for didactic purposes:

> To regard the ancient writer as a possible source of knowledge – to anticipate that what
> he said could possibly modify your thoughts or your behaviour – this would be rejected
> as unutterably simple-minded.
>
> (*Screwtape Letters*, 151)

In other words, the choice seems to be between a rather anodyne and apparently unideological approach to a text, an approach that can, however, also yield political effects – as Lewis suggests, it can be used as a weapon in the professional rivalry between the "learned men", on the one hand, and an overtly political or ideological method of interpretation that has the ambition to provide an answer to the burning question of "what should be done?", on the other.

In this particular case, we are invited to consider Boethius as a source of knowledge that can resolve the modern man's problem with ineffective prayers, or rather prayers that seem, in our eyes, to have been unanswered. Instead of racking our brains and trying to solve this problem ourselves, Lewis suggests we had better have recourse to Boethius. In Screwtape's words: "It may be replied that some meddlesome human writers, notably Boethius, have let this secret out" (*Screwtape Letters*, 150). In what way can our acquaintance with Boethius help us? Principally, Boethius, speaking through the mouth of his Lady Philosophy, refutes the common impression that evil people prosper while the good ones are persecuted, for he suggests that the evil, already during earthly existence, are punished with their evil, while the good are rewarded with their goodness, and that this goodness can be identified with authentic happiness:

> Goodness is happiness, and therefore it is obvious that all good men obtain happiness in
> virtue of their being good. But we agree that those who attain happiness are divine. The
> reward of the good, then, a reward that can never be decreased, that no one's power can
> diminish, and no one's wickedness darken, is to become gods. ... The reward we see to the
> good must be balanced by a corresponding punishment of the wicked. Therefore, just as
> goodness is its own reward, so the punishment of the wicked is their very wickedness.
>
> (Boethius 1982: 124)

The doctrine based on the assumption that "goodness is its own reward" is indeed clever enough. Lewis represents the devil as an individual who, concerning the question of prayer, uses the "'heads I win, tails you lose' argument" (*Screwtape Letters*, 148), that is, argues that a prayer that has been granted is irrelevant, for what happened would have happened anyway as a result of a natural and logical course of events, while a prayer that has not been granted is highly relevant because it shows that God is powerless and therefore probably nonexistent. If this is so, then Boethius's Lady Philosophy is some kind of "anti-devil" that uses a symmetrically opposed "heads you win, tails I lose" argument in that she seems to be arguing that there is no such run of bad luck that can show that God has turned his back on man, or on a particular person, for this bad luck can bear no relationship to the "true happiness" which is entirely moral and spiritual. On the other hand, good luck, or prosperity, can quite easily be taken for a sign of "true happiness", as there is no way to prevent a good man from thinking that his material prosperity can be read as a token of God's grace, that is, of his being in God's good books, which is something that Boethius seems to understand perfectly well when he says, for example:

> Another man may be perfect in every virtue, holy and very close to God: Providence judges that it would be outrageous for him to meet with any adversity to such an extent that he is not even allowed to be upset by bodily illness.
>
> (Boethius 1982: 139)

Thus, Boethius appears to be preaching a doctrine according to which whatever happens can and should be interpreted as a sign of God's perfect love and infallible justice, which is of course the opposite of Screwtape's doctrine of the God who can never do well, but also its mirror reflection. Screwtape's teaching once again reveals itself to be a traditional theology and ethics with a twist. As a result, he seems unable, for example, to criticise or distance himself from Boethius's theology of prayer, he can only superficially distort it by standing it on its head.

Screwtape is a devil who seems to be playing an angel's advocate in the sense that what he says is hardly an intellectual position that can be rationally taken by anyone. In his twenty-seventh letter to Wormwood, a junior and subservient devil, Screwtape embarks on explaining, as far as this is at all possible, God's idea of time. The purpose of this explanation seems to be to "justify the ways of God to men", in particular, to show that God's foreknowledge does not limit or invalidate man's freedom, so that man should not imagine foolishly that it does not matter what he does, or fails to do, everything being "predestined" in God's infallible mind:

> *Why* that creative act leaves room for their free will is the problem of problems, the secret behind the Enemy's nonsense about 'Love'. *How* it does so is no problem at all; for the Enemy does not *foresee* the humans making their free contributions in a future, but *sees* them doing so in His unbounded Now. And obviously to watch a man doing something is not to make him do it.
>
> (*Screwtape Letters*, 150; original emphasis)

Of course the usual Christian position on this matter is exactly the opposite, the Christians have usually little trouble envisaging God as a loving Father, but they certainly have trouble understanding how God's mind works. For the devil, on the other hand, this is easy as falling off a log, after all, he is a pure spirit endowed with the intelligence of an angel. It is in connection with this theory of God's mind that Screwtape evokes "the meddlesome" Boethius, who "let the secret out". The relevant passage in Boethius seems to be the following and it is one of the last statements of *The Consolation of Philosophy*:

> Since, therefore, all judgement comprehends those that are subject to it according to its own nature, and since the state of God is ever that of eternal presence, His knowledge, too, transcends all temporal change and abides in the immediacy of His presence. It embraces all the infinite recesses of past and future and views them in the immediacy of its knowing as though they are happening in the present. If you wish to consider, then, the foreknowledge or prevision by which he discovers all things, it will be more correct to think of it not as a kind of foreknowledge of the future, but as the knowledge of a never ending presence. So that it is better called providence or "looking forth" than prevision or "seeing beforehand". For it is far removed from matters below and looks forth at all things as though from a lofty peak above them.
>
> (Boethius 1982: 165)

Boethius's argument is largely linguistic and it hinges, in a high degree, on the difference between the Latin prefixes "pro" in *provideo* and "pre" in *prevideo*, which Lewis freely translates as the distinction between 'seeing' and 'foreseeing'. Both distinctions are meant to obliterate the temporal or chronological aspect of God's "vision" in favour of a non-chronological simultaneity that somehow manages to include in itself what we perceive as chronological sequence of events.

The main problem here seems to be how to reconcile the Boethian vision of a God who sits "on a lofty peak above the matters below and far removed from them" with the Christian idea of a loving God who takes interest in His creatures. Boethius, even though he no doubt was a Christian, did not write his *Consolation of Philosophy* as a Christian, but rather as a philosopher, and the philosophy that he knew, even though it did not have to be necessarily incompatible with Christianity, clearly was the fruit of a non-Christian tradition and environment. This is probably why Boethius did not feel obliged to harmonize his philosophical God with the God of the Christians, but Lewis does not make this effort either and prefers to pretend that there is no difference between those two visions of God, that Boethius's God is the Christian God. Screwtape, being a devil, and a pretty intelligent one, could have easily made use of this discrepancy in, for example, instructing Wormwood that he should sow the seeds of religious doubt in the mind of the man he tries to waylay by pointing out to a real or apparent logical incoherence in the traditional views on God, but Screwtape does not think of such a possibility, which may make the reader think that Screwtape, in fact, is a typical "sheep in wolf's clothing", an "unfallen" angel, who speaks as if he were a fallen one, only to make his argument appear more interesting for the people who are too blasé to accept a straightforward teaching on sin and virtue from a person who is understood to side with virtue.

But Boethius is an important thinker in the context of *The Screwtape Letters* and *Mere Christianity* also as somebody who talks about Lady Philosophy in a manner resembling William Langland's description of the lady representing Holy Church in the fourteenth-century *Vision of Piers Plowman*. This is the way Lady Philosophy is shown in *The Consolation of Philosophy*:

> ... I became aware of a woman standing over me. She was of awe-inspiring appearance, her eyes burning and keen beyond the usual power of men. She was so full of years that I could hardly think of her as of my own generation, and yet she possessed a vivid colour and undiminished vigour. It was difficult to be sure of her height, for sometimes she was average human size, while at other times she seemed to touch the very sky with the top of her head, and when she lifted herself even higher, she pierced it and was lost to human sight.
>
> (Boethius 35-36)

In Langland we encounter, or rather the Dreamer encounters:

> A lady lovely of lere [face], in linen clothed
> Came down from a castle and called me fair ...
> I was afraid of her face, though she was fair ...
> (Langland 1973, 1: 357; B-text, Passus I, 4-5,10)

Both ladies combine good looks with a rather formidable majesty. A moment later, Langland's Lady Church in her sermon on the "plant of peace" gives the Dreamer a paradoxical vision of changeability and unity that is quite compatible with the Boethian Lady Philosophy's wonderfully telescoping height:

> And also the plant of peace, most precious of virtues.
> For Heaven might not hold it, it was heavy in itself.
> Till it had of the earth, eaten its fill.
> And when it had of this fold [earth], flesh and blood taken,
> There was never leaf upon linden lighter thereafter
> A portative [rapid] and piercing as the point of a needle,
> So that no armour might let [stop] it, and no high walls
> (Langland 1973, 1: 361-362; B-text, Passus I, 152-157)

Screwtape's method of temptation in The Screwtape Letters consists exactly in making the "patient", that is an Everyman-like character who is the object of the devils' interest, fail to see the link between the Church with the capital 'C' and the church with the lower case 'c', the link between "the Church ... terrible as an army with banners" (*Screwtape Letters*, 5) and "the half-finished, sham Gothic erection on the new building estate" (*Screwtape Letters*, 5). If Lady Philosophy represents a force that brings together practice and theory symbolized by the Greek letters "Pi" and "Theta" embroidered on the Lady's dress:

> On the bottom hem could be read the embroidered Greek letter Pi, and on the top hem the Greek letter Theta. Between the two a ladder of steps rose from the lower to the higher letter
>
> (Boethius 1982: 36)

then Screwtape's whole cunning is focused on confirming the patient in his inability to move from "Pi" to "Theta" and back again, that is from "spiritual" to "material" Church:

> At his present stage ... he has an idea of 'Christians' in his mind which he supposes to be spiritual but which, in fact, is largely pictorial. His mind is full of togas and sandals and armour and bare legs and the mere fact that the other people in church wear modern clothes is a real – though of course an unconscious – difficulty to him.
>
> *(Screwtape Letters*, 6)

Lewis, speaking through Screwtape, his paradoxical mouthpiece, characteristically belittles the difference between those two aspects of reality, and suggests that neither the "spiritual" ideas are truly spiritual, nor the "material" aspects are so common and despicable.

In conclusion, I would like to say that Screwtape, the protagonist of C.S.Lewis's *Screwtape Letters*, turns out to be a singularly religious devil. In a sense, Screwtape describes himself when he talks about Father Spike, a local, presumably Anglican, vicar who puzzles his congregation with clever views on any subject, and who is politically very volatile. The common denominator of Father Spike's attitudes is, as Screwtape discovers, hatred, which of course is very good from the hellish point of view: "But I must warn you that he has one fatal defect: he really believes. And this may yet mar all" (*Screwtape Letters*, 84). It is clear enough that Screwtape also "really believes", he is constantly harping on "the Enemy", that is, God, and he has quite an intimate knowledge of God's ways and of His mind, even though he cannot understand the ultimate motives of God's decisions. Of course Screwtape himself is motivated, just like Father Spike, by hatred, but his hatred of God, and of everything else, makes him focus his mind on God in a way that is reminiscent of the highest forms of religious passion. Screwtape seems indeed too obsessed with biblical themes to be able to hold a distanced and flippant view on matters religious that is typical of atheists and freethinkers. All this does not naturally mean that Screwtape can be saved, after all, as St. James said in his epistle, "the devils also believe, and tremble" (2: 19).

Screwtape is also, in a sense, a Protestant devil, or, to be more precise, a devil whose temptational project seems to be well suited to a Protestant sensibility and mentality. This is why Screwtape tries to take advantage of the difference, already great enough in the Protestant doctrine, between immanence and transcendence, between things material and things spiritual. Screwtape's method of tempting consists in exaggerating the above mentioned difference, in making, for example, the spiritual dimension of the Church appear as absent and inaccessible in the church seen as a specific congregation that includes all kinds of people, also such that may easily get on other people's nerves, or in suggesting that an "ordinary" prayer based on a set text is not spiritual enough and should be replaced by "devotional mood" (*Screwtape Letters*, 15-16). In Catholicism, at least theoretically, the gap between transcendence and immanence is much narrower, which is why, a Catholic, again theoretically, should find it much easier to remain convinced of the holiness of the Church, in spite of the unholiness, or even unworthiness, of its specific members, including the clergy.

It is possible that Lewis wrote this book with mainly an Anglican, or post-Anglican, reader in mind, or that he made his devil a quasi-Protestant because he thought, together with such critics as Max Weber, that it was the Protestant mentality that gave our civilization its modern face, the face he rather detested. The exasperation of Screwtape at the fact that "the patient has continued to attend one church" (*Screwtape Letters*, 81) seems, at any rate, to reflect, paradoxically and metaphorically, Lewis's desire to see the Christian Church united, at least in the sense of bringing together Roman Catholicism and the traditional and established Protestant denominations. The frequent medieval allusions in the *The Screwtape Letters* reflect its author's scholarly speciality, but, indirectly, they seem to conjure up the spirit of the age when the Western Christianity was more or less in unity.

References

Aquinas, Thomas
1988   *An Aquinas reader. Selections from the writings of Thomas Aquinas.* (Edited by Mary T. Clark.) New York: Fordham University Press.

Bible
1997   *Authorized King James Version.* (Edited by Robert Carrol – Stephen Prickett.) Oxford – New York: Oxford University Press.

Boethius
1982   *The Consolation of Philosophy.* (Edited by V.E. Watts.) Harmondsworth, Middlesex: Penguin Books.

Coleridge, Samuel Taylor
1973   *The Rime of the Ancient Mariner*, in: Frank Kermode – John Hollander (eds.), vol. 2: 238-254.

Hyman, Arthur – James J. Walsh (eds.)
1983   *Philosophy in the Middle Ages. The Christian, Islamic and Jewish traditions.* Indianapolis: Hackett Publishing Company.

Kermode, Frank – Hollander, John (eds.)
1973   *The Oxford anthology of English literature.* 2 vols. New York – London – Toronto: Oxford University Press.

Langland, William
1973   *Vision of Piers Plowman*, in: Frank Kermode – John Hollander (eds.), vol. 1: 351-363.

Lewis, Clive Staples
2002   *Mere Christianity* (A revised and amplified edition with a new introduction of the three books *Broadcast Talks*, *Christian Behaviour* and *Beyond Personality*). London: HarperCollins Publishers.

2002   *The Screwtape Letters* (with *Screwtape Proposes a Toast*). London: HarperCollins Publishers.

Livingstone, E.A. (ed.)

1996   *Concise Dictionary of the Christian Church* (based on F.L. Cross's The-Oxford *Dictionary of the Christian Church*). Oxford – New York: Oxford University Press.

Todd, John M.

1974   *Reformacja* [Reformation]. (Translated by J.S. Łoś.) Warszawa: Instytut Wydawniczy PAX.

Tuwim, Julian

1986   *Wiersze* [Poems]. 2 vols. (Edited by Alina Kowalczykowa.) Warszawa: Czytelnik.

Blind Hary's *The Wallace* and Mel Gibson's *Braveheart*: what do
medieval romance and Hollywood film have in common?

Władysław Witalisz, Kraków

Introduction

Since the revival of interest in the Middle Ages in the nineteenth-century medieval themes and stories have continued to inspire novelists, poets and artists who
willingly borrowed from the rich repertory of medieval history, literature and art.
Medievalism has grown into a full-blown artistic phenomenon and a separate field
of research. The new media, especially film and television, have made the Middle
Ages truly popular by reaching numbers of audiences that literature never could.
For better or for worse, the popular vision of the Middle Ages is being constructed
by "the movies," lavish international productions which combine artistic ambition
with demands of the market. The evaluation of films on medieval subjects has
been variously approached by medieval scholars. Purists scoff at their inaccurate
presentation of historical facts, misrepresentation of social relations or the anach-
ronisms of costume and setting. Those with a more apologetic attitude focus on
the transformations that medieval constructs of thought have to undergo when
they are retold through a new medium to a modern audience in a new context.
They complain about what is lost in the translation but admit that it is no longer
possible to cross what Paul Zumthor called the "unbridgeable abyss" (1992: 24)
between our mentality and that of medieval authors and audiences. Others, like
the present author, whose job and passion is to teach medieval literature to readers
at this side of the abyss, commend the medievalist moviemakers for their use of
medieval meanings, metaphors and references in telling their own modern stories
to modern audiences as this shows that at least some of the old constructs of human thought are still alive and universally communicable. Besides, it is quite possible, and thus reassuring, that films like *Excalibur* or *First Knight* have encouraged a few audience members to read fragments of Malory.

The purpose of this paper is to examine and evaluate the medievalism of *Braveheart*, Mel Gibson's 1995 Hollywood story of the Scottish hero William Wallace. The term medievalism will be understood here in its broadest sense as the
filmmakers' reception and use of medieval sources, meanings and themes. In order that the present author's love of cinema does not blind his critical eye the paper shall combine the three approaches to medievalism in popular culture mentioned above: the scoffingly historical, the apologetically contextual and the
commendingly universal. Medieval history and the popular medieval poetic romance on the life and deeds of the Scottish leader, *The Wallace*, by Henry the

Minstrel also known as Blind Hary, will be used as a point of reference in this discussion of the film's reception and vision of the Middle Ages.

1. The history

The over-forty-year-long rule of the Scottish king Alexander III, also called the Glorious, came to an end with his death in an accident in 1286. His only heir was his three-year-old granddaughter Margaret, known as the maid of Norway. After Margaret's unexpected death on the Orkney Islands in 1290, two Scottish claimants to the throne emerged: Robert the Bruce and John Balliol, both deriving their claims from their ancestors' relation to the twelfth-century King David I. The English Edward I Longshanks was asked for arbitration and gave his support to Balliol, who was crowned King in 1292. On the strength of his help to Balliol's coronation Edward started treating the king as his vassal. Edward's claim to suzerainty over Scotland had earlier roots in his father's, Henry III's, demand of homage from Alexander III, who had married Edward's sister, Margaret of England, in 1251. As those demands had remained unanswered, Edward again saw his opportunity in the new political situation in Scotland and pressured John Balliol into obedience. But King John soon stood up for his nation and, in 1295, allied himself with England's enemies, Norway and France. That move brought about an invasion of Edward's forces and commenced the Wars of Scottish Independence which lasted until 1328, when Edward III recognized Robert the Bruce as king and Scotland as an independent state (Barrell 2000: 50-77).

William Wallace's career as soldier and commander falls on the initial years of the Wars of Independence, when Edward defeats King John, places him in the Tower and then exiles him in France. For ten years, until 1306, Scotland remains a country without a monarch, a country rent by internal political struggle and devastated by the English occupying army. Such was the political situation which shaped the young William Wallace. Not much can be gleaned from early Scottish and English documents about this undeniably historical figure. Early historiography offers 1270 as the year of his birth and associates him with the commoner family of a Scottish landowner in Kilmanrock, the County of Ayshire. Wallace's military career began before 1297, soon after the English invasion. His name is associated with the major battles of the Wars of Scottish Independence: Stirling Bridge in 1297 and Falkirk in 1298. His death is more definitely recorded in 1305, when he was put on a show trial and cruelly executed at the order of King Edward I (MacKay 1996: 16-23). Hardly anything more is known of his life in terms of documented historical facts, but the medieval tradition of oral legend and then literary romance, supplied the details and constructed a life story of a hero appealing to the patriotic demands of medieval Scotland.

2. The legend and the romance

Hary composed his romance between 1471 and 1479 and claimed to have based it on an eye-witness account of the life of Wallace written by John Blair, Wallace's chaplain and former schoolmate (McKim 2003: 1). However, no such text survives. The mention, indeed, invention of John Blair, is a known medieval device used by authors to construct the text's authority. When Hary sat down to write his poem, the life of Wallace had already become the stuff of legends on which he largely based his story. Yet, as textual analysis shows (McKim 2003: 1-5) he also used the available works of medieval historiography other than John Blair's: (1) the late fourteenth-century annals by John de Fordun (*Gesta Annalia* caps. 98-103), later included in his *Chronica Gentis Scotorum* (c. 1380) (edited by Skene 1871); (2) the vernacular chronicles of Andrew of Wyntoun (c. 1420) (edited by Laing 1872-1929) and (3) the Latin *Scotichronicon* of Walter Bower (c. 1440) (edited by Watt et al 1987-1998). An important source of a different nature was *The Bruce* (edited by McDiarmid and Stevenson 1980-1985), a verse romance biography of the other Scottish national hero, Robert the Bruce, written by John Barbour, the archdeacon of Aberdeen in 1375. Hary refers to John Barbour several times in the text and is full of praise for the merits of his biography of the king. But he makes it clear that the hero of his story, William Wallace, was a better man, braver and more patriotic. In his preference for Wallace he goes as far as to borrow a few heroic episodes from *The Bruce* and assign them to Wallace (McKim 2003: 1-2). This daring narrative measure reveals the intentions of his work fully: rather than writing historiography he is set on composing a hagiography, which for the sake of its patriotic appeal freely mixes fact with legend and popular belief. His aim is clearly to memorialize and to eulogize his hero. References to Arthur, Brutus, Caesar, Hector, Alexander the Great and other heroes of Antiquity and the Middle Ages place the Scottish leader in the company of the "Nine Worthies" celebrated in art and literature of the times (*The Wallace,* Book 8, ll. 961-970, Book 12, ll. 835-848).

Blind Hary's poem is not exactly a conventional romance, an aristocratic tale of chivalry and courtesy. It is more an account of the military history of the Scottish War of Independence with an emphasis on Wallace's role in it. The martial and strategic skills of Wallace make him an ideal soldier and a commander hero. He is governed primarily by his sense of justice, or rather injustice, done to the Scotsmen by the English army-revenge becomes a noble motive of his war. His role as leader of Scotland is divinely ordered, which St. Andrew confirms in a prophetic dream Hary assigns to Wallace (*The Wallace*; Book 7, ll. 68-152). The rules of romance require also that Wallace shows some respect for the refined rules of the code of chivalry. Not only is he presented as brave and strong, but also as prudent (he avoids open battle when outnumbered), generous to his followers, and magnanimously chivalrous when he repeatedly refuses to harm noncombatants (women, children and priests). Hary makes his hero exhibit perfect courtly decorum in the completely unhistorical meeting between the English queen and Wallace (*The Wallace*; Book 8, ll. 1215-1466). There, refined speech and courtly manners match Wallace's martial prowess. As required of a medieval hero, he is a lion in the field and a lamb in the hall.

Hary's largely imaginative account of Wallace has exerted enormous influence on the popular memory and representation of the Scottish War of Independence and of its hero for centuries to come. In the late Middle Ages the book was known through numerous copies and, in 1507 or 1508, it was one of the first books to be printed in the newly established printing press in Edinburgh. Twenty two other editions would be published before 1707 (McKim 2003: 4). The popularity of the story of William Wallace in Scotland continued well into the late nineteenth century when the book was said to have been owned by every Scottish home (Fraser 1873: 111). The book's influence on shaping the Romantic vision of Scottish history, indeed, shaping the anti-English element of Scottish national identity, is undeniable. Robert Burns wrote in one of his letters, "The story of Wallace poured a Scottish prejudice in my veins which will boil along there till the floodgates of life shut in eternal rest" (Burns, 1: 106-107).

3. The film

Hollywood films are as likely to eulogize an ideal hero as medieval romances did. Turning the story of William Wallace into a film the screenwriter (Randall Wallace) and the director offer an impassioned vision of Wallace's noble patriotism set against the cunning and cruelty of Edward the Longshanks. The good guy and the bad guy are in place from the start of the film and its authors remain poised for any occasion that drives the contrast home: the physiognomies of the handsome blue-eyed hero and the evil-looking anti-hero, images of Wallace enjoying friendship and love in the Scottish village and scenes of the corrupt family links of King Edward, Wallace's sparing the lives of enemy soldiers (at least at the beginning of the war) and Longshanks' enraged killing of his son's male lover. All these are part of a clearly valuating discourse that guides the audience's identification with one and not the other character. The hagiographically didactic tone of Hary is echoed in the interplay between the ideal hero created by Mel Gibson and the Machiavellian King Edward played by Patrick McGoohan. The medieval tendency of moral categorizations and allegorizations achieved by the use of contrast, emblematic emphasis and exaggeration, is not alien to the modern film version of the story of Wallace. Of course, the morally transparent appeal of the film narrative cannot be seen as just an effect of its medieval source. Such valuating devices can be found in the western, the war or the adventure film, based on sources other than medieval. It should rather be proposed that simplified and patterned moral valuation is a genre quality of all popular story-telling, whether medieval or modern, whether literary or cinematic. Such a valuation, however patterned and simplified, ensures a proper identification of, and a stronger emotional attachment to the ideals represented by the hero.

Another convention used by medieval authors to make sure that their message was accepted and taken seriously was the construction of the authority of their texts. Especially in historical narratives this was often done by way of defining and praising their sources. Entire exordia, or prefaces, were offered where the authors traced the origins of their stories: most telling examples can be found in medieval narratives of the Trojan War which almost always show the literary route the story had traveled before it reached their books. Quite expectedly, Blind Hary spends a number of lines on historiographic authorization of his narrative. However fictitious the figure of Wallace's chaplain, John Blair, the confidence with which Hary speaks of him is persuasive and achieves its purpose. Indeed, for a medieval writer and reader, historiography was a respected body of knowledge from which much learning could be gleaned. In the modern age history and historiography have lost their earlier prestige, partly because we are now aware that all history is an interpretation of facts and that most interpretations are biased or mistaken. It is probably in keeping with this modern perception of history that the film Braveheart bluntly brushes the work of historians aside. A voice-over narrator, who is not identified as yet, says "Historians of England will say I am a liar. History is written by those who have hanged heroes". The phrase immediately brings to mind Winston Churchill's famous, "History is written by the victors". But the film narrator's introductory comment on history and politics has a much more sinister touch to it: it renders victory anti-heroic. The heroes are not political victors who win their power to write and thus to shape history. As the discourse of the film implies, the hero's victory may be a moral one, but in political terms he will always be a loser. Such an attitude to the concept of heroic life marks a significant difference between medieval and modern perceptions of the justice of history. Most Germanic epics, *chansons de geste* and medieval romances, see fame and victory as a natural reward for the individual courage of the hero, who often continues to fight against all odds, in the teeth of common sense. However unpredictable the Anglo-Saxon vision of Wyrd may be, the ominous decrees of fate can be overcome by acts of true heroism. Beowulf wins against Grendel and becomes king of the Geats; Havelok the Dane wins back the usurped Danish throne and then regains the English crown for his wife. In medieval literature the heroes are usually the winners. Mel Gibson's Wallace is, as if, doomed from the beginning. The world he lives in is not a world of romantic idealism, but a world of pragmatic compromise. Heroism is seen as madness, indeed a holy madness, and this is clearly expressed by the scene in which the character of a strangely-behaved Irish warrior joins Wallace's troops. "You are out of your mind," says one of the warriors to him. "Then I am in the right company," answers the Irishman.

Another aspect of the textual authority upon which medieval writers of historical romances grafted the voices of their narrators was the presumed historicity of the events they narrated. The avowal of historical truth, often confirmed by references to known authors, served as a conventional prefatory discourse for the narration of the most incredible feats of the hero. Medieval heroes were meant to be received as real and historical even though their literary lives were concoctions of fact, legend and hearsay. The film *Braveheart* offers an interesting meta-narrative comment on the interplay between history, legend and heroic fame. From the beginning of the film, when the narrator assumes his critical stance towards written history, the audience is invited to give their ear to an unofficial, private story. The character of the hero is thus made more real and tangible, unlike the hypostatized figures of epic and heroic discourse.

The beginnings of the cinematic William Wallace seem altogether too domestic and unheroic. As a boy he runs and plays children's games among the fields of Scotland. As a young man he falls in love with a village girl and proves to be a truly romantic lover. On his return to Scotland from his travels with his uncle he declares, "I came back to live in peace, raise a family and reap my crops". Yet from the start he is seen suffering from the hands of the English. The realism with which the film shows the massacre of his family and the death of his beloved builds the necessary psychological framework for his later reaction of revenge. His future defiance of the English is a result of this suffering, a natural reaction that needs time to come to the fore. Wallace's first use of force against the English soldiers happens when he tries to defend his beloved and then, full of rage, revenges her death. His heroism is then a result of circumstances that from now on will push him into battle after battle. In the continuous bloody and violent skirmishes on the screen there is little room for the medieval high-mindedness of heroic motivation. Revenge, rage and the will to survive are emotions painted on the faces of Wallace and the other warriors in battle. Stratagem, cunning and sheer force are the means of survival and victory. How does this relate to the ancient or the medieval concept of the noble, almost superhuman hero, refusing, as Beowulf does, to fight with a sword against an enemy that does not know how to use it? Mel Gibson clearly intends to de-romanticize the figure of the hero, by showing him primarily as a soldier on his bloody duty. Heroic fame, Gibson seems to suggest, is the product of imagination and legend. At least twice in the film Wallace's identity is doubted by the people he meets. "You cannot be William Wallace", they say. "He is seven feet tall". Thus the legend of the hero grows independently of his deeds and requires no authoritative support of history.

Hary's medieval biography of Wallace is already a romantic fabrication. Gibson and his screenwriter let their fancy play with the hero's life even more fantastically. One of the most outrageous, though aesthetically pleasing, manipulations of history offered by the film is the episode with Isabella. The unhistorical meeting of Wallace and Marguerite, Edward I's wife, which Hary had put into his narrative, is in the film turned into a second romantic affair that the hero experiences. Here, though, we encounter not the queen Marguerite, who would have to be shown as a middle-aged woman, but King Edward's daughter-in-law, the young and beautiful Isabella (played by Sophie Marceau), daughter of the French king Phillip. In the film she is sent by Edward to negotiate with Wallace and the meeting, in the end, gives the film authors the opportunity to show some nudity on the screen. The historical Isabella, the neglected wife of the homosexual king Edward II, had not come to England until after the execution of Wallace in 1305. But in a modern romance chronology does not matter and no authority needs to be summoned. Her role in the story is of paramount importance. Even if the screenwriter allows his Wallace to die young without achieving freedom for Scotland, his idea of poetic justice makes him invent a masterly revenge of fate on Edward the Longshanks. On his deathbed the king learns that the wife of his son, the future queen of England, bears an illegitimate child in her womb – the obvious implication is that this is the child of William Wallace.

Yet another interesting fabrication of the filmmakers is the Irish episode in the battle of Falkirk, where King Edward's Irish footmen, charging against the Scots, stop right in front of them, shake hands with their enemies and join the army of Wallace. A possible historical suggestion for this scene may have come from a real rebellion of Edward's Welsh longbow units before the battle, though they never joined the Scots.

However free the film is in its treatment of history, it appears surprisingly historical in the depiction of medieval warfare. For example, Wallace's film footmen are organised into what seems to be the Scottish *schiltrons* - crowded phalanx formations carrying 12-foot spears used against cavalry, raised when the enemy horsemen are too close to slow down. The initial success of Wallace's army at Falkirk came primarily from the use of schiltrons, which decimated the English cavalry by killing their horses (Armstrong – Mcbride 2003: 20). The violence and bloody realism of the battle scenes effectively creates the image of the madness and confusion of war.

Conclusion

Mel Gibson's *Braveheart* is altogether a story of war with a focus on the life and death of the war's major soldier, who, through the workings of human imagination, gains the fame of a hero. The world of Wallace is believably medieval in some of its aspects and completely modern in some other. Such a combination is unavoidable to, first of all, bridge Zumthor's gap, and secondly, relate a popular story to a popular audience through a modern medium. Bernard Cerquiglini calls the study of medieval literature "the mourning for a text" and adds that "it is the quest for an anterior perfection that is always bygone, that unique moment in which the presumed voice of the author was linked to the hand of the first scribe, dictating the authentic, first, and original version, which will disintegrate in the hands of all the numerous, careless individuals copying a literature in the vernacular" (Cerquiglini 1999: 34). Whether we like it or not popular film is the vernacular of today. But the act of watching, and possibly making, a popular film about the Middle Ages must not sound like a dirge for the Middle Ages. It should, as *Braveheart* tries to do, celebrate and translate into a new medium what is still communicable of the medieval discourse and give up on what is not. Incidentally, medievalisation and a sort of cultural translation were the two major strategies of many medieval artists, who like the authors of *Braveheart*, used history, legend and fantasy as sources of equal importance. It is therefore much more appropriate to view the film's medievalism not from the perspective of Cerquiglini's funerary metaphor, but through a much more encouraging definition proposed by Richard Glejzer, who understands that "medievalism acknowledges the fictional structure of history, going beyond simple historical understandings, to focus instead on a mythic structure that ties us to history" (1995: 220-221). Thus, the medievalism of *Braveheart* and many other films inspired by medieval texts can be seen to lie exactly in the filmmakers' ability to freely combine the three sources (history, legend and fantasy) in order to achieve the result of a narrative rather than a historical credibility that, in many ways, ties us to the medieval world.

References

Andrew of Wyntoun
   1929   *The Orygynale Cronykil of Scotland by Androw of Wyntoun.* (Edited by
             David Laing.) 3 vols. (The Historians of Scotland 2, 3, 9.) Edinburgh:
             Edmonston and Douglas.
Armstrong, Peter – Angus Mcbride
   2003   *Stirling Bridge and Falkirk* 1297-98: *William Wallace's rebellion.* London: Osprey Publishing.
Barrell, A. M. D.
   2000   *Medieval Scotland.* Cambridge: Cambridge University Press.
Bower, Walter
   1998   *Scitichronicon.* (Edited by D.E.R. Watt et al.) 9 vols. Aberdeen University Press.
Barbour, John
   1985   *Barbour's Bruce: A Fredome is a Noble Thing!* (Edited by Matthew P.
             McDiarmid – James A. Stevenson.) 3 vols. Edinburgh: Scottish Text Society.
Braveheart
   1995   Directed by Mel Gibson. 20th Century Fox Home Entertainment.

Burns, Robert
    1931   *The letters of Robert Burns.* (Edited by J. De Lancey Ferguson.) 2 vols. Oxford: Clarendon Press.

Cerquiglini, Bernard
    1999   *In Praise of the Variant.* (Translated by Betsy Wing.) Baltimore, MD: Johns Hopkins University Press.

Fordun, Johannis de
    1871   *Chronica Gentis Scotorum.* (Edited by W.F. Skene.) (The Historians of Scotland 1.) Edinburgh: Edmonston and Douglas.

Fraser, John
    1873   *The humorous chap-books of Scotland.* New York: Hinton.

Glejzer, Richard
    1995   "Medievalism and New Historicism", *The Year's Work in Medievalism* X: 219-227.

Hary, Blind
    2003   *The Wallace. Selections.* (Edited by Anne McKim.) TEAMS Middle English Text Series. Kalamazoo: Medieval Institute Publications.

MacKay, James
    2003   *William Wallace: Brave Heart.* Edinburgh: Mainstream Publishing.

McKim, Anne
    2003   "Introduction", in: Anne McKim (ed.), 1-7.

Zumthor, Paul
    1992   *Toward a medieval poetics.* (Translated by Philip Bennett.) Minneapolis: University of Minnesota Press.

Studies in English Medieval Language and Literature

Edited by Jacek Fisiak

Vol. 1 Dieter Kastovsky / Arthur Mettinger (eds.): Language Contact in the History of English. 2nd, revised edition. 2003.

Vol. 2 Studies in English Historical Linguistics and Philology. A Festschrift for Akio Oizumi. Edited by Jacek Fisiak. 2002.

Vol. 3 Liliana Sikorska: *In a Manner Morall Playe*: Social Ideologies in English Moralities and Interludes (1350-1517). 2002.

Vol. 4 Peter J. Lucas / Angela M. Lucas (eds.): Middle English from Tongue to Text. Selected Papers from the Third International Conference on Middle English: Language and Text, held at Dublin, Ireland, 1-4 July 1999. 2002.

Vol. 5 Chaucer and the Challenges of Medievalism. Studies in Honor of H. A. Kelly. Edited by Donka Minkova and Theresa Tinkle. 2003.

Vol. 6 Hanna Rutkowska: Graphemics and Morphosyntax in the *Cely Letters* (1472-88). 2003.

Vol. 7 The *Ancrene Wisse*. A Four-Manuscript Parallel Text. Preface and Parts 1-4. Edited by Tadao Kubouchi and Keiko Ikegami with John Scahill, Shoko Ono, Harumi Tanabe, Yoshiko Ota, Ayako Kobayashi and Koichi Nakamura. 2003.

Vol. 8 Joanna Bugaj: Middle Scots Inflectional System in the South-west of Scotland. 2004.

Vol. 9 Rafal Boryslawski: The Old English Riddles and the Riddlic Elements of Old English Poetry. 2004.

Vol. 10 Nikolaus Ritt / Herbert Schendl (eds.): Rethinking Middle English. Linguistic and Literary Approaches. 2005.

Vol. 11 The *Ancrene Wisse*. A Four-Manuscript Parallel Text. Parts 5–8 with Wordlists. Edited by Tadao Kubouchi and Keiko Ikegami with John Scahill, Shoko Ono, Harumi Tanabe, Yoshiko Ota, Ayako Kobayashi, Koichi Nakamura. 2005.

Vol. 12 Text and Language in Medieval English Prose. A Festschrift for Tadao Kubouchi. Edited by Akio Oizumi, Jacek Fisiak and John Scahill. 2005.

Vol. 13 Michiko Ogura (ed.): Textual and Contextual Studies in Medieval English. Towards the Reunion of Linguistics and Philology. 2006.

Vol. 14 Keiko Hamaguchi: Non-European Women in Chaucer. A Postcolonial Study. 2006.

Vol. 15 Ursula Schaefer (ed.): The Beginnings of Standardization. Language and Culture in Fourteenth-Century England. 2006.

Vol. 16 Nikolaus Ritt / Herbert Schendl / Christiane Dalton-Puffer / Dieter Kastovsky (eds): Medieval English and its Heritage. Structure, Meaning and Mechanisms of Change. 2006.

Vol. 17 Matylda Włodarczyk: Pragmatic Aspects of Reported Speech. The Case of Early Modern English Courtroom Discourse. 2007.

Vol. 18 Hans Sauer / Renate Bauer (eds.): *Beowulf* and Beyond. 2007.

Vol. 19 Gabriella Mazzon (ed.): Studies in Middle English Forms and Meanings. 2007.

Vol. 20 Alexander Bergs / Janne Skaffari (eds.): The Language of the Peterborough Chronicle. 2007.

Vol. 21 Liliana Sikorska (ed.). With the assistance of Joanna Maciulewicz: Medievalisms. The Poetics of Literary Re-Reading. 2008.

www.peterlang.de